Heike Hartung, Roberta Maierhofer, Christian Schmitt-Kilb (eds.)
Masculinities Ageing between Cultures

Aging Studies | Volume 21

The series is edited by Heike Hartung, Ulla Kriebernegg and Roberta Maierhofer.

Heike Hartung is an independent scholar who has earned her PhD in English studies at Freie Universität Berlin and her PhD habil. at Universität Potsdam, Germany. She is affiliated as senior researcher at the Center for Inter-American Studies at Universität Graz, Austria. In her publications she applies the methods of literary theory and cultural studies to the interdisciplinary fields of ageing, disability and gender studies. She is a founding member of the European Network in Aging Studies (ENAS).
Roberta Maierhofer is a professor of American studies and Director of the Center for Inter-American Studies (C.IAS) at Universität Graz, Austria. She is a founding member of the European Network in Aging Studies (ENAS), supported the establishment of the North American Network in Aging Studies (NANAS), and has been a member of the Humanities and Arts Committee of the Gerontological Society of America. Her research focuses on American literature and cultural studies, gender studies, Transatlantic cooperation in education, and age/aging studies.
Christian Schmitt-Kilb is a professor of English literature at Universität Rostock. He received his MA from the University of Keele (UK), PhD from the Goethe-Universität Frankfurt am Main on early modern rhetoric and poetics and habilitated at Universität Rostock with a thesis that resulted in a monograph on the theme of absent fathers in the contemporary novel. His current research interests, editorships and essay publications are in the field of ecocriticism, ecopoetry and New Nature Writing.

Heike Hartung, Roberta Maierhofer, Christian Schmitt-Kilb (eds.)

Masculinities Ageing between Cultures

Relationality, Kinship and Care in Dialogue

Bibliographic information published by the Deutsche Nationalbibliothek
The Deutsche Nationalbibliothek lists this publication in the Deutsche Nationalbibliografie; detailed bibliographic data are available in the Internet at https://dnb.dnb.de/

This work is licensed under the Creative Commons Attribution 4.0 (BY) license, which means that the text may be remixed, transformed and built upon and be copied and redistributed in any medium or format even commercially, provided credit is given to the author. https://creativecommons.org/licenses/by/4.0/ Creative Commons license terms for re-use do not apply to any content (such as graphs, figures, photos, excerpts, etc.) not original to the Open Access publication and further permission may be required from the rights holder. The obligation to research and clear permission lies solely with the party re-using the material.

First published in 2024 by transcript Verlag, Bielefeld
© Heike Hartung, Roberta Maierhofer, Christian Schmitt-Kilb (eds.)

Cover layout: Maria Arndt, Bielefeld
Cover illustration: Emil Filla, "Hlava starého muže/Hlava starce", 1914. Copyright: The Gallery of West Bohemia in Pilsen.
Proofread: Nicole Haring
Printed by: Majuskel Medienproduktion GmbH, Wetzlar
https://doi.org/10.14361/9783839469064
Print-ISBN: 978-3-8376-6906-0
PDF-ISBN: 978-3-8394-6906-4
ISSN of series: 2702-7996
eISSN of series: 2702-8003

Printed on permanent acid-free text paper.

Contents

Acknowledgements 7

Introduction: Masculinities Ageing Between Cultures
Bringing Relationality, Kinship and Care into Dialogue
Heike Hartung, Roberta Maierhofer, Christian Schmitt-Kilb 9

Male Ageing and Migrancy
sevā and the Indian Diaspora in the US
Rüdiger Kunow 25

Masculinity, Aging, and Reversion
An Essay on Losing Direction
Annette Leibing 43

The Age and Gender of Homesickness
Mother Russia's Prodigal Sons
Dagmar Gramshammer-Hohl 69

Ageing as Emasculation?
Rethinking the Father Image in Ang Lee's "Father Trilogy"
Yumin Zhang 87

A Journey in Reverse
Myths of a Foreign Father in Aris Fioretos' *Halva solen*
Katharina Fürholzer 109

Queer Kinship
Masculinity, Age and the Closet in the Windrush Generation in
Bernardine Evaristo's *Mr Loverman* (2013)
Kristina Weber 127

**Formen männlicher Identität in Spielfilmen
von Ines Tanović**
Renate Hansen-Kokoruš 149

Aging Behind Bars
Perspectives from Incarcerated Men in the United States
Andrea Zittlau 173

Man Plants, Woman Nurtures
Reflections of Older German Men
Lisa-Nike Bühring 191

**Health Care and Ageing Masculinity in the Performance
of *Notaufnahme – Hospitali***
Pepetual Mforbe Chiangong 211

Contributors 233

Index 239

Acknowledgements

The contributions of this volume are based on a virtual workshop that has taken place at the University of Rostock, Germany, in April 2021. The general research framework for this work is the European research project "Gendering Age: Representations of Masculinities and Ageing in Contemporary European Literatures and Cinemas" (MASCAGE), funded by Gender-Net Plus ERA-Net; and it was funded in part by the Austrian Science Fund (FWF) [I4187].

The scope of this volume reflects the possibilities of scholarly exchange within the European research project MASCAGE, facilitated also by the European and North American Networks of Aging Studies (ENAS & NANAS). It brings together experts within the fields of Masculinity and Age Studies with early career researchers. In response to the great cultural variety of essays we have left the choice of language (British English, American English, German) open to the contributors.

Introduction: Masculinities Ageing Between Cultures
Bringing Relationality, Kinship and Care into Dialogue

Heike Hartung, Roberta Maierhofer, Christian Schmitt-Kilb

This book aims to bring together perspectives from Masculinity Studies and cultural Age Studies in order to explore multiple ways in which men age between different cultures, examining also how concepts of gender and masculinities are affected by cultural exchange.

Addressing a broad geographical framework in response to global mobility and migration, the essays in this volume examine exilic and transcultural experiences of ageing men from Northern and Eastern Europe, British and North American diasporic relationships including the Indian diaspora in the US, Chinese father images in the US-American context and Black British queer kinship, drawing its examples for conceptualizing relationality, care and kinship 'in-between' cultures also from Brazilian society and African European contexts.

Our first premise is that mobility is one of the crucial, perhaps even the prototypical experience of our time. As a "post-disciplinary" phenomenon in contemporary societies worldwide, the 'mobilities turn' or 'mobilities paradigm' encompasses "various kinds and temporalities of physical movement," which extend both to the vertical movement of upward or downward "*social* mobility" and the horizontal kind of geographical movement involved in migration (Urry 2007, 6, 8; emphasis in original), which may extend over people's lifetime. John Urry's analyses of the forms and social functions of mobilities have introduced new ways of thinking about societies beyond clearly defined spatial boundaries, foregrounding "networks, mobility and horizontal fluidities" (Urry 2000, 3) as of central importance in conceptualizing social interactions and relationships.

In the context of COVID-19, which affected work on this edited collection by shifting personal encounters primarily to the virtual format, mobilities have been revalued. If the mobilities turn in the 1990s responded to "a theoretical devaluing of mobility" in the humanities and social sciences with the implication that 'cultures' were frequently seen as "the properties of groups of people with clear territories who shared common identities", so that the "mobility (real and imagined) of the homeless, the migrant, the refugee" were equally devalued (Cresswell 2020, 52, 53), in a post COVID-19 world 'viral mobilities' have been associated with the pathological. As Tim Cresswell points out, this constitutes a regressive return to disease metaphors which have historically been "at the heart of violent reactions to mobility and displacement" (2020, 54). While acknowledging that the mobility of people and infrastructures has crucially enabled the spread of the COVID-19 pandemic, Cresswell argues that it is the metaphorical link between disease and mobility that leads to a devaluing of mobility as "wasted time" or "dysfunction": "COVID-19 and its mobilities are not an aberration but, instead, evidence of the way 'normality' has been spatially rendered" (55).

Mobilities in a post COVID-19 world have implications for thinking about cultures in general, and they affect our spatial metaphor of 'masculinities ageing between cultures' in particular. In addition to postcolonial critiques of the spatial and Homi Bhabha's sense of "In-betweenness" as a cultural condition (1994, 2), there is also the liminal aspect of temporality in 'ageing'. Also, an 'in-between' is, according to the *Oxford English Dictionary*, 'a person who intervenes', while the adjective 'in-between' is associated with both the temporal interval and with spatial intervention; and these different forms of 'intervention' figure in the essays of this volume. Cultural 'in-betweenness' brings up the further association with travel, theorized by James Clifford as "Culture *as* travel,", who redefined cultures "as sites of dwelling *and* travel" and as encounters between people on the move and in fixity (1992, 103, 105; emphasis in original). While travel in this broad sense is associated with negative ("as transience, superficiality, tourism, exile, and rootlessness") as well as positive meanings ("as exploration, research, escape, transforming encounter"; Clifford 1992, 105), this is also true for mobilities. In the halting of mobilities in the various political responses to the COVID-19 virus, one of the negative meanings of travel – its environmental aspects – were frequently observed, while the push which the enforced fixity of lockdowns gave to digital exchanges were also experienced as positive. However, the negative aspects of the prevalence of digital over embodied encounters were experienced most forcefully by the very young and the very old, while poorly paid workers renamed as 'key workers' and refugees falling ill in camps around the Mediterranean were predominantly exposed to "mobility inequities" (Cresswell 2020, 55).

Travel and mobilities *as* culture and *in-between* cultures have not only a multitude of positive and negative meanings, but are also marked by the intersections of gender, sexualities, class, race and age. In this collection, we focus primarily on intersections of masculinities and age, because it is our second premise that the cultural constructions of masculinities as they change across the life course have received too little critical attention. This is related to the even more punitive cultural constructions of female old age, which have therefore been analyzed primarily in feminist age studies.[1] Constructions of male ageing, then, constitute a blind spot in humanities research, which this volume begins to address in the context of mobilities. In bringing together gendered aspects of movement and non-movement, forced or deliberate, with representations of ageing masculinities, the essays in this volume begin to map a variety of cultural narratives of male ageing.

The two opening essays sketch out a theoretical framework for these narratives by conceptualizing respectively the links between spatial

---

[1] For work in Age Studies that reflects on the gendered "double standard of aging" (Sontag 1972), see, for instance, Maierhofer 2003, 2019, Maierhofer and Haring 2023, Haller 2005, Hartung 2017, Vedder 2018, and Woodward 1999.

movement and male ageing as migrancy and by reflecting on the directions male ageing may take. With few exceptions, among them Rüdiger Kunow's work[2], cultural Age Studies have focused primarily on Western cultures and literature, an over-emphasis that is in the process of being redressed[3]. From a materialist perspective, Rüdiger Kunow brings his expertise in postcolonial theory and Age studies to bear on the connection between population ageing, migration and masculinities. If capital-driven mobility has more frequently been associated with the young, old age and older people have been constructed as the 'leftover' of global migration, he argues. Regarding this as a misconception in view of millions of labour migrants growing old "between cultures" in the United States, Kunow maintains that old age does matter in migration in multiple ways, promoting in his essay a "multi-generational understanding of migration". To illustrate the implications of a necessary change in our understanding of mobility and later life, Kunow turns to Indian literature in English in the United States for its awareness of cultural 'in-between-ness'. He focuses on the Sanskrit term "sevā", which designates a complex of services due to older men as part of a non-Western way of regulating relations between generations as well as male ageing inside the Indian family. Reading Jhumpa Lahiri's short story "Unaccustomed Earth" (2008) as an exemplary text that addresses key issues of Indian diasporic culture, Kunow shows how the story about the middle-aged Ruma and her retired father revolves around unspoken issues of filial obligation, intimacy as distance, intergenerational relations and generational difference, in which "sevā" is not an option. Contextualizing Lahiri's story within older Indian men's migration to the United States, Kunow concludes that capitalist globalization uncou-

---

2   See Kunow 2010 and 2016.
3   See the special issue on "Postcolonial Perspectives in Aging Studies" of *Journal of Aging Studies* 2016 (co-edited Silke van Dyk and Thomas Küpper), Sweta Rajan-Rankin 2018, Sweta Brosius and Roberta Mandoki 2020, and work by Ira Raja and Emily Timms, forthcoming in *The Bloomsbury Handbook to Ageing in Literature and Film* 2023.

ples cultural traditions and relationships to an extent that "age itself, as an idea and ideal" becomes migratory.

From the perspective of medical anthropology, Annette Leibing tackles issues of belonging, citizenship and the complex identitary issues of masculinity constructions by thinking through the directions taken within Masculinity Studies. Leibing's pioneering comparative work on dementia in Brazil and Canada illustrates that a fruitful dialogue can be initiated between anthropological research on ageing, on the one hand, and literary and cultural perspectives, on the other.[4] In her essay in this volume, Leibing introduces the analytical concept of "reversion" to define social, political and cultural responses to value systems achieved over time that are in the process of being lost. With reference to such deeper changes within societies as "regression, backwardness and devolution", "reversion" reveals the surprising (structural) absence of older men from cultural narratives of masculinities, which contrasts with the strong presence of older male actors in current world politics. Drawing on the narrative of political masculinities in Brazil after the election of Jair Bolsonaro as president, Leibing illustrates the impact of gendered politics with reference to images and metaphors used by Bolsonaro and his followers to reinforce heteronormative and homophobic values. Reminiscent of older models for being male, the new scenarios redirect images of illegal leadership and violence – for instance, in Bolsonaro's posing with firearms – into 'positive' signs of masculine power. Furthermore, in the context of Bolsonaro's response to the COVID-19 pandemic illness and the receiving of medical care is linked to frailty and a loss of masculinity.

Conceptualizing links between mobility, age and masculinity as multi-generational migrancy and as reversion, the two opening essays introduce many of the terms that reverberate with other contributions in this volume. In order to knit the observations in the case studies that follow closer together, we invited contributors to engage in cultural comparison by drawing on the concepts of relationality, kinship and care. In this way, insights from the broad geographical and intercultural

---

4   See Leibing 2006 and 2015.

framework, from which the essays draw, may be put into dialogue. The "need" of ideas, concept and theories "to be ever on the move" is one further dimension of mobility (Urry 2007, 16), while the idea that theories travel in time and space is a metaphor introduced by Edward Said, who links conceptual travel to a "a distance traversed" and "conditions of acceptance [...] or resistances" (1983, 127). As a flexible tool of transcultural research, Mieke Bal defines narrative as a travelling concept and concepts as "sites of debate, awareness of difference, and tentative exchange" (2002, 13), which she regards as the "basis for an intellectual adventure" (2009, 18). In this sense, we offer the concepts of relationality, kinship and care as mobile sites of dialogic exchange between cultures.

Beginning with the broadest, but also most encompassing term 'relationality', the essays in this section address mobility, age and masculinity from the perspectives of Russian literary writers in exile reflecting on their homeland and from the angle of Ang Lee's filmic (re-)construction of the Chinese-American father-son relationship. Dagmar Gramshammer-Hohl shows in her essay how discourses of home and belonging by male Russian literary writers in exile during the twentieth century are shaped by (re-)configurations of both age and gender. Relationality is at stake in this essay as it investigates how concepts of gender and masculinities itself are affected by movement and migration. While exile is associated with age, even an accelerated ageing process imagined as "turn[ing] grey overnight", the exile's longing for home is also gendered. As Gramshammer-Hohl illustrates in her analyses, the relationship between the exiled writer and his homeland is conceived in familial and gendered terms, in the trope of "homesickness" or the longing of a prodigal son for his (aged) mother.

Yumin Zhang investigates in her essay on the Taiwanese filmmaker Ang Lee's "Father Trilogy" how the changes in the depicted relationships between ageing fathers and their sons or daughters portray generational and cultural conflict, while they challenge hegemonic views and stereotypes in American society concerning perceptions of Chinese masculinities. Lee's films do this, Zhang argues, by representing a variety of positions taken by these only apparently traditional older men, thus suggesting that ageing men's experiences are "anything but monolithic". With the story of the retired Master Chu in *Pushing Hands* (1991), who moves to the US to join his son, Lee uses conflicts in filial obligations to dismantle the stereotypes of emasculated Chinese men in American culture; in *The Wedding Banquet* (1993), the Confucian father Mr. Gao is shown as a complex figure who embraces his son's homosexuality as well as alternative family arrangement to the surprise of his own family; while the protagonist of *Eat Drink Man Woman* (1994), the retired Chef Chu, a widower who has raised his three daughters alone, represents 'caring masculinity'.

As both these essays illustrate in their different cultural contexts, representations of masculinities ageing between cultures rely on different forms of relationality, which involve also forms of kinship – as Dagmar Gramshammer-Hohl shows in her essay by highlighting the connection between images of home and belonging with kinship relations – and those of care – as Yumin Shang indicates with reference to the various forms of caring, but also un-caring, masculinities in Ang Lee's films.

The next section addresses the interrelations of 'kinship' with ageing masculinities and migration in three case studies on Swedish literature, Black British literature and Bosnian film. The concept of kinship itself has travelled from anthropology to gender, queer and diaspora studies. In response to universalist claims in structuralist anthropology which associated kinship with nature and biology, the concept itself was challenged, following David Schneider's *A Critique of the Study of Kinship* (1984), who rejected kinship studies as forcibly imposing "European categories on other cultures, thereby distorting them" (Adair 2019, 13). In response to Schneider's critique, a more complex understanding of the relationship between the biological, social and cultural in kinship has evolved, which traces its links to other cultural phenomena, identity categories and biopolitical developments (Franklin and McKinnon 2002, Carsten 2004, Sahlins 2013).

From the perspective of queer studies, Kath Weston foregrounded the aspect of choice in homosexual relationships which recast close friends as kin. As she argues, the aspect of choice is determined by social aspects such as "material circumstances, culture, history, habit and imagination", intending with her approach to undercut "the dangerously utopian fantasies of harmony" in concepts of family which ignore that families are "sites of conflict as well as support, violence as well as love" (1991, xv, xviii). In her examination of the link between sexualities and kinship, Judith Butler considers the implications of the concept for our understanding of cultures as exchanges between provisional rather than "self-standing entities or unities", suggesting that we think of kinship as "a kind of *doing*, [...] as an enacted practice," which makes it possible to "consider how modes of patterned and performative doing bring kinship categories into operation and become the means by which they undergo transformation and displacement" (2002, 34; emphasis in original).

Emphasizing the performative and relational aspects of kinship, these considerations foreground the spatial and temporal movement of the concept, which makes it possible to move beyond the binaries of nature and culture, the normal and the pathological in terms of gender and sexualities. Similarly, recent work on diasporic kinship draws specifically on "structural queerness" in arguing for both a spatial displacement "of the national" and a temporal redirection "in a desire to be and relate otherwise" (Adair 2019, 10). Gigi Adair describes the "double bind of kinship discourse" in her study of diasporic kinship as "an awareness of the privileges accorded to normative kinship forms", on the one hand, and as "a diasporic longing to find alternative ways of being in the world", on the other (2019, 10). Arguing that contemporary forms of migration, and mobility more generally, are part of kinship, Janet Carson shows that both models of kinship – the more static one that "emphasizes *being* over doing, origins over attainment, the past over the future", and the more dynamic one which "stresses the importance of processual and performative ways of *becoming* kin" (2020, 321; emphasis in original) – have important implications for a politics of mobility and the multidimensionality of kinship as "imaginative, material and relational" (332).

Taking up the imaginative link between kinship, male ageing and migration, Katharina Fürholzer analyses in her essay the Swedish-born writer Aris Fioretis' book about his father, a Greek physician who migrated to Sweden, *Halva solen* (2012; "Half the sun"). The dementia and death of the father motivates the son's intercultural narration, looking back at the father's youth, his immigration to Sweden during the Greek Civil War in the 1940s, and at his professional and personal life in the new country. Linking key moments in the father's past to his illness, the narrative oscillates between intimacy and distance, revealing the double bind of kinship, as Fürholzer points out, in the "paradoxical dichotomy of the foreign in the familiar and the familiar in the foreign".

In her essay on the British writer Bernardine Evaristo's novel *Mr Loverman* (2013), Kristina Weber considers implications of queer kinship for older black men of the Windrush generation, who migrated to Britain from the Caribbean between 1948 and 1971. Set in 2010, the novel focuses on the protagonist Barrington "Barry" Walker and his long-term secret partner, Morris, both in their seventies. As Weber argues, the rigid standards of "hegemonic masculinity" (R. W. Connell 1995) lead to the two closeted queer men's "internalised homophobia, shame and self-hate", while their relationships to their (biological) families are conflicted. In response to the loneliness the two men face in their old age, the novel portrays their eventual coming out as gay and their adopting a queer kin network, thus contributing to a "redefinition of what kinship means for elderly queer diasporic men".

Renate Hansen-Kokoruš turns to narratives of male identity in two films by the Bosnian director Ines Tanović, *Our Everyday Life* (*Naša svakodnena priča*, 2015) und *The Son* (*Sin*, 2019), which focus on family relationships and generational conflicts in post-war Bosnia. In contradistinction to the "toxic masculinity" of the stereotypical martial war hero in other post-war films, Hansen-Kokoruš argues, the two films by Tanović foreground generational aspects, showing how male gender roles evolve in familial connections and intergenerational interactions across different stages of the life course. Just like kinship itself (Carsten 2020, 326), these familial roles in their effect on masculinities across the ages may be conflicted and exclusionary, but can also be supportive and beneficial. Leaving the future of the younger generations of men open in the films' ending, as Hansen-Kokoruš suggests, Tanovic's films nevertheless invite a conciliatory perspective.

Turning to the concept of 'care', the last section brings this concept, which has historically been associated more frequently with women and femininity, to bear on ageing masculinities. Stereotypes such as the 'uncaring male' have been deconstructed in a feminist care ethics, which has foregrounded the importance of relationships and responsibilities rather than rights and rules in matters of care (Gilligan [1983] 2003, 19). From the perspective of metaethical political theory, Joan Tronto has analysed two forms of social care as the traditional domain of men: those of the "protection" of society and "productive economic activity", for instance in providing for the family (2013, 91). As she argues, these engagements, which traditionally granted men "a pass from caring" are no longer adequate in response to changing gender and care conceptions in contemporary societies (93). The traditional focus on the public realm within which care has been defined as a feature of hegemonic masculinities, has also been questioned in sociology, in which the concept of 'caring masculinities' has been employed to shift the emphasis instead on familial care, to promote fatherhood as a realm for male care beyond the paradigm of protection and productivity (Scholz and Heilmann 2019, Tholen 2018).

Nevertheless, male care – whether extended to others or to the self – is still perceived as unusual in many social contexts, while gender implications in care encounters may be complicated in intercultural contexts, as the essays in this section illustrate. In the opening essay on a group of men who have grown older in correctional institutions in the United States, Andrea Zittlau explores the opposite end of the mobilities paradigm in her focus on male imprisonment, drawing out the implications that forced fixity also has on care. Excerpting texts written in creative writing workshops and in personal communications, her essay presents some of the voices of imprisoned men themselves on how ageing affects their self-images. With reference also to a senior center behind bars that is in the process of being created at the State Correctional Facility of the city of Chester, Zittlau addresses the complex contradictions of masculinity images and ideas of care, self-care and the lack of both that are at stake at the personal and institutional level within the prison, which leaves little room for physical frailty or vulnerability.

In her interview-based study of older German men, Lisa-Nike Bühring illustrates from a different angle how hegemonic masculinity constructions continue to associate care predominantly with women and femininity. Conducting semi-structured interviews with four white, heterosexual and married German men in retirement, whose successful careers mark them as belonging to a hegemonic class of men, Bühring is interested in how they respond to the loss of their professional roles and how this affects their gender identity. While their responses indicate a relatively stable self-image, with which they carry their traditional gender concepts into older age, Bühring suggests a "potential revaluation" as part of the retrospective life review. However, confirming a traditional view of the gender binary in the identity constructions of these older German men, Bühring points out, crucially illustrates also the limits to gender equality in Western cultural settings.

Pepetual Mforbe Chiangong's closing essay brings migration to bear on male ageing and care, focusing specifically on *Notaufnahme – Hospitali*, an intercultural theatre project, written and directed by Christoph M. Gosepath and Robert Schmidt and performed in 2018 at Vierte Welt (Berlin). Exploring the intersections of health care, elderhood, and African masculinity as points of diasporic encounter – a relationship that has received little critical attention, as Chiangong points out –, the play centers on an older Tanzanian artist with mental illness who has moved to Berlin and his struggles with the German medical system. Chiangong illustrates how the older performer as artist embodies different identities – as storyteller, restaurant owner and traditional healer – in order to tell "multiple narratives about diasporic experience, elderhood and masculinity". At the point in the plot when the artist has a mental breakdown, he encounters a young and unfriendly female medical doctor, a moment in the performance that stages the conflict between gender and age within the framework of Western medical authority. However, as Chiangong argues, the hybridized performance structure in the multiple roles of the artist-performer as well as his silence to the doctor's intrusive questions serve to deconstruct these power relationships within modern medicine by providing a counter-discourse of ageing African masculinities.

As the broad range of intercultural encounters analysed in the essays in this volume proves, the contemporary spaces for masculinities ageing between cultures are multidimensional, encompassing both imaginary and material travel; they can be disruptive and disturbing experiences, but also instructive and expansive journeys in space and time. We consider the heterogeneity of approaches, methods and materials that the essays in this volume display and address as a strength. It is a necessary outcome of the intersectionality that the amalgamation of different academic fields – Masculinity Studies, cultural Age Studies – and theoretical perspectives – such as gender studies, postcolonial studies, migration studies – demands. "Masculinities always have an age", writes Edward H. Thompson (2019, 1) in the introduction to *Men, Masculinities, and Aging: The Gendered Lives of Older Men*. They also have a transcultural and a diasporic dimension, a postcolonial and a class dimension, a geographical, performative and a social dimension. All of these dimensions need to be thought of as dynamic and interdependent, they are as mobile as so many people in a transcultural world characterized by globalization and mass migration. In this framework, masculinities and age emerge as contingent and changeable concepts, an understanding that the editors share, and the volume reflects, hopefully to offer a wide variety of possible pathways for further investigation.

Works Cited

Adair, Gigi. Kinship Across the Black Atlantic: Writing Diasporic Relations. Liverpool: Liverpool University Press, 2019.

Bal, Mieke. "Working with concepts." European Journal of English Studies 13.1 (2009): 13–23.

Bal, Mieke. Traveling Concepts in the Humanities. A Rough Guide. Toronto: University of Toronto Press, 2002.

Bhabha, Homi K. The Location of Culture. New York: Routledge, 1994.

Brosius, Christiane, Roberta Mandoki, eds. Caring for Old Age. Perspectives from South Asia. Heidelberg: Heidelberg University Publishing, 2020.

Butler, Judith. "Is Kinship Always Already Heterosexual?" differences: A Journal of Feminist Cultural Studies 13.1 (2002): 14–44.

Carsten, Janet. "Imagining and Living New Worlds: The Dynamics of Kinship in Contexts of Mobility and Migration." Ethnography 21.3 (2020): 319–334.

Carsten, Janet. After Kinship. Cambridge: Cambridge University Press, 2004.

Clifford, James. "Traveling Cultures." Cultural Studies. Ed. Lawrence Grossberg, Cary Nelson, Paula A. Treichler. New York: Routledge, 1992. 96–116.

Connell, R. W. Masculinities. [1995] Second Edition. Cambridge: Polity Press, 2005.

Cresswell, Tim. "Valuing mobility in a post COVID-19 world." Mobilities 16.1 (2020): 51–65.

Dyk van, Silke and Thomas Küpper. "Postcolonial perspectives in Aging Studies: Introduction." Special Issue. Journal of Aging Studies 39 (2016): 81–82.

Franklin, Sarah and Susan McKinnon, eds. Relative Values: Reconfiguring Kinship Studies. Durham: Duke University Press, 2002.

Gilligan, Carol. In a Different Voice: Philosophical Theory and Women's Development. Cambridge, MA: Harvard University Press, [1983] 2003.

Haller, Miriam. "'Unwürdige Greisinnen'. 'Ageing Trouble' im literarischen Text." Alter und Geschlecht. Repräsentationen, Geschichten und Theorien des Alter(n)s. Ed. Heike Hartung. Bielefeld: transcript, 2005. 45–63.

Hartung, Heike. "Alter und Geschlecht im kulturellen Diskurs. Zur Doppelmoral in Alternsnarrativen und Altersbildern./Age and Gender in Cultural Discourse. The Double Standard in the Narratives and Images of Aging. "Die Kraft des Alters/Aging Pride. Ed. Stella Rollig, Sabine Fellner. Wien: Verlag für Moderne Kunst, 2017. 256–274.

"In-between." Oxford English Dictionary Online. December 2022 update. 24 January 2023. https://www.oed.com/.

Kunow, Rüdiger. "Old Age and Globalization." A Guide to Humanistic Studies in Aging. What Does it Mean to Grow Old? Ed. Thomas R.

Cole, Ruth E. Ray, Robert Kastenbaum. Baltimore: The Johns Hopkins University Press, 2010. 293–318.

Kunow, Rüdiger. "Postcolonial theory and old age: an explorative essay." Journal of Aging Studies 39 (2016): 101–108.

Leibing, Annette. "Alzheimer's disease, the person within, and death in life." Thinking about Dementia. Culture, Loss, and the Anthropology of Senility. Ed. Annette Leibing, Lawrence Cohen. New Brunswick: Rutgers University Press, 2006. 240–268.

Leibing, Annette. "Dementia in the making. Early detection and the body/brain in Alzheimer's disease." Popularizing Dementia. Public Expressions and Representations of Forgetfulness. Ed. Aagje Swinnen, Mark Schweda. Bielefeld: transcript. 2015. 275–294.

Maierhofer, Roberta, and Nicole Haring. "Feminism, gender, and age." The Bloomsbury Handbook to Ageing in Contemporary Literature and Film. Ed. Sarah Falcus, Heike Hartung, Raquel Medina. London: Bloomsbury, 2023.155-166.

Maierhofer, Roberta. "Feminism and Aging in Literature." Encyclopedia of Gerontology and Population Aging. Ed. Danan Gu, Matthew E. Dupre. Cham: Springer 2019. 1–8.

Maierhofer, Roberta. Salty Old Women. Frauen, Altern und Identität in der amerikanischen Literatur und Kultur. Essen: Blaue Eule, 2003.

Raja, Ira. "Nation and ageing: Mother India's mutable body." The Bloomsbury Handbook to Ageing in Contemporary Literature and Film. Ed. Sarah Falcus, Heike Hartung, Raquel Medina. London: Bloomsbury, 2023. 239–254.

Rajan-Rankin, Sweta. "Race, embodiment and later life: Re-animating aging bodies of color." Journal of Aging Studies 45 (2018): 32–38.

Sahlins, Marshall. What Kinship Is ... And Is Not. Chicago: The University of Chicago Press, 2013.

Scholz, Sylka and Andreas Heilmann, eds. Caring Masculinities? Männlichkeiten in der Transformation kapitalistischer Wachstumsgesellschaften. München: oekonom, 2019.

Sontag, Susan. "The Double Standard of Aging." The Saturday Review September 23, 1972: 29–38

Tholen, Toni. "Narrating the Modern Relation between Masculinity and Care. Perspectives on a Transdisciplinary Problem." Internationales Archiv für Sozialgeschichte der deutschen Literatur 43.2 (2018): 387–402.

Thompson, Edward H. *Men, Masculinities, and Aging: The Gendered Lives of Older Men*. Lanham, MD: Rowman & Littlefield, 2019.

Timms, Emily. "Postcolonial ageing studies: Racialization, resistance, re-imagination." The Bloomsbury Handbook to Ageing in Contemporary Literature and Film. Ed. Sarah Falcus, Heike Hartung, Raquel Medina. London: Bloomsbury, 2023. 225–238.

Tronto, Joan. C. Caring Decmocracy. Markets, Equality, and Justice. New York: New York University Press, 2013.

Urry, John. Mobilities. Cambridge: Polity Press, 2007.

Urry, John. Sociology beyond Societies: Mobilities for the Twenty-first Century. London: Routledge, 2000.

Vedder, Ulrike. "Literarische Altersbilder und ihre Geschlechterordnung." Alter und Geschlecht. Soziale Verhältnisse und kulturelle Repräsentationen. Ed. Elisabeth Reitinger, Ulrike Vedder, and Pepetual Mforbe Chiangong. Wiesbaden: Springer, 2018. 187–201.

Weston, Kath. Families We Choose: Lesbians, Gays, Kinship. New York: Columbia University Press, 1991.

Woodward, Kathleen, ed. Figuring Age: Women, Bodies, Generations. Bloomington: Indiana University Press, 1999.

Male Ageing and Migrancy
sevā and the Indian Diaspora in the US

Rüdiger Kunow

Introduction

In this chapter I would like to bring together two signature experiences of our time, population ageing and migration. Both phenomena are well-known but have not often been seen as in any way connected. In 2005, in a much-quoted statement, Shelley Fisher Fishkin spoke of the "proverbial migrant" (24) and both this figure and the mobility for which it stands have been haunting literary and cultural studies for some time now. But that emblematic person has mostly been imagined as young or at least as somehow "ageless." After all, it seems to be part of the eternal order of things that the young are mobile whereas older people either stay or are left behind. In such a scheme, ageing and old age are seen as the local other, the leftover, in quite a literal sense, of global migration. I think this is and has always been a misconception; it is a misconception especially today, as capital-driven globalization has over the last 50 years "mobilized" people of all ages in hitherto unprecedented ways. Recent data from the United Nations Department of Economic and Social Affairs indicate that an estimated 12.2 percent of all global migrants are 65 and older (DESA, Migration Data Porta, update Jan. 2021). In addition, the first generations of (often male) labour migrants that once came in great numbers to the United States (and other countries of the Global North) as unskilled labourers have been getting old. Not only are they getting old far away from "home," they are also ageing in ways that are vastly different from the "home" ways.¹ Millions with various social and cultural backgrounds thus not only spend most of their lives living between cultures, they also grow old between cultures. What this means is that at some point in their life course they will have to contend with the problem of how and where to age best at the crossroads of intercultural and intergenerational differences. For this reason, old age does matter in migration, in multiple, complicated and even contradictory ways, and it is the purpose of this essay to trace some of these ways and to promote *a multi-generational understanding of migration*.

Putting "age" (back) into our debates about migrancy requires, inter alia, that we develop a sustained focus on a number of constellations, in both the Global South and North, in which the mobility of older people, real or imaginary, requires changes in our understanding of both migration and later life. Literary texts offer important reference points for such a project, not least because they are usually not held in thrall by epistemologies of power or practicability but are concerned instead with "repairing what has been broken in the relation between individuals and worlds" (Berlant 2009: 1090). There is no space here to present a panoramic view of literary representations of the nexus of old age and migrancy from various cultural contexts. In what follows, I will focus instead on one complex and well-documented example, the literature in English of the subcontinental Indian community in the United States which speaks about and for the age-migrancy-nexus.

Such a choice justifies itself on a number of grounds. First and most obviously, intellectuals with a subcontinental background such as Arundhati Roy, Gayatri Spivak, or Nobel Prize winner Amartya Sen

---

[1] In response to this situation, "culture sensitive" care facilities for ageing migrants have sprung up all over the Global North. These facilities are run by staff who speak the migrants' language and are familiar with cultural traditions such as religiously mandated dietary restrictions. They include institutions such as the Paulo Agabayani Retirement Village set up by the United Farm Workers for aging Filipino field workers near Delano, CA, or Nikkei Manor for Japanese seniors in Seattle, WA. These institutions have often been praised as a solution for the quandary of ageing "away from home". On the ambivalences of this perspective see Kunow 2016, esp. 104–106.

have been taking a leading role in the conversation in the academy but also the general public about migration, diasporic life and issues of political and cultural advocacy.[2] Secondly, the migration of people from the Indian subcontinent to the United States and Canada since the 1960s has produced a rich and distinct body of literary texts committed to exploring what it means to be living (and ageing) between two cultures. Almost all of this literature is written in English, is therefore widely accessible and has become recognized even in the popular culture of the United States.[3] The most visible author here is of course Salman Rushdie who moved to the United States in the 1990s, began to write pieces for the *New York Times* and has become a vigorous advocate of US culture and (sometimes) politics. Aside from him, a sizable number of other writers, many of them women, have also gained popular and critical attention.[4] South Asian American women writers have performed cultural work as "interpreters of transnationalism" (Schlote 2006) in their representations of the gendered traumas of identity crises and gender discrimination in both traditional Indian and US-American culture. As Inderpal Grewal argues, "The immigrant novel written by or about the 'Asian' or 'Asian American' woman . . . revealed a great deal about the transnational circulation of knowledges of nation, race, and gender" and, as I hope to show, also age (2005: 62).

---

2   I am referring here *inter alia* to Roy's *Public Power in the Age of Empire* (2004), Spivak's *Critique of Postcolonial Reason* (1999) and Sen's *The Argumentative Indian* (2005). But see also Robert JC Young "Postcolonial remains." New Literary History 43, (2012): 19–42.

3   On this development and also the possible price to be paid for Indians writing in English see Salman Rushdie's "Introduction" to *The Vintage Book of Indian Writing 1947–1997*.

4   Aside from the boom of Bollywood movies, Indian writers in the US have attained national popularity as scripts for movies. Chitra Banerjee Divakaruni's novel *The Mistress of Spices* (1997), for example, when turned into a film, became a major box-office success. This development has recently been critically reviewed, for example in interventions from scholars positioned in India; cf. here the recent overview in *Diasporic Inquiries into South Asian Women's Narratives*, ed. Shilpa Dithota Bhat. Lanham: Lexington Books, 2020.

The third reason for the focus in this chapter on literature produced by Indians living in the United States (non-resident Indians, or "NRIs") is that in its representations of the age-migrancy nexus this literature engages with a clearly circumscribed and religiously sanctioned, non-Western mandate regulating the understanding of age and the relations between generations. Going back to the sacred Hindu text, the *Bhagavad Gita* (2nd century BCE), the Sanskrit term *sevā* designates a complex of services and respect due to older men, especially inside the family, during the *sannyasa*, the fourth and last stage of renunciation of worldly pursuits within the Hindu system of age-based life stages (https://slife.org/s annyasa/). Such services would include material and symbolic gestures, ranging from serving food, combing hair and washing, to touching an elder's feet as a sign of respect (Cohen 115, 180, Lamb 32–33). The principal recipient of *sevā* is the family patriarch.[5] In this way, *sevā* became an integral part, if not the idealized emblem, of male ageing in Indian families. And aside from introducing a temporality of ageing which in its emphasis on acceptance, even renunciation is markedly different from the current western model of forever active "best agers," *sevā* also invokes an alternative economy of belonging inside the family. In the context of the Indian migration to the West since the 1960s the moral imperatives of *sevā* came to interact and intersect with competing concepts of late life, most obviously those produced by Western modernity. Literary texts and other cultural practices such as photographs and films enter public conversation as case studies or case histories of this confrontation.

Male Migration and Indian Family Life: A Fictional Portrait

Jhumpa Lahiri's fictions are particularly relevant for the present inquiry because they trace the "predicaments of the hyphen" (Visweswaran 1993:

---

5   Interestingly, a similar concept can be found in Muslim cultures and the figure of the *murabbi*. For an extensive discussion of the changing positionality of this figure in migratory contexts see Gardner 2002.

301): the problems of lived interculturality for Indian migrants to the US, in a migration or rather post-migration setting, with a sustained emphasis on intergenerational relations. Lahiri, whose debut collection *Interpreter of Maladies* won the 2002 Pulitzer Prize for fiction, is a widely acclaimed writer whose texts do not simply lament the cultural losses incurred by migration. Instead, they are meant to perform "simultaneous translations in both directions, of characters who literally dwell in two separate worlds" (Lahiri qtd. in Kumar 2002: 178). Many of her characters are shown at a crucial moment of their diasporic lives, as they are beginning to distance themselves from their parents' beliefs and traditions, without rejecting them wholesale, and negotiate new social and cultural subject positions, or what Lahiri calls an "amalgamated domain". "My writing," she says, "is less a response to my parents' cultural nostalgia, and more an attempt to forge my own amalgamated domain" (179). Nevertheless, cultural nostalgia is everywhere in her writing but often to be found at unexpected moments and not only among older people.[6]

A good example of all this is the short story collection *Unaccustomed Earth* (2008; the title is an echo of Nathaniel Hawthorne's "Custom House" chapter of *The Scarlet Letter*), which debuted as number 1 on the *New York Times* bestseller list. In the title story Ruma, a well-to-do NRI suburbanite married to an American hedge-fund manager expects a visit from her ageing widowed father. Ruma's father, a first-generation immigrant and now retired pharmaceutical company executive, has spent his retirement traveling. This is his first visit to his daughter's suburban life, and it is overshadowed by the death of his wife. After giving birth to a son, Akash, she decided to give up her career at a law firm and become a homemaker instead. The story is told from the two alternating subject positions of Ruma and her father, allowing an insight into the secret thoughts of both protagonists. So we learn that Ruma's

---

[6] Meanwhile, her interests and her writing have taken a decidedly different turn: *Dove mi trovo* (2018) is her first novel in Italian. Lahiri is proving an important point in debates about diasporic literature, namely that authors from such backgrounds are not at all restricted to dwelling on issues connected with migration.

father has a new love interest which he is afraid to reveal to his daughter, while she is apprehensive about her father's age and the demands Indian traditions might bring. She looks at him as the unchanged embodiment of Indian paternalism even in his adopted country:

> Ruma feared that her father would become a responsibility, an added demand ... It would mean an end to the family she'd created on her own ... She couldn't imagine tending to her father, serving the meals her mother used to prepare. Still, not offering him a place in her home made her feel worse. It was a dilemma Adam [her husband] didn't understand. (7)

Lahiri organizes her narrative around a key issue in Indian culture, intergenerational relations and obligations, more precisely the moving of older parents into the households of their children, and the concomitant obligations of *sevā*. What frightens Ruma is exactly this, that the generational relations grounded in the Indian tradition of sevwould be transplanted into her American life, adding new obligations to an already challenging routine with a demanding child and another one to be born soon. As it turns out, her apprehensions are unfounded, as her father has no intention of moving in with his daughter. Although *sevā* is part of his considerations, he has decided to opt for independent older life, more along American lines: "[H]is wife," he muses, "would not have thought twice about moving in with Ruma ... The isolation of living in an American suburb ... had been more solitude than she could bear" (29). But this was not for him: "He did not want to live in the margins of his daughter's life" (53). And going back to India is not an option, either. In the course of a successful business career he has assimilated to US culture and customs more than his daughter had realised. His outer appearance is a first indication of that. When they meet, Ruma is "struck by the degree to which her father resembled an American in his old age." (11)

As the story unfolds, Lahiri stages the encounter between two generations of Indian migrants as a complex, highly gendered play of open declarations and secret assumptions, of competing cultural scripts and commitments, assimilations and diasporic identities. Thus, in spite of the comforts of her upper middle-class life, Ruma is haunted by a sense of failure, even of cultural betrayal, as her Indian cultural heritage seems to be slipping away from her. Food is of crucial importance here:

> She [Ruma] had spent the past two days cooking [in preparation for the father's visit], and the labor had left her exhausted. When she cooked Indian food for Adam [her husband], she could afford to be lazy. ... Her mother had never cut corners; even in Pennsylvania she had run her household as if to satisfy a mother-in-law's fastidious eye. (22)[7]

But her mother is dead now and her Indian ways of life cannot be reenacted by her daughter. Aside from cooking, Ruma is also losing the ability to speak her native Bengali[8] and worst of all, she cannot pass her language and cultural heritage on to her son Akash: "In spite of her efforts he [Akash] was turning into the sort of American child she was always careful not to be, the sort that horrified and intimidated her mother: imperious, afraid of eating things," (23).

India, together with the cultural traditions of Hindu culture, remains clearly separated from the everyday life of the characters by a distance that they are both aware of, a past that is irrevocably lost and that can be conjured up at best as a receding horizon of reference of which the characters become aware, on certain occasions, almost in spite of themselves. This is not a tale of two cultures, nor of the rewards

---

7   Food is a crucial everyday praxis as migrants seek to organize their diasporic life. I have discussed this at some length in "Eating Indian(s): Food, Representation, and the Indian Diaspora in the United States" (2003, 151–75).

8   Like her fictional character, Lahiri is very much concerned about losing her native language: "Because of my divided identity, or perhaps by disposition ... I consider myself an incomplete person, in some way deficient. Maybe there is a linguistic reason – the lack of a language to identify with." She grew up with Bengali as her mother tongue but has never been able to identify with it: "I was ashamed of speaking Bengali and at the same time I was ashamed of feeling ashamed" (qtd. In Hardley).

of living a model minority life.[9] Instead, different responses to the experience of migrancy and their aftermath have a way of seeping into the narrative, and they are mediated along generational lines, but not in the expected way. In "Unaccustomed Earth," it is the children of Indian immigrants who lose the sense of connectedness with the culture their parents had brought with them to the US but that loss occurs without causing emotional troubles: "It was one of the many habits of her upbringing which she'd shed in her adult life, without knowing when or why" (14). Here, as in many Lahiri stories, intercultural differences are re-coded in terms of intergenerational differences. Ruma's father is keenly aware of the rewards and losses of diasporic life[10], and with a distinct tone of resignation, he realizes that the widening gap that separates him from his daughter cannot be bridged and that his migratory background is not just passed on to the next generation: "The more the children grew, the less they had seemed to resemble either parent—they spoke differently, dressed differently, seemed foreign in every way, from the texture of their hair to the shapes of their feet and hand" (54). The realization of this distance is painful for both Ruma and her father, but this is not the cause for drama, it is the way life goes.

In the intimate framework of the nuclear family, of a father-daughter relationship, Lahiri stages a role reversal between genders and generations. *Sev* is not an option here, not even an issue. Ruma's father does

---

9 On the concept of the Indian "model minority", its history and its vicissitudes see Venugopal 2021. There is a hidden economic argument behind the relative prosperity of Indian immigrants: In 2019, immigrant households had a median income of $132,000, compared to $64,000 and $66,000 for all immigrant and U.S.-born households, respectively (https://www.migrationpolicy.org/article/indian-immigrants-united-states-2019).

10 To help identify the position I am writing from I want to mention that my reading here is resourced by Rushdie's well-known reflections on the abiding power of the "imaginary homelands, Indias of the mind" (10) but more especially by James Clifford's *Routes: Travel and translation in the late twentieth century* (1999) and Pheng Cheah's *What is a world? On postcolonial literature as world literature* (2016). Cf. also my "Postcolonial theory and old age: An explorative essay" (2016).

not expect it, and Ruma is not prepared to give it. Throughout she remains insecure about her status as the daughter of Indian immigrants, and has been so for quite some time, as her deceased mother had noted: "You are ashamed of yourself, of being Indian, that is the bottom line" (26), and her marriage to an American had not been able to change that. It falls to Ruma's father to try and stabilize her identity by invoking the values and gender roles of US, not Indian, culture. His own wife had been totally bound by traditional Indian gender roles, but now he tries to encourage his daughter to follow American ways. When Ruma explains to him that she wants to remain a mother and a housewife — a role sanctified, according to Cohen (1998: 119–120), by the traditional Joint Indian Family — he raises objections which have their roots in US achievement culture, including its veiled ageisms: "Now is the time for you to be working, building your career" (36). In a long conversation with his daughter he tries to encourage her to plan her life on the American model of the successful career woman with its own inbuilt bias against women's age. When Ruma explains she wants to see her children grow up, he points to the rigid rules of business: "Then what will you do? . . . You will be over forty. It may not be so simple." (36) As is often the case in Lahiri's fictions, the difference of opinions between generations will not mature into an open conflict. As the story ends, Ruma's father is at the airport for departure, and Ruma returns to her homemaker routine. In this story, and especially in the subject positions which it organizes, Lahiri subverts widely held assumptions about the age-migrancy-nexus by a realignment of subject positions: it is Ruma's father who in his late life has found a way to strike a balance between the demands of Indian traditions and of the culture of his adopted country, while his daughter is caught in an uneasy and unsatisfying "in between." "In-betweenness" is of course a loaded term in postcolonial critique, but Lahiri's approach to this condition is far removed from Bhabha-style celebrations of this condition.

Transnational Realities and new Global Frameworks for Ageing Indians

Overall, it would be tempting to read this story in terms of postcolonial critique and its orthodoxies as an exploration of hybridity, third spaces, or contestation. Such a reading would be even more suggestive because of the autobiographical overtones. But Lahiri and her text do not follow the well-traveled postcolonial conceptual routines focused on "inter cultural and outer national social and political processes" (Gilroy 1994: 19) or "the emergence of the interstices – the overlap and displacement of domains of difference" (Bhabha 1994: 2). Rather, Lahiri here, as elsewhere in her stories, presents a carefully circumscribed world where intergenerational relations are crosshatched by conflicting cultural allegiances. They can be read as the fictional *mise-en-scene* of the age-migrancy-nexus and the new relationalities emerging in the aftermath of Indian migration to the United States.

In the world outside fiction, these cultural politics have stimulated a wave of late-life migration from India to the US, as NRIs are asking their ageing parents still living in India to join them. Economic considerations are not important in this context. Subcontinental immigrants are eligible for SSI (supplementary security income), but most children are both willing and able to support their parents financially anyway. Rather, this late-life migration is the expression of a deep sense of cultural unease among affluent Indians who have "made it" in the US. This unease centers around intergenerational relations and the cultural tradition of the Great Indian Joint Family (GIJF) and its transgenerational bonds of love and support.[11] According to GIJF ideals, caring for ageing parents is the

---

11 My argument here is indebted to Sarah Lamb's rich and theoretically sophisticated anthropological work which explores the intersection of culture and social science. Aside from *Aging and the Indian Diaspora* see also "Assemblages of Care and Personhood: "Successful Ageing" across India and North America" (2020) where she offers a detailed account of how "globalizing ageing models are increasingly circulating within India" (330). She also notes that "diverse and often contradictory models for living and ageing" are circulating in the transnational and transcultural spaces opened by migration (333).

children's *dharma*, their moral-religious duty, and so the transnational dispersal of Indian families is cause for anxieties, often intensely felt. These anxieties have been repeatedly taken up (and reinforced) by Indian popular culture, notably by Bollywood. In *Baghban* (2003), for example, the protagonist, Raj Malhotra (played by Bollywood legend Amitabh Bachchan), offers the conventional wisdom on the GIJF: "life does not move up like a ladder. Life grows like a tree. . . If a father can help his son to take the first step in life, then why can't that son help his father the last step of his life?" (qtd. In Lamb 2009: 43–44).[12]

The answer to that question lies in the new transnational realities of Indian life, realities which are dedicated to maintaining the arrangements essential for the moral integrity of families by bringing ageing parents to live with children and receive their *sevā* outside India but in an Indian milieu (Lamb 2009: 32–33, 206–235). As one NRI says about bringing his old father to the US: "culturally, I cannot imagine it any other way." (Lamb 2009: 209) Thus, bringing one's elders to the US can be read as a *reparative move*, an attempt to rescue intergenerational relations and especially the entitlements of male elderhood in the new international and intercultural framework created by capitalist globalization and world-wide labour markets. This reparative gesture is often mirrored on the elders' side by an equally restorative impulse. As Sarah Lamb has shown, Indian elders view their own late-life migration to the United States as an effort to stem the tide of Americanization, to assist their children in keeping attuned to their Indian roots and, even more importantly, their grandchildren. Says one of them: "in the Indian way I looked after the grandchildren—one of the greatest joys. [and after a great pause, he added, wistfully] But then the grandkids grow up and go the American way" (qtd. Lamb 2009: 217). And Lahiri's story has both characters reflect on the seemingly inevitable Americanization of Ruma's son. Late-life migration to the US can thus be understood as a way of "claiming culture," endowing older Indians with a new role

---

12   The tree metaphor is deeply rooted in Indian cultural memory, it goes back to Sanskrit narratives such as the *Bhagavad Gita* and is also often invoked to idealise material dependencies (Cohen 1998: 104–106).

and a new status: they are not elderly migrants, they are migrant elders, custodians of traditions and gate-keepers to the right life prescribed by Hinduism and Indian cultural traditions.[13]

But the opposite is also true: a still small but growing number of Indians are deciding to forego the comforts and privileges of *sevā* in favor of other privileges imported from Western ways of late life. In the context of the burgeoning Indian middle-class, new retirement facilities have emerged all over India, first in the southern states but now also around big cities in the North. Some sources say that the current demand is for 3 million units. They are part of the fast-growing senior living industry which caters to the needs and wishes of a growing cohort of 60+ Indians.[14] Their senior lifestyle is characterized not, as might be expected from the perspective of *sevā*, by neglect or abandonment but by new and alluring creature comforts modeled on the West. Unsurprisingly, perhaps, there is a strong class (and in the Indian context also a caste) index to these new forms of living. Only people of the upper middle classes/castes can afford to live a Western-style late life.[15] The reasons for choosing this way of living, most often a choice made by men, are no different from the motives of seniors living in US retirement communities: safety, companionship, independence (Desai 2019). The growing demand for such facilities is the indirect and often unintended result of the continuing wave of migration and the resultant disintegration of GIJF.

---

13   A similar argument has been made by Katy Gardner in her study of Bangla Deshi elders in London (Gardner, Katy. *Age, Narrative and Migration: The Life Course and Life Histories of Bengali Elders in London*. Oxford: Berg, 2002).

14   All this is part of a changing demography. The numbers of Indians 65 and older are expected to grow from ca. 76 million to 173 million in the next five years alone. Estimates of future demand are often described in terms of market opportunities (https://www.tomorrowmakers.com/retirement-planning/living-home-versus-living-retirement-home-india-article).

15   There are only very few facilities for the less wealthy. HelpAge India operates 6 homes across the country. Ashima Saini, Director of Resource Development at HelpAge says "Our homes are free of cost for the residents. We sometimes charge a nominal fee for healthcare services, but only if the residents can afford it" (Desai 2019).

Although the quality of these facilities for senior life will vary as largely as the financial resources of their residents, the trend toward a fundamental change in the life circumstances of older Indians is unmistakable. Ten years ago, the emergence of Western-style retirement homes was still heralded as a quite astonishing feature by an Indian quarterly:

> While retirement homes for the elderly are commonplace in the US, they are a new, and growing, phenomenon in India. Fountains tumble in manicured gardens. Gray haired retirees shuffle along on afternoon walks. Inside the activity center, card players pair up in the early evening. And elderly spectators gather as a ping pong rally heats up. While it may seem like a Florida retirement village with its leisurely pace, this one is located two hours south of New Delhi in the Indian state of Rajasthan. And the 600-unit complex has a few features you won't find in Ft. Lauderdale. ("Western Style Retirement Homes")

The reference to Florida in this article certainly was no accident. The retirement homes for the wealthy signal, local variations aside, the advent of the Western concept and praxis of late life in India, and they are there to stay. This is not an Indian idiosyncrasy but marks a global trend, a trend that is unsurprisingly heralded by pundits of capitalist globalization. A few years ago, *Forbes* magazine, with a special reference to India, offered a celebratory account of how the "globalization of senior living" offered unlimited new opportunities for investments and revenue.

Conclusion

In this paper, I have tried to offer brief reflections on how "age," more particularly male age, figures in the context of migration (also broadly understood). The present argument marks a departure from previous reflections, including my own, in that it no longer focuses on Euro-American older people and their trials and tribulations, but instead on people from the Indian subcontinent and the multiple determinations at work at the intersection of two of their trajectories: that of the human life course in time and also the courses across the global manifold. Literary texts like the one discussed above may help in creating a better understanding of this broader perspective by presenting a cultural imaginary of these trajectories and their impact on migrant life across multiple generations, as in Lahiri's tentative representation of *the ur-scene* of the Indian ideal of good ageing, the moving in with the children in the name of *sevā*. Here as elsewhere over the last decades it has become increasingly clear that migrancy is putting not only different cultures, but different cultures of age and ageing, into contact and contestation with one another. Lamb is speaking here of "deterritorialized images" of a good old age for men intersecting with one another (2020: 322). Lamb's notion of deterritorialization reflects a situation in which cultural traditions and ideals of a good late life are becoming "traveling cultures" (Clifford 1997: 17–46) moving from the Global North to the South, as the growing popularity of the Western concept of age for emerging middle-classes in India but also the world over makes abundantly clear. Sometimes, as with the Indian diaspora in the United States, this movement also goes in the opposite direction. Not only do ageing people migrate, "age" itself, as an idea and ideal, has become migratory. Uncoupled from the cultural locations and traditions which have sustained it, it can traverse the wide spaces created by capitalist globalization both from South to North and inversely, all the while recruiting people into its framework of expectations and obligations.

What the present argument, in its combination of literary and cultural-critical analysis, has furthermore shown is that the age-migrancy nexus can also present theoretical challenges. Our overall understanding of migration is often eventual, guided by what I would here call a "cultural politics of the instant," the moments when migrants actively enter different places and cultures. But "age" is a longitudinal idea and ideal which spans generations, and as the Lahiri story has reminded us, its multigenerational norms and prospects impact even those who are far from being old. What the age-migrancy-nexus thus adds to the presentist eventual view of migrancy is a sense of what Fredric Jameson in a different context called a cultural "politics of duration" (Jameson 13), a duration characterized not only by the immediate co-presence of cultural others but also by the never-ending, inchoate and inconclusive processes of mapping personal experience onto different and competing cultural frameworks of late life.

Works Cited

Berlant, Lauren. "Eve Sedgwick, Once More." *Critical Inquiry* 15 (2009): 1089–1091.

Bhabha, Homi. K. *The Location of Culture*. New York: Routledge, 1994.

Bhagban. Directed by Ravi Chopra. Produced by B. R. Chopra. B.R. Films, 2003.

Bhat, Shilpa Daithota. *Diasporic Inquiries into South Asian Women's Narratives*. Lanham: Lexington Books, 2020.

Chan, John. "Mass protests in China point to sharp social tensions." 1 November 2004. https://www.wsws.org/en/articles/2004/11/chin-n 01.html.

Cheah, Pheng. *What is a world? On postcolonial literature as world literature*. Durham, London: Duke University Press, 2016.

Clifford, James. *Routes: Travel and Translation in the Late Twentieth Century*. Cambridge, MA: Harvard University Press, 1997.

Cohen, Lawrence. *No Aging in India: Alzheimer's, the Bad Family, and Other Modern Things*. Berkeley: University of California Press, 1998.

Desai, Ketaki. "Why these seniors prefer old-age homes." *Times of India* 24 April 2019. https://timesofindia.indiatimes.com/home/sunday-t imes/why-these-seniors-prefer-old-age-homes/articleshow/69028 391.cms.

Fisher-Fishkin, Shelley. "Crossroads of Cultures: The Transnational Turn in American Studies – Presidential Address to the American Studies Association. 12 November 2004." *American Quarterly*, 51.1 (2005): 17–57.

Gardner, Katy. *Age, Narrative and Migration: The Life Course and Life Histories of Bengali Elders in London*. Oxford: Berg, 2002.

Gilroy, Paul. *The Black Atlantic: Modernity and Double Consciousness*. Cambridge: Cambridge University Press, 1993.

Grewal, Inderpal. *Transnational America: Feminism, Diaspora, Neoliberalisms*. Durham: Duke University Press, 2005.

Grewal, Inderpal. "Reading and Writing the South Asian Diaspora: Feminism and Nationalism in North America." *Our Feet Walk the Sky: Women of the South Asian Diaspora*. San Francisco: Aunt Lute Books, 2008. 226–36.

Hardley, Tessa. "In Other Word by Jhumpa Lahiri: A Review" *The Guardian* 30 January 2016. https://www.theguardian.com/books/2016/jan/30/in-other-words-jhumpa-lahiri-review-learning-italian.

Jameson, Fredric. "An American Utopia." *An American Utopia: Dual Power and the Universal Army*. New York: Verso, 2016. 1–104.

Kumar, Amitava. *Bombay – London – New York*. New York: Routledge, 2002.

Kunow, Rüdiger. "Eating Indian(s): Food, Representation, and the Indian Diaspora in the United States." *Eating Cultures: The Poetics and Politics of Food*. Ed. Tobias Döring, Markus Heide, and Susanne Mühleisen. Heidelberg: C. Winter, 2003. 151–75.

Kunow, Rüdiger. "Postcolonial theory and old age: An explorative essay." *Journal of Ageing Studies* 39 (2016): 101–108.

Lahiri, Jhumpa. *Unaccustomed Earth*. New York: Alfred Knopf, 2008.

Lamb, Sarah. *Ageing and the Indian Diaspora: Cosmopolitan families in India and abroad*. Bloomington: Indiana University Press, 2009.

Lamb, Sarah. "Assemblages of Care and Personhood: "Successful Ageing" across India and North America." *Caring for Old Age: Perspectives from South Asia*. Ed. Christiane Brosius and Roberta Mandoki. Heidelberg: Heidelberg University Publishing, 2020. 322–336.

Migration Data Portal. "Older persons and migration. Last updated on 2 November 2020." https://migrationdataportal.org/themes/older-persons-and-migration.

Roy, Arundhati. *Public Power in the Age of Empire*. New York: Seven Stories Press, 2004.

Rushdie, Salman. *Imaginary Homelands: Essays and Criticism*. Islington: Granta Books, 1992.

Rushdie, Salman. "Introduction." *The Vintage Book of Indian Writing*. Ed. Salman Rushdie and Elizabeth West. London: Random House, 1997. Ix-xxii.

Schlote, Christiane. "Interpreters of Transnationalism: South Asian American Women Writers." *Amerikastudien/American Studies* 51.3 (2006): 387–409.

Schobert, Benjamin. "The Globalization of Senior Living" *Forbes* 25 February 2016. https://www.forbes.com/sites/benjaminshobert/2016/02/25/%C2%AD%C2%AD%C2%ADthe-globalization-of-senior-living/?sh=1496d14312fc.

Sen, Amartya. *The Argumentative Indian: Writings on Indian History, Culture and Identity*. London: Allen Lane, 2005.

Spivak, Gayatri Chakravorty. *A Critique of Postcolonial Reason: Toward a History of the Vanishing Present*. Cambridge, Mass.: Harvard University Press, 1999.

United Nations Department of Economic and Social Affairs. Migration Data Portal. Updated 20 January 2021. <https://migrationdataportal.org/?i=stock_abs_&t=2020>.

Venugopal, Arun. "The Notion of the Model Minority family in America." *The Takeaway* December 21, 2020. https://www.wnycstudios.org/podcasts/takeaway/segments/notion-model-minority-family-america.

Visweswaran, Kamala. "Predicaments of the Hyphen." *Our Feet Walk the Sky: Women of the South Asian Diaspora*. Ed. Women of South Asian Descent Collective. San Francisco: Aunt Lute Books, 1993. 301–12.

"Western Style Retirement Homes in India, A New Phenomenon." *Hinduism Today* 18 January 2010. <https://www.hinduismtoday.com/blogs-news/hindu-press-international/western-style-retirement-homes-in-india--a-new-phenomenon/9538.html>.

Young, Robert R. C. "Postcolonial remains." *New Literary History* 43 (2012): 19–42.

Masculinity, Aging, and Reversion
An Essay on Losing Direction

Annette Leibing

> "Tenho tão nítido o Brasil que pode ser, e há de ser, que me dói o Brasil que é."
> "I am so clear about the Brazil that can be, and that should be, that the Brazil that is hurts me."
> (attributed to anthropologist and politician Darcy Ribeiro [1922–1997])

The starting point for this essay is my impression that there is a general tendency – a directionality – in masculinity studies. This is, of course, a simplification of an increasingly diversified field. Yet an example for a common underlying narrative could be the title of feminist journalist Liz Plank's recent book *For the Love of Men* (2019), and the sub-title she chose, *From Toxic to a More Mindful Masculinity*. Here, what I call directionality starts with a narrative of insufficiency. The detected male 'defect', in such tales, needs to be pushed towards an improved masculinity in a future, in which men, through a reflexive act of conscientization, ideally accept other types of gender and themselves as equal in rights and, at the same time, improve their way of living gender. But what if this desired evolutive and emancipatory idea – from bad to better, from traditional to modern – gets turned around or even loses direction?

I am not talking here about recent discussions found in countries like Germany where a major wave of immigration has come from countries in which parts of the population do not acknowledge equal rights for women (or LBGT+ individuals) – which, of course, aren't fully acknowledged by many Germans, either. Complaints about sexist assaults of women (as in the 2015 New Year's Eve attacks in Cologne)[1], is not what this essay is primarily about, although parts of it can be read as such. Even though these sexual assaults of German women by men from Muslim backgrounds were considered by one local politician a *"momentary* breakdown of civilization" (*zeitweiliger Zivilisationsbruch*; emphasis added; see note 1), the evolutive direction from bad to better is generally not questioned. For many Germans, immigration-related sexism is a – momentary – step backward in an imagined local gender equality, but not a return in itself. Solutions like sexual education courses for immigrant Muslims (also in other countries, like Belgium) can be seen as vectors pushing into one direction – here towards a culture-bound 'better', 'modern' man. Yet, following Corrigan (2018), this kind of "educational fix", based on "educational positivism", is a naïve way of trying to change complex identitary issues, in this case, issues of belonging and citizenship, in which masculinity models are embedded.[2]

What I want to call *reversion*[3] (in line with masculinities) results in deeper changes in societies, affecting underlying structures and value-systems that are generally perceived by those critical to such changes as regression, backwardness, and devolution, and as involving dominant forces in society, like the way of doing politics. The fact that politics is

---

1   https://de.wikipedia.org/wiki/Sexuelle_%C3%9Cbergriffe_in_der_Silvesternacht_2015
2   On "Male citizenship" in so-called Western societies, see Dudink, Hagemann and Clark (2012).
3   Here 'reverse anthropology' comes to mind. This approach developed by Roy Wagner (2016 [1975]), means a radical change of perspective and, after Viveiros de Castro (2013: 477), "the art of determining the problems posed by each culture, not of finding solutions for the problems posed by our own". 'Reversion' in this essay is, first of all, the general feeling of fought-for value systems getting lost, and its consequences.

deeply gendered has been discussed by many scholars but, as Marx Ferree (2020) argues, this insight is rarely acknowledged. The author observes that "[g]ender (...) attaches the identifications of individuals, each with their own masculinity, femininity, sexuality, and nationality, to the postures leaders display, consciously or not, in the theater of democratic politics" (p. 899). In the specific case of reversion and masculinity, older men are practically absent from such narratives, as if while getting older, masculinity as an attribute fades away. This might be because masculinity is often associated with sexuality and performance, and aging men, in many societies, are more easily perceived as a-sexual (or, otherwise, as 'dirty old men') and as less performant (Kenny 2013).

It is the absence of old age in the following discussion on masculinity – the 'un-masculinity' so to say – that is the underlying issue, although this point will only be articulated towards the end of this text. And this absence is astonishing since powerful examples from current affairs are based on aging actors in politics. Examples are based on masculinity models many thought of as long overcome but that are on full display in countries like the US (a central figure being former president Trump, born in 1946) or Brazil (president Bolsonaro was born in 1955). In these places, the resurgence of "macho" role models, displayed in political enactments, are based on attributes linked to the young and aggressive, invulnerable body (and with the help of much younger wives in the case of the two politicians).

To make my point, I will provide, in the next section, a short and certainly incomplete narrative of political masculinities in current Brazil – at the time of writing this text situated specifically after the election of current president Jair Bolsonaro. This will be followed by a discussion of 'reversion' and its pitfalls as an analytical framework for certain masculinities, and, as a conclusion, I will highlight the aspect of aging within the chosen perspective.

Brazilian masculinities and 'obscene' current politics

For several years, Brazil had a leftist government lead by presidents Luis Inácio Lula da Silva (2003–2011), followed by his successor Dilma Rousseff (2011–2016). And although not all was perfect,[4] during this period, several important social programs were implemented. Some followed programs already established by the prior (social-democratic) Cardoso government (1995–2002), but an important number of new policies allowed even the most marginal and impoverished in the country to have better access to food, education, housing, and health, to a more dignified life (de Almeida 2005, Ansell 2011). Important laws protecting minorities against discrimination and violence were implemented (e.g., the 'Maria da Penha law' from 2006 targeting domestic violence against women)[5], but also more tolerant attitudes in general toward LBGT+ and other minorities were widely propagated (Machado 2016, Rodrigues 2021). Improved rights for LBGT+ individuals became firmly associated with the Lula/Roussef governments and, paradoxically, exploited as a sign of anomy by the opposition, which constructed a great part of its rhetoric on criticizing the, in their view, immoral new age. This reading of what some called an improvement (of rights) as a (re)turn towards anomy by far-right ideologists was, at least partially responsible for Bolsonaro's election (Cavalcanti 2017).[6]

---

4   See, for example, an analysis of recent Brazilian politics in https://www.youtube.com/watch?v=Aomyj6_KnKc. A major critique of the Lula/Roussef governments was the frenetic consumerism that went hand in hand with a financial empowerment of poorer Brazilians. The tragic side of this is captured in Fernando Bonassi's novel *Luxúria* (2016), in which hope, class-related hierarchies, desire and consumerism get entangled in a narrative of despair and destruction.
5   See https://www.bbc.com/news/magazine-37429051
6   In between the Lula/Roussef and the Bolsonaro governments, interim conservative president Michel Temer started already abolishing some of the protective institutions in Brazil, such as the SPM (*Secretaria para Políticas das Mulheres*) – the Secretary for Women's Rights, as he implanted his central political program that he called "the bridge to the future" (*uma ponte para o futuro*). Again 'directionality' captures historical changes: after Cavalcanti and Venerio (2017),

On January 1, 2019, Jair Bolsonaro became Brazil's president with a political agenda that, as Assis and Ogando (2018) observe,

> *marks the return of white, male, sexist and authoritarian politics in Brazil [...]* Although over the years, his rhetoric targeting women, the LGBTQI community and minorities grew increasingly obscene, it in no way upset his political career. In fact, it seemed to strengthen it.

Well-known examples that appeared regularly in the news and that did not affect the president's popularity, were, for instance, that

> [d]uring a parliamentary debate in 2014, he told MP Maria do Rosario that he would not rape her because she "was not worth it" [in terms of femininity]. The same year, he suggested during a TV interview that spanking a son who "showed signs" of being gay was the best way for parents to change his behaviour and assure he would grow up as a "proper" man. In 2017, he claimed that after having four sons, having a daughter was the result of a moment of "weakness". (Assis and Ogando 2018)

Among the multiple co-existing masculinity models in Brazil, those based on heteronormative and homophobic values, but also on an image of the man as the aggressive protector of women and children – modes that never were extinguished – became reinforced due to the growing number of people adhering to ultra-conservative groupings, but also because of a greater visibility and communication platforms of these groupings in recent years. Brazilians further became regularly exposed to media images showing the smiling president and his sons posing with firearms or, making with their fingers the sign of a pistol that became Bolsonaro's 'trademark'. These kinds of images were previously reserved for powerful bandits, who posed with weapons as a sign of their illegal leadership. Weapons here stand for a kind of masculinity

---

"there is really a bridge here – but a bridge to the past, especially because it leads directly back to the end of the 18th Century" comparable to the accumulation of capital among the rich elite in Europe (p. 158; my translation).

that not only goes hand in hand with a banalization of violence, but that has now also become a material and symbolic sign of *positive* power – however only when linked to the country's (contested) elite. Forms of violence found in poorer communities continued to be a problem that, at the same time, legitimated the elite's violence, as indicated by one solution that Bolsonaro propagated, namely, to arm the entire general population. In the opinion of the president and many of his followers, Brazilians had "the right" to defend themselves against bandits and to protect women and children, the sacred family (Noblat 2021, Kalil, Pinheiro-Machado and Scalco 2021). These necropolitics (Mbembe 2003) offered a philosophy allowing violence for all, bandits and non-bandits, although with an important new line drawn between good and bad kinds of predominantly male violence (cf. Rouse 2021 for the US).

The heterosexual, white, and armed Brazilian male, as an ideal, stands for the legitimization of violent attacks against and the killing of members of sexual minorities and members of religious groups other than fundamentalist evangelical and neo-Pentecostal groups (*The Guardian* 2021, Henning 2021). Homophobia especially, in line with the new Bolsonaro government – although historically not a new phenomenon in Brazil (e.g., Mott 2001) – was turned into a virtue. Fake statements made by the president that "homosexual fundamentalists" were brainwashing heterosexual children so they could "satisfy them sexually in the future", helped to change the moral meaning of homophobia. "I have [parliamentary] immunity to say: yes, I'm homophobic – and very proud of it," Bolsonaro declared in a filmed interview (Phillips 2020).

Like Bolsonaro, his cabinet members, many from fundamentalist evangelical churches,[7] showed a stark obsession with sexual themes and

---

7   In fact, it was the "BBB" (*boi, bala, bíblia* – bulls, bullets, bible) – meaning elected politicians and institutions linked to the powerful agri-food industry, to pro-weapon and military movements and to fundamentalist evangelical and neo-Pentecostal churches – that supported Bolsonaro's election. The majority of these groups were also involved in the impeachment of former president Dilma Roussef that many called a *coup d'état* (Cavalcanti 2017).

gender issues, which have occupied a large part of public discussions in recent years. Some topics were so absurd that it is hard to believe (for me) that anybody took them seriously: the Brazilian carnival was considered immoral and debauched, and it was suggested that this important cultural institution be abolished. The minister for women, family and human rights, who received her master's degree – as she finally admitted after a lot of public questioning – from her church and not from a university, defended the idea that baby boys should be dressed in light blue and girls in pink, manifesting her disapproval of more fluid gender definitions. She further plead for sexual abstinence before marriage, said that sex was something for leftist people, and sex between gay men she described as an aberration.[8] These churches had already become extremely powerful in Brazil before Bolsonaro's election and increasingly occupied strategic posts in radio, TV, and the government (deputies, senators, governors), so that even the previous leftist governments had been forced to make deals with evangelicals, in order to keep votes (Zanatta et al. 2016).

And when right after the elections, still in shock, I started talking to taxi drivers, clerks and other people one meets randomly when in Brazil – many told me they voted for Bolsonaro because, in their opinion, the previous leftist government's success was based on a loss of family values. The words of an older taxi driver who admitted that Bolsonaro might not be the ideal president, but who added that the previous situation had been intolerable, could stand for many of those I talked to: "Sodom and Gomorrah! My granddaughter is traumatized because she saw two men kissing each other in public, in plain view! One sees that all the time now, no shame at all – the family isn't worth anything anymore, the sacred family was destroyed by the PT [Lula's workers' party]."

---

8   See https://www.telesurenglish.net/news/Brazil-Minister-Says-Her-Masters-Degree-Granted-By-Her-Church-20190131-0027.html; and https://www.buzzfeednews.com/article/alexandreorrico/brazil-boys-wear-blue-girls-wear-pink-damares-alves (downloaded April 12, 2021)

These heteronormative family values are linked to another example of the changing – or 'inversion' (cf. Leibing 2001)[9] – of moralities. Recently, and paradoxically, well-known bandits and drug-dealers, declaring themselves evangelical, took part in this culture war and attacked members of Afro-Brazilian religions. Stories surged about "the rise in violent attacks by narcotics gangs claiming to be Christians – the so-called "drug traffickers of Jesus" (Bunker, Sullivan and Da Cruz 2017). The same story, though with different social actors, might be told about the president. When Bolsonaro first entered his residence in the *Palácio do Planalto*, in Brasilia, his wife Michelle, a member of an evangelical church, banned the famous paintings by Brazilian artist Djanira that were part of the palace, showing Afro-Brazilian deities, *orixás*. She had previously announced that she would also hide any reference to the Catholic church (Ferreira 2020).

A last example of the specific way politics (here of public health) and masculinity models are intertwined under the Bolsonaro government, can be found in responses to the Corona pandemic. Brazil has had one of the worst outcomes in terms of deaths worldwide as a result of the virus (607 000 in October 2021[10]). However, using masks is "coisa de viado" – something for fairies, gays – the president declared. He ostentatiously continued to shake hands and meet people without wearing a mask, and when he personally contracted COVID-19, he dismissed it as a "little flu", evoking his athletic condition. The recent exclamation by president Bolsonaro that Brazil is a "land of *maricas* [effeminate persons, sissies],"[11] referring to the fear of Brazilians preoccupied with uncon-

---

9   In this article about inversion (not reversion) I show how in some discourses (e.g., media, auto-biography) the traditional negative image of bandits in Rio de Janeiro gets renegotiated in positive, even heroic terms.

10 See https://www.google.com/search?client=firefox-b-d&q=brazil%27s+covid+deaths

11 Quote (our translation): "I am sorry for the deaths, but we all have to die one day. There is no sense in fleeing from this [COVID] reality, we have to stop being a country of *maricas* [sissies]." (Folha de São Paulo, 10 November 2020; https://www1.folha.uol.com.br/poder/2020/03/veja-o-que-bolsonaro-ja-disse-sobre-coronavirus-de-certa-histeria-a-fantasia-e-nerouse.shtml)

trolled COVID-19 numbers in the country, shows the denigration of men who care too much about health issues.[12]

A common stereotype of Brazilian men is the *machista*, although this notion needs, obviously, to be situated and relativized, depending on the context and the multiple masculinity models at work in this very heterogenous society. In terms of class, Heilborn and da Silva Cabral (2013), in their study of young Brazilians, gender and sexual practices, arrive at the conclusion that notions of gender equality, even in more educated parts of society, are less commonly accepted and less put into practice by men as compared to women. The authors write that even

> ... highly educated men demonstrate a weak adherence to the principles of gender equality, while their female peers show a remarkable flexibility in their attitudes toward and beliefs about sexuality. This unexpected disparity provokes us to suggest that there is a reinvigorated expression of gender inequality in a social stratum, in which the real progress of egalitarianism could easily be imagined (2013: 40).

However, a general growing acceptance of minorities and more fluid masculinity models in the country over time – especially under the Lula/Roussef governments – coincide with an increased organization and visibility of minority groups. Examples include the growing number of feminist organizations (e.g., Magalhães 2017), but also minority groups among older Brazilians which have lately become more mainstream, especially in the big urban centers, as for example the "gray pride" movement (cf. Henning 2021).

However, many of the issues that contrast so 'obscenely' with the previously growing rights and discourses of recognition and equality regarding minorities – for instance, the 'uncaring' male that is predominant in Bolsonaro's discourses – are not new phenomena. Now these issues have become condensed and reinforced as an overarching, but still

---

12 This denigration of male self-care needs to be seen nevertheless within a general high acceptance and desirability regarding health technologies and medications in the Brazilian population (Leibing, Engel, and Carrijo 2019).

contested, cultural model that reminds us of older models, in a new scenario for being male. As an example, Coelho, Giacomin and Firmo (2016) show in their study on older men, that most men – just like in other national contexts – often avoid receiving medical care, and link illness, as well as the aging body, to frailty and a loss of masculinity. Male self-care, like elsewhere, is typically enacted through practices located outside of the medical domain, although such activities – playing sports, sexual activity, or physical work in general – can easily get medicalized, when declining functionality is perceived as pathological (Katz and Marshall 2003, Medeiros et al. 2014, Pereira 2009). This reliance on activity, force, and performance as signs of masculinity was also part of the study by Brigeiro (2000) who introduced a category that was frequently employed by the older middle-class urban men he studied in Rio de Janeiro, nicknamed "the pyjamas". Different from the men Brigeiro observed and who regularly met in public spaces, a man described as a 'pyjama' is passive and stays mostly at home (imagined as wearing pyjamas and slippers all day); he is pitied and perceived as being dominated by his wife.

And in contrast to the often-encountered notion of older men as asexual, Debert and Brigeiro (2012), in their study, show that happening especially after the introduction of Viagra to the Brazilian market in the late 1990s, a major "eroticization of old age" took place, with a concomitant quasi-obligation – more for men than for women – of talking constantly about and ideally also having (heterosexual) sex in order to prove one's youthfulness.

In a recent study, Engel and Leibing (2022) observed that within such rather normative role models there was strong "identity tinkering" – a negotiation of what is (typically) male and female for the men who in that study were taking care of a dependent family member:

> In fact, there are various kinds of masculinity being disputed in these encounters that vary depending on the generation, but also on conflicting images of what it is to be a man. (...) As shown in many more recent masculinity studies (...; Santos and Rifiotis 2004), Brazilian men also adhere to multiple masculinities (...). In our two vignettes, men and women compose narratives in which there is

a tension between the desire to increase men's caring side, while trying equally to avoid creating too feminine behaviors, within a strong homophobic paradigm. (Engel and Leibing, 49)

Can the fact that among the many existing masculinity models in Brazil, the reinforcement of a certain uncaring, aggressive and heteronormative way of being male surged especially under Bolsonaro, be seen as a reversion?

Reversions

As I will argue in the following, the dramatic changes in Brazil, here illustrated by anecdotes[13] mirroring ultra-conservative and aggressive masculinity models, can be read as a re-enactment of values of the past that have been changed over time, often through major fights within feminist and human rights movements. Several scholars have thought about such historical and societal changes that I want, for the moment, to gather under the umbrella term 'reversion' (see for instance, Heinze and Vogel (2016) on German bio-farmers returning to conventional agriculture).[14] Reversion, after the Merriam-Webster dictionary (n.d.), touches on the aspect of "returning… to a former condition", which of course, is an illusion, since the past cannot be the present, even if elements (values, objects, fashions etc.) from the past may get re-acknowledged and re-enacted (from neo-Nazis to back-to-nature movements). Reversions like those seen in Brazil can be defined, at least for the moment, as referring to a "…lasting degradation of material, health, and cultural conditions in a formerly modernized society, a return to premodern forms of life and collective identities", as Rabkin (2018: 23) defines what he calls 'demodernization'.

---

13   For a deeper analysis of Brazil's recent history, see, for example, Carvalho (2018) and de Souza (2019a, 2019b).
14   Agriculture here is a targeted example, not one that necessarily shows a wider, societal change as in our definition of reversion.

In recent years, the concept of demodernization has been used by several authors, to describe a historical backwards movement – a "future in the past", after Rabkin and Minakov (2018). Rabkin, in his chapter "Undoing years of progress" about contemporary Russia, explains that "the clock appears to be turned back" and that "demodernization means regression on the scale of modernity." (2018: 17) This, of course, raises the question of what modernity exactly means, whether it is a single and universal entity, if we all should eventually get there, and whether modernity is something like a civilizing process that can be measured "on the scale [of modernity]".

Demodernization needs to be seen in context, explains Rabkin (2018: 17)); it can co-exist with modernization movements and is not restricted by national boundaries. The result, according to Rabkin, is leading, among other manifestations, to growing inequalities, a degradation of public services, a loss of tolerance regarding diversity, and a resurgence of irrational religion-like authoritarian manifestations. Alain Touraine (1997), in a similar vein, described demodernization as a process in which (in France) a market economy leads to de-socialization, de-politization and de-institutionalization.

'Decivilization' is a similar concept; it means a reverse movement of a civilizing process – although 'civilization' itself is rarely defined – characterized principally by the destruction of more elaborated attitudes (with reference to Norbert Élias), but also of community and institutions, leading to a "savagization" of societies.[15] As Aramini and Gulli (2016) observe, this process can be described at an individual micro-level, as an increasing lack of self-control – the authors use the psychoanalytical term of "pulsations" – that often results in a brutalization of and an increase of

---

15 "'Décivilisation' désigne donc d'une part le processus de destruction des communautés et d'autre part, le retournement du processus de civilisation, le reflux des comportements civilisés, le relâchement du contrôle des pulsions, le retour de la violence notamment, le retour de l'immédiateté et l'indifférence pour le présent et l'avenir, etc. 'Décivilisation' réfère donc aux incivilités, à l'accroissement de la délinquance, aux nouvelles formes de violences particulièrement barbares, aux multiples formes d' tournée contre soi telle que la toxicomanie, etc." (Aramini and Gulli 2016)

violence among people. On a societal level, this process is linked to the weakening of institutions that regulate how individuals live together (US American individualism is an example here). Contemporary neo-capitalism is considered a central vector for such processes, destroying and uniformizing cultures, ways of being and local psychologies – "devaluing values" (2016).

Bolsonaro's enactment of politics can be easily described in these terms: the interaction of a weakening of institutions and a social net, with an increase in violence,[16] the empowerment of a specific kind of religious world-making, and the destruction of more inclusive rights for minorities. The impact of such a 'turn' of masculinity models on many Brazilians, but by far not all, is also easy to show. However, since "devaluing values" as a general tendency depends on the observer, current affairs under Bolsonaro can easily be described as a "savagization" of Brazilian society; but also, as mentioned above, Bolsonaro's huge number of followers had the opposite impression, namely that former, leftist social politics resulted in anomy, in 'savagization'. Yet it is not so much the relativity of positions that is at stake, but more so the absolute moral and directional positions that impede further discussions.

In fact, regarding the specific case of gendered reversion, after Paternotte (2020) this kind of "backlash" perception is a misleading narrative of the history of extensive nets of value systems:

> This perspective generally regards sexual politics as a long march towards a bright future and imagines the latter as necessarily more progressive. Opponents would therefore come from the darkness of the past, and backlash is understood as a resistance to change. Erasing the complexity of politics, it assumes that history has a direction. (n. p.)

---

16   As we have seen, certain kinds of violence have gained a positive connotation in Brazil, so that some might perceive current measures like less restrictions to gun ownership and the symbolic and concrete campaigns in favor of its use, as limiting violence, although, it has been clearly shown that the contrary is the case (cf. Eisele 2021).

Along with history's problematic "direction", Paternotte argues that "the Right", "feminists", "LGBTQ+ individuals", among other groupings, are in such accounts often considered homogenous movements with unified positions and recommends that it would be better instead to pay more attention to diversity and frictions within and among groups. Marx Ferree makes a similar point, when she argues that "[b]ecause these [gendered] relations change, it is disingenuous to describe current assertions of masculine privilege in the language of patriarchy, *as if they were throwbacks to some prior age*. Instead, what appears is a new form of racialized hegemonic masculinity." (2021: 900; emphasis added).

A similar though even wider perspective is Bruno Latour's (2021) who, like other scholars working on the Anthropocene, sees 'decivilization' as caused by the gap between the world we live *in* and the planet we live *from*. Latour (2016) alerts us to the fallacy of thinking only in moralizing directions (e.g., backwards = negative, reactive, archaic). He suggests transcending the value-laden directivity in modernization and civilization processes located between two poles and suggests "attractor" as a third. By doing this, the directionality towards and away from modernity has vanished, which could then result in situating phenomena by looking at their (among others, ecological) *impact*, before attributing labels that immediately end discussions locked in morally opposed positions.

Within the context of this essay, this would mean looking, first of all, at the impact of the described masculinity models in Brazil. In line with Latour's preoccupation, there are, for instance, concrete ecological consequences linked to how masculine gender regimes are enacted (e.g., Hultman and Pulé 2018). In Brazil, those who support Bolsonaro, are also often those who are in favor of exploiting and destroying ecologies, for instance the so-called 'ruralistas' who need huge spaces for their cattle or soya plantations (one of the three "Bs" mentioned in note 6). Although not a new phenomenon, the destruction of the Amazon under Bolsonaro (and of indigenous land) became highly dramatic in the last years:

> Despite evidence that fire, drought and land clearance are pushing the Amazon towards a point of no return, they say the far-right lea

der is more interested in placating the powerful agribusiness lobby and tapping global markets that reward destructive behaviour. (...) Amazon deforestation reduced 80% between 2004 and 2012 under the Workers party administration of Luiz Inácio Lula da Silva. Bolsonaro has steadily dismantled or discredited the mechanisms that achieved that (Watts 2021).

Dunlop and Jacobsen (quoted in Menezes and Barbosa 2021) call this attitude "total extractivism", defined as "a global imperative of the capitalist economy that occurs through the use of violent technologies" (Menezes and Barbosa 2021: 231). Bolsonaro, for whom the environment is "only for vegans who only eat vegetables" (cf. Simões 2019), and who despised and ridiculed ecological concerns by recommending as a solution "to poop only every other day" (Simões 2019), represents exactly what Marx Ferree observed, when the environment is part of an entanglement of gendered, aggressive politics: "Environmental protection, science-based decision making, police accountability, mass incarceration, international diplomacy, and even a nonpartisan civil service all have now become aligned with the reproductive politics of gender itself" (p. 911).

What about aging masculinities? This aspect has until now been largely absent from the discussion of reversion.

Reversion and older men

Jair Bolsonaro was elected president at an age when many men are already retired. Yet he communicates explicitly youth-inspired values and attitudes through his enactment of politics, in which aging individuals are rarely mentioned. Seniors only appear as a counterpoint to what in extreme neo-liberalism is considered a good citizen, as "un-masculine".[17] This is astonishing, since in the past a number of political careers

---

17 Although neoliberalism has been criticized for being a too imprecise category as a single explanation for a variety of existing economic and social State models, extreme neoliberalism is nevertheless helpful as a notion. After Dutta (2020), it is "the free market ideology pushed beyond its organizing limits,

in Brazil have been built by adopting aging as a political cause, like the then federal deputy (and later governor) Sérgio Cabral, who in 1994 had the highest numbers of votes nationwide due to his political program aimed at older people (he is now in prison due to a major corruption scandal). It is possible that Bolsonaro's neglect of seniors might be the source of major changes in the near future, as some of the older people, who are an important constituency of Bolsonaro's voters, seem to change who they support quite readily (IPESPE 2022 in: Amado 2022). Within the current context, in which older people are easily denied a meaningful citizenship, this concluding section sketches two intermingled examples of aging-related reversion: one in terms of rights and politics, the other one in line with models of masculinity, including issues of identity and biography.

At least since the 1980s, Brazilian gerontologists (in the wider sense) have adopted the cause of rights for older people and, over the years, have established several highly advanced policies of inclusion, although, according to some observers, the actual implementation of many measures is lagging (e.g., de Mendonça 2016). Nevertheless, and especially since the Senior Citizen's Statute (*Estatuto do Idoso*) from 2003, older people receive several important benefits, including a pension that, in many cases, make the older person the main breadwinner in the family and, as a result, shift power relations within a great number of households.

With the Bolsonaro government (and the interim government of Temer before him), a steady attempt at dismantling achieved rights and care for older people can be shown to have occurred and, in this sense, reversion here can be understood as a return to a state when older people are/were more marginalized, and especially those in need. When thinking in terms of reversion, this kind of discourse can clearly be seen as a 'savagization' of society with regard of older people being a matter of concern. In fact, as Galvão, Resende and Resende (2021) write, older persons became central in Bolsonaro's necropolitics during

> with the structuring of the state as an authoritarian instrument of control [...], generating precarity while simultaneously deploying the logics of business-friendliness to enable the mobility of capital across spaces/borders".

the Covid-10 pandemic as a counter-category of State concern. In his communications, seniors are understood to be disposable – they are seen as consuming resources, and, following an extreme neo-liberal line of thought, do not contribute to society in a meaningful way. Only older persons, according to the president, should be isolated due to COVID-19, because they are the fragile ones in the context of the pandemic, as if they were living lives that are disconnected from society. Social aid programs helping older people in need (e.g., "BPC")[18] were rejected or dismantled, and State responsibility clearly denied: "Each family has to protect its elderly, not throw that on the State," Bolsonaro said in a television interview in April 2020 (Canineu and Brown 2020).

More specifically regarding masculinity models, reversion can mean the resurgence and revaluation of those models that many thought were part of the past. Interesting here is the fact that within the wider landscape of the many overlapping and dynamic kinds of masculinities, two in particular have often been reinforced in recent years in Brazil: the aggressive, uncaring, white male briefly described above, and the 'neo-pentecostal or evangelical male' – two ways of being that would appear to be mutually exclusive. The predominant values of neo-Pentecostal churches, of which more than half of the members are female and Black (cf. Balloussier 2020), demand attitudes that are opposed to violence, drinking, and approve of sex only after marriage. In her insightful analysis of men adhering to the Universal Church of the Kingdom of God in Rio de Janeiro, Lima (2010) described how the 'divine' and, at the same time, this-wordly entrepreneurship that is central to such churches, improves in many cases the financial situation of its members (who then also contribute more to the church). And although opposed to the aggressive machismo, this is linked to the important positive image of a man as being able to take care of his family, as doing honest work, and as living in an orderly world that otherwise is often a chaotic and violent universe, especially in many poorer neighborhoods. The church identity based on doing the right thing, of leading a quiet, moral life, is much

---

18 See, on the social protection program for older Brazilians (BPC): https://www.socialprotection-toolbox.org/practice/brazils-continuous-benefit-programme

closer to the general image of older men in many societies than is the aggressive, youth-oriented one propagated by Bolsonaro. And yet both are linked to major groups of voters of the current president.

Sawin (2013), in the US-American context, describes how in his study young men who are part of an evangelical Bible group creatively navigate between conflicting role models, between "godly masculinity" and the more hegemonic American model for young men, by creating a third model that integrates elements of both. In Brazil, this might also be the case. There, the centrality of the 'sacred family' in Bolsonaro and his followers' discourses became a unifying factor for both 'godly' as well as 'aggressive' men. A central common cause of both models – a heteronormative family model and an opposition to "too-fluid" gender models—was an important reason for many especially older Brazilians to vote for the president. It might have been as important as the "Carwash scandal" that connected the former PT government to corruption and played in favor of Bolsonaro, as did his contested anti-violence promises (cf. Machado and Franco 2018).[19] However, the idea that he might not be the ideal president – as already mentioned above – is possibly changing the current voter landscape, as a good number of evangelical voters after three years of government seem less inclined to vote for Bolsonaro (*O Estado* 2021). In this sense, in both masculinity models – the aggressive macho and the virtuous evangelical man – the idea of reversion is in constant movement and might even become a source of renewal and change (as the more recent voting intentions show).

The specific case of LGBTQ+ men is even more telling, since they are excluded from both hegemonic masculinity models. In Henning's (2021) sensitive study about older LGBTQ+ individuals, reversion as a loss of rights and recognition is not only embedded in current increases in numbers of violent attacks of LGBTQ+ people, but mean an especially traumatizing déjà vu for these individuals:

---

19   Beyond the scope of this article, the "Carwash scandal" (*Lava Jato*) is well explained in Laura Carvalho's book "Valsa Brasileira" (2018). An English explication can be found here: https://www.youtube.com/watch?v=A0myj6_KnKc

> Having lived part of their lives during the military dictatorship in Brazil (1964–1985), their narratives in general terms highlighted their experiences with previous totalitarian regimes. They also addressed their daily hardship of having to deal with homophobia, lesbophobia, and transphobia, as well as, in some cases, racism and poverty during their entire lives in relation to the "struggles of the present". (2021: 196)

> Thus although they liked to assert their lives as marked by courage and resilience to adversity, such "old warriors" (…) were also largely impacted by undeniable vulnerabilities that became even more worrisome after Bolsonaro's victory. (2021: 203)

Henning's interlocutors' narratives point to the struggle they had fought already, during the military dictatorship, as a "baggage" within an aesthetic of courage and resilience, that prepared them for current struggles, while at the same time framing their life history as one of constant struggle, and in which current homophobic and, to a certain extent, ageist politics impact dramatically on LGBTQ+ lives and identities.

Final remarks

Reversion as an analytical tool means acknowledgment that something valued and achieved over time (often through struggles) is in the process of being lost or is already lost. And although reversion is deeply embedded in history, it is not an historical de-evolution. By transcending the very tentative impulse to call certain phenomena retrocession or backlash (and similar notions), the "matter of concern" (cf. Latour 2004)[20] that is at stake can be studied in its multiple manifestations, and especially how it is impacting on the enactment of (here gendered) politics and peoples' lives.

---

20   See also Gordon (2012) who argues in favor of "matters of concern", in order to avoid locked-in oppositions in arguments, or "rhetorical warfare".

In this sense, studying masculinities should, ideally, be longitudinal, in order to see how cultural change reflects on identitary tinkering, practices of recognition and the making and unmaking of glocal worlds. Extreme changes in hegemonic value systems – like the one in Brazil that strongly depends on images, metaphors and prescriptions based on masculinity – can then be analyzed as impacts on individual, collective and planetary lives and, in this way, we might avoid moralizing accounts (as tempting as they are)[21]. Looking at central discursive knots and how they are put into practice, for instance through matters of care and self-care, or the enactment of force (violence, arms) – the impact of masculinity models can be studied at different levels and ideally, over a longer period of time, in order to follow changes and ruptures, as has happened recently, dramatically, in Brazil.

Acknowledgments

This essay is in part of a research funded by SSHRC (the Canadian Social Sciences and Humanities Research Council). I am grateful to Till van Rahden who sent me the inspiring article written by Marx Ferée, to Abel de Castro Cavalcanti who reminded me of the important program "A bridge to the future" by interim president Michel Temer, to Oscar Lima, who sent me the link to Laura Carvalho's excellent book, and to Adam Lock for revising my German English.

Works Cited

Amado, Guilherme. "PT incentiva voto jovem, bolsonarismo faz apelo a idosos." *Metropoles* (14 February 2022); https://www.metropoles.com/colunas/guilherme-amado/pt-incentiva-voto-jovem-bolsonarismo-faz-apelo-a-idosos.

---

21 Many of such words come to mind.

Ansell, Aaron. "Brazil's Social Safety Net Under Lula." *NACLA Report on the Americas*, 44:2 (2011): 23–26, https://doi.org/10.1080/10714839.201 1.11725533.

Aramini, Aurélien et Florian Gulli. "Du concept de 'décivilisation.'" *Philosophique* [En ligne], 19 (2016). http://journals.openedition.org/p hilosophique.

Assis, Mariana P.randini and Ana Carolina Ogando. "Bolsonaro, 'gender ideology' and hegemonic masculinity in Brazil." *Aljazeera* 31 October 2018. https://www.aljazeera.com/opinions/2018/10/31/bolsonar o-gender-ideology-and-hegemonic-masculinity-in-brazil.

Balloussier, Anna Virginia. "Cara típica do evangélico brasileiro é feminina e negra, aponta Datafolha." *Folha de São Paulo* 13 January 2020). https://www1.folha.uol.com.br/poder/2020/01/cara-tipica-d o-evangelico-brasileiro-e-feminina-e-negra-aponta-datafolha.sht ml.

Bonassi, Fernando. *Luxúria*. Rio de Janeiro: Record, 2016.

Brigeiro, Mauro. *Rir ou chorar? Envelhecimento, sexualidade e sociabilidade masculina*. Rio de Janeiro, Master's thesis in Social Medicine, Instituto de Medicina Social, State University of Rio de Janeiro, 2000.

Bunker, Robert J., John P. Sullivan and José de Arimatéia da Cruz. "Third Generation Gangs Strategic Note No. 6 – Holy War in Rio's Favelas: Bandidos Evangélicos (Evangelical Bandits)." Small Wars Journal 15 November 2017. https://smallwarsjournal.com/jrnl/art/third-gener ation-gangs-strategic-note-no-6-holy-war-rios-favelas-bandidos- evangelicos.

Calasanti, Toni. "Feminist Gerontology and Old Men." *The Journals of Gerontology: Series B* 59.6 (2004): S305–S314.

Cavalcanti, Bernardo Margulies and Carlos Magno S. Venerio. "Uma Ponte para o Futuro? Reflexões sobre a Plataforma Política do Governo Temer." *RIL Brasilia* 54.215 (2017): 139–172.

Cavalcanti, Roxana Pessoa. "How Brazil's far right became a dominant political force." The Conversation 25 January 2017. https://theconver sation.com/how-brazils-far-right-became-a-dominant-political-fo rce-71495.

Carvalho, Laura. *Valsa Brasileira, Uma Análise sobre a Economia Recente do País*. São Paulo: Todavia, 2018.

Corrigan, Patrick W. "Beware the educational fix." *The Stigma Effect: Unintended Consequences of Mental Health Campaigns*. Ed. P. W. Corrigan. New York, NY: Columbia University Press, 2018. 125–154.

De Almeida, Maria Herminia T. "The social policies of Lula's administration." *Novos Estudos – CEBRAP*, 1(se). 2005. http://socialsciences.scielo.org/scielo.php?script=sci_arttext&pid=S0101-33002005000100002&lng=en&tlng=en. (29 November 2021).

De Mendonça, Jurilza Maria B. *Idosos no Brasil, Políticas e Cuidados*. Curitiba: Juruá, 2016.

De Souza, Jesse. "O que significa Bolsonaro no poder." *Brasil De Fato* 8 May 2019 (a). https://www.brasildefato.com.br/2019/05/08/artigo-or-o-que-significa-bolsonaro-no-poder-por-jesse-souza.

De Souza, Jesse. A Elite do Atraso: Da Escravidão a Bolsonaro. Rio de Janeiro: Estação Brasil, 2019 (b).

Debert, Guita Grin. "Metamorfoses da Velhice." Agenda brasileira – temas de uma sociedade em mudança. Ed. A. Botelho and L. M. Schwarcz. São Paulo, Companhia das Letras, 2011. 542–553.

Debert, Guita Grin and Mauro Brigeiro. "Fronteiras de gênero e a sexualidade na velhice." Rev. Bras. Ci. Soc. 27.80 (2012): 37–54. http://www.scielo.br/scielo.php?script=sci_arttext&pid=S0102-69092012000300003&lng=en&nrm=iso.

Dudink, Stefan, Karen Hagemann and Anna Clark, eds. *Representing Masculinity: Male Citizenship in Modern Western Culture*. Palgrave Macmillan, 2007.

Dutta, Mohan Jyoti. "COVID-19, Authoritarian Neoliberalism, and Precarious Migrant Work in Singapore: Structural Violence and Communicative Inequality." *Frontiers in Communication* 5 (2020): 58.

Eisele, Ines. "Brazil: relaxed gun laws could lead to more violence." *Deutsche Welle* 11 February 2021. https://www.dw.com/en/brazil-relaxed-gun-laws-could-lead-to-more-violence/a-56529162.

Engel, Cintia and Annette Leibing. "Masculinities in Brazil: Identity tinkering and dementia care." *Ageing Masculinities, Alzheimer's and De-*

mentia Narratives. Ed. Heike Hartung, Rüdiger Kunow and Matthew Sweeney, London, Bloomsbury, 2022. 37–52.

Ferreira, Yuri. "Governo retira obra clássica dos Orixás do Palácio do Planalto em novo ataque contra religiões negras." *Hypeness* 21 October 2020). https://www.hypeness.com.br/2020/08/governo-re tira-obra-classica-dos-orixas-do-palacio-do-planalto-em-novo-ata que-contra-religioes-negras.

Galvão, Flavia Motta de P., Glariston Resende and Fernanda Motta de P. Resende. "A representação do idoso em tempos de pandemia: Bolsonaro e o enfrentamento neoliberal da Covid-19 no Brasil." *Gláuks – Revista De Letras E Artes* 21.1(2021): 59–82. https://doi.org/10.47677/gl uks.v21i01.229.

Gordon, Jonathan. "Rethinking Bitumen: From 'Bullshit' to a 'Matter of Concern.'" *Imaginations* 3.2 (2012): 170–187.

Heilborn, Maria Luiza and Christiane da Silva Cabral. "Youth, gender, and sexual practices in Brazil." *Psicologia & Sociedade* 25 (2013): 33–43.

Henning, Carlos Eduardo. "LGBTTI Elders in Brazil, Subjectivation and Narratives about Resilience, Resistance, and Vulnerability." *Precarious Democracy, Ethnographies of Hope, Despair, and Resistance in Brazil*. Ed. Benjamin Junge, Sean T. Mitchell, Alvaro Jarrin and Lucia Cantero. New Brunswick: Rutgers University Press, 2021. 195–205.

Hultmann, Martin and Paul M. Pulé. *Ecological Masculinities: Theoretical Foundations and Practical Guidance*. New York: Routledge, 2018.

Kalil, Isabela, Rosana Pinheiro-Machado and Lucia Mury Scalco. "Dreaming with guns, Performing masculinity and imagining consumption in Bolsonaro's Brazil." *Precarious Democracy, Ethnographies of Hope, Despair, and Resistance in Brazil*. Ed. Benjamin Junge, Sean T. Mitchell, Alvaro Jarrin and Lucia Cantero. New Brunswick: Rutgers University Press, 2021. 50–61.

Katz, Stephen and Barbara Marshall. "New sex for old: lifestyle, consumerism, and the ethics of aging well." *Journal of Aging Studies* 17.1 (2003): 3–16.

Kenny, Roisin. "A Review of the Literature on Sexual Development of Older Adults in Relation to the Asexual Stereotype of Older Adults." *Canadian J Family and Youth* 5.1 (2013): 91–106.

Latour, Bruno. "Why Has Critique Run out of Steam? From Matters of F act to Matters of Concern." *Critical Inquiry* 30.2 (2004): 225–248.

Latour, Bruno. "Why Gaia is not the Globe – and why our future depends on not confusing the two." Invited talk at The School of Culture and Society, Aarhus University, Denmark, 02 June 2016.

Latour, Bruno. "From one lockdown to the next, A change in cosmology and one political consequence." Lin Center invited talk, McGill University, Canada, 8 April 2021.

Leibing, Annette. "Marcinho et Mauricinho, Violence et les nouveaux héros de Rio de Janeiro, Brésil." *Anthropologie & Sociétés* 25.3 (2001): 51–68.

Leibing, Annette. "The Old Lady from Ipanema: Changing Notions of Old Age in Brazil." *Journal of Aging Studies* 19.1 (2005): 15–31.

Leibing, Annette, Cintia Engel and Eisangela Carrijo. "Life through Medications – Dementia Care in Brazil." *ReVista, Harvard Review of Latin America*, Winter 2019 (part II), https://archive.revista.drclas.harvard.edu/book/leibing-change-title.

Lima, Diana. "Prosperity and Masculinity: Neopentecostal Men in Rio de Janeiro." *Ethnos* 77.3 (2012): 372–39.

Machado, Lia Zanotta. "Feminismos brasileiros nas relações com o Estado. Contextos e incertezas." *Cadernos Pagu* 47 (2016). https://doi.org/10.1590/18094449201600470001.

Machado, Leandro and Luiza Franco. "Eleições 2018: voto anti-PT; por segurança e pela família tradicional." *BBC News* 4 October 2018. https://noticias.uol.com.br/ultimas-noticias/bbc/2018/10/04/voto-anti-pt-por-seguranca-e-pela-familia-tradicional-o-que-pensam-as-mulheres-que-escolheram-bolsonaro.htm.

Magalhães, Livia. *Lugar de Mulher: Feminismo e Política no Brasil*. Rio de Janeiro: Oficina Raquel, 2017.

Marx Ferré, Myra. "The crisis of masculinity for gendered democracies: Before, during, and after Trump." *Sociological Forum* 35.S1 (2020): 898–917.

Mbembe, Achille. "Necropolitcis." *Public Culture* 15.1 (2003): 11–40.

Medeiros, Paulo Adão de et al. "Participação masculina em modalidades de atividades físicas de um Programa para idosos: um estudo longitudinal." *Ciência & Saúde Coletiva* [online]. 198. (2014): 3479–3488. https://doi.org/10.1590/1413-81232014198.16252013.

Menezes, Roberto G. and Ricardo Barbosa Jr. "Environmental governance under Bolsonaro: dismantling institutions, curtailing participation, delegitimising opposition." *Z Vgl Polit Wiss* 15(2021): 229–247.

Mott, Luiz. "Memória Gay no Brasil: O Amor que não se Permitia Dizer o Nome." *Devorando o Tempo, Brasil, o País sem Memória*. Ed. Annette Leibing and Sybille Benninghoff-Lühl. São Paulo: Mandarim, 2001. 190–204.

Pereira Erik Giuseppe B. "Reflexões sobre práticas corporais, identidades e masculinidades." *Rev Bras Psicol Esporte Motricidade Hum* 1 (2009): 37–43.

Noblat, Ricardo. "Avança o plano de Bolsonaro de armar os brasileiros, O crime organizado e as milícias agradecem." *Veja* 9 January 2021. https://veja.abril.com.br/coluna/noblat/avanca-o-plano-de-bolsonaro-de-armar-os-brasileiros.

O Estado de São Paulo. "Pesquisa IPEC: Lula e Bolsonaro empatam no voto evangélico." 15 December 2021. https://politica.estadao.com.br/noticias/geral,ipec-pesquisa-lula-jair-bolsonaro-sergio-moro,70003926761.

Paternotte, David. "Backlash: A misleading narrative." *Engenderings*, Blog by the London School of Economics' Department of Gender Studies. 30 March 2020. https://blogs.lse.ac.uk/gender/2020/03/30/backlash-a-misleading-narrative/

Plank, Liz. *For the Love of Men: From Toxic to a More Mindful Masculinity*. New York: St. Martin's Press, 2019.

Rabkin, Yakov and Mikhail Minakov, eds. *Demodernization A Future in de Past*. Stuttgart: Ibidem, 2018.

Rabkin, Yakov. "Undoing years of progress." *Demodernization A Future in de Past*. Ed. Y. Rabkin and M. Minakov. Stuttgart: Ibidem, 2018. 17–45.

Rodrigues, Julian. "Lula é ícone das LGBT." *Forum* 21 November 2021. https://revistaforum.com.br/rede/lula-e-icone-das-lgbt/#.

Phillips, Tom. "Brazil: Bolsonaro reportedly uses homophobic slur to mock masks." *The Guardian* 8 July 2020. https://www.theguardian.com/world/2020/jul/08/bolsonaro-masks-slur-brazil-coronavirus.

Rouse, Carolyn M. "Necropolitics versus Biopolitics: Spatialization, White Privilege, and Visibility during a Pandemic." *Cultural Anthropology* 36.3 (2021): 360–67.

Sawin, Tom "The Habit of Meeting Together: Enacting Masculinity in a Men's Bible Study." *Crossroads of Language, Interaction and Culture*, 9.1 (2013). https://escholarship.org/uc/item/6683w3fs.

Simões, Mariana. "Brazil's Bolsonaro on the Environment, in His Own Words." *New York Times* 28 August 2019. https://www.nytimes.com/2019/08/27/world/americas/bolsonaro-brazil-environment.html.

The Guardian. "'Epidemic of violence': Brazil shocked by 'barbaric' gang-rape of gay man, Activists fear that an increase in attacks on the country's LBGT community is fuelled by a culture of homophobia at the very top." 9 January 2021. https://www.theguardian.com/global-development/2021/jun/09/epidemic-of-violence-brazil-shocked-by-barbaric-gang-rape-of-gay-man.

Touraine, Alain. *Pourrons-nous vivre ensemble? Égaux et différents*. Paris: Fayard, 1997.

Viveiros de Castro, Eduardo. "The relative native." *HAU: Journal of Ethnographic Theory* 3.3 (2013): 473–502.

Wagner, Roy. *The Invention of Culture. Second Edition*. Chicago: The University of Chicago Press, 2016 [1975].

Watts, Jonathan. "Amazon rainforest will collapse if Bolsonaro remains president." *The Guardian*, 14 July 2021. https://www.theguardian.com/environment/2021/jul/14/amazon-rainforest-will-collapse-if-bolsonaro-remains-president.

Zanata, Luiz Fabiano et al. "Igualdade de gênero: por que o Brasil vive retrocessos?" *Cad. Saúde Pública* 32.8 (2016). http://dx.doi.org/10.1590/0102-311X00089616.

The Age and Gender of Homesickness
Mother Russia's Prodigal Sons

Dagmar Gramshammer-Hohl

1. Introduction: The Exile's Age

Literary representations of the exilic experience widely make use of images of ageing.[1] Emigration is depicted as "existential rupture" (Grübel 2006), as it always is involuntary, even if the émigré is not forced to leave his home country by expulsion but feels forced to leave in order to save his life or to be able to live with dignity.[2] When losing his former home, the émigré also appears to irretrievably lose part of his own self: The loss of the places of one's childhood, of the places of youth or first love are imagined as the loss of one's youth itself. Just like for the émigré returning home is impossible, one cannot revisit one's past; in the same way as exile is perceived as irreversible, the experience of ageing is linked to notions of irretrievable loss and irrecoverability. It is, thus, not surprising that in literary representations of exile, protagonists seem to grow old almost all of a sudden and sometimes turn grey nearly immediately after passing the threshold to the foreign land.

This topos is, for instance, revisited – and deconstructed – in Efraim Sevela's 1975 novella *Ostanovite samolet – ia slezu!* (Stop the plane – I'm getting off!). The first-person narrator, a Soviet-Russian Jew like the author himself, relates his encounter with Soviet Jews at New York airport – he himself being a remigrant on his way back 'home', to the USSR, whereas

---

[1] See Gramshammer-Hohl 2015, 2017, 2019.
[2] See, e.g., Neubauer 2009, 8.

the new arrivals are on their way into emigration. The narrator comments on how his compatriots must feel:

> Ведь уже проливали они слезы, прощаясь с Россией, седели и старились на глазах, когда с кровью рвали все нити – друзья, родня – что связывали их с прошлым. (Sevela 1980, 186)

> For they already spilled tears when bidding farewell to Russia, turned grey and grew old for all the world to see, when sorely breaking all the bonds (with friends, kin) that connected them with their past.[3]

Representations of 'exile as ageing' are not confined to Russian émigré literature. For instance, the French writer Albert Camus, in his notebooks, describes exile as a vanishing of youth (cited in Camus 1995, 12). Catalin Dorian Florescu, a Swiss author of Romanian origin writing in German, depicts the change that his protagonist undergoes when arriving in Switzerland – after his flight from Romania – as having "turned grey overnight" (Florescu 2002, 46). The Romanian writer Norman Manea even speaks of the "leap years" of exile: Every year in exile was equal to four years of "normal" existence (Manea 2003, 44). The émigré, in Manea's view, thus grows old more quickly than do those who have stayed in their home country. Apparently, the exiles' longing for home has a certain age; does it also have a gender?

2. The Gender of Homesickness

The poet Konstantin Bal'mont, having gone into exile in 1920 in the wake of the so-called 'first wave' of Russian emigration, published the collection *Gde moi dom?* (Where is my home?) in 1924; it contains an essay entitled *Bez rusla* ([River] without bed), written in 1923, where he says:

---

3   Unless otherwise indicated, all translations are mine.

Но нет дня, когда бы я не тосковал о России, нет часа, когда бы я не порывался вернуться. [...] Я полон беспредельной любви к миру и к моей матери, которая называется Россия. [...] я на чужбине, я вне действительной связи с душой здешней жизни, и я вне действительной связи с моей Матерью, с моей Родиной [...]. (Bal'mont 1990)

But there is not a single day where I would not long for Russia, not a single hour when I would not strive to return. [...] I am full of boundless love for the world and for my mother, who is called Russia. [...] I am in a foreign land, I do not have any true bond with the soul of this country's life, and I do not have any true bond with my Mother, my Motherland [...].

In many texts of exilic literature written in that key, one cannot help noticing that homesickness seems to be a gendered experience – at least, in its literary treatment. The major part of the works that I have thus far analysed features a male protagonist longing for, imagining or even attempting a homecoming, and desperate about its impossibility and failure. In exilic poetry, we also seldom meet a homesick female persona.

Similarly, the journey in the "monomyth" described by Joseph Campbell – which necessarily ends with the adventurer's return home – is generally undertaken by a male hero.[4] Referring to Russian literature, Aleksei Podchinenov and Tat'iana Snigireva state that in the nineteenth century, the one who comes home usually is the Son (*Syn*, capitalised) as opposed to the Father (*Otets*), who is the primary homecomer of Soviet literature (Podchinenov and Snigireva 2011, 162). However, there does not seem to exist any prototype of the homecoming daughter or mother. There are examples to rather support the contrary: E.g., in Aleksandr Pushkin's story *Stantsionnyi smotritel'* (*The Stationmaster*, 1830), the eponymous hero's daughter Dunia does not return, though the pictures on

---

4   Adopting James Joyce's term of "monomyth" from *Finnegans Wake* (1939), Campbell argues that all the myths of the world share the same basic structure. See Campbell 1968.

the wall described at the narrative's beginning, which display scenes of the biblical prodigal son's homecoming, might make the reader expect Dunia to do so (see Schmid 2014, 34).

In her *Kniga o rodine* (Book about the Homeland, 2001), Russian linguist Irina Sandomirskaia also points to the fact that in Russian discursive practices, the theme of the 'homeland' does not unfold in 'female' stories. The author explains this by the distinctly patriarchal character of the 'homeland' discourse:

> Интересно задуматься […] над тем, почему тема родины не порождает отдельную "женскую" историю и не очень приветствует в качестве своего протагониста персонаж женского рода. Причины кроются, по-видимому, в патриархальном характере дискурса. […] малая родина – это отношения матери и сына. В дискурсе о родине "женский" сюжет уже отведен родине, и это сюжет материнства. Кроме того, родина […] – это сюжет странствия, а образ странствующей женщины (вообще сочетание образа женщины с образом дороги) грубо противоречит патриархальному идеалу женственности и женскому назначению сидеть "в доме", "в тереме", на месте. (Sandomirskaia 2001, 60)
>
> It is interesting to reflect […] upon the question of why the theme of the 'homeland' does not generate a distinctive 'female' story and does not embrace as its protagonist a female character. The reasons obviously lie in the patriarchal nature of the discourse. […] home is the relationship between mother and son. In the discourse about the homeland, the 'female' storyline already pertains to the 'homeland' itself, it constitutes the maternal theme. Furthermore, the homeland […] develops the plot of peregrination, and the image of the wandering woman (generally, the conjunction of the image of the woman with that of the road) grossly contradicts the patriarchal ideal of femininity and a woman's destiny to sit 'in the house', secluded in the 'terem' [i.e., the Old Russian women's chamber], to stay in place.

In the patriarchal worldview, the 'female' space is the house; a woman who leaves the house and sets out to peregrinate or go *tramping* (Russ.

bluzhdaet), becomes a 'public' woman, that is, a prostitute or *tramp* (Russ. *bludnitsa*).

As a cultural concept, the house epitomises the Self: It provides protection from the threatening Other, warmth, security, the feeling of belonging and intimacy, thus connoting motherliness or the maternal womb itself. Etymologically, the house (Russ. *dom*, Lat. *domus*, Gr. δόμος) is linked to Indo-Eur. **dem(ǝ)-* or **dom(ǝ)-* 'to tame, to force' and is thus opposed to nature, which is untamed and threatening. The protecting, enclosing and enwombing aspect of the house is conspicuous in the etymological link of, e.g., Germ. *Haus* 'house', Germ. *Hose* 'trousers', Eng. *hose*, Eng. *hide* (the noun and the verb), Germ. *Haut* 'hide' or Russ. *kryt'* 'to cover' und *krysha/krov* 'roof' (see Baak 2009, 25–28).

The garden represents a transition zone which belongs to the sphere of the Self: a natural, although – unlike untamed nature – built environment. It is cultivated and taken care of, thus providing man with nourishing fruits, which is why it belongs to the realm of the mother. The father, by contrast, is the one who moves outwards and passes the threshold of the house to the road, towards the unknown.

The 'homeland' is an extended 'home': It fulfils the same role as the built house and the fenced-in and cultivated garden, offers security, a familiar organisation, and nourishment. The homeland constitutes the outermost of a number of protecting layers which man creates or imagines and which can be conceived of as concentric circles, at whose very centre is the individual himself: body/hide, womb, house, garden fence, village/town boundaries and the country's frontiers. In representations of the 'homeland', analogies drawn between the home country and the house are therefore frequent. Imaginations of the homeland as house or home are so widespread in Russian émigré literature, that Joost van Baak, in his seminal study on the mythopoetics of the house, stated that treatment of emigrant literature was beyond the scope of his book (Baak 2009, 13). The equation of home with the mother or of the motherland with the womb, which can also be observed in the previously mentioned quotation by Konstantin Bal'mont, is a result of the same metonymical process.

In general, the personification of a national community as a female character – most frequently a mother figure[5] – is very common. 'Mother Russia' (*matushka-Rus'/matushka Rossiia*), a myth revived in Soviet times in the shape of 'Mother Motherland' (*Rodina-mat'*), is just one among a number of examples – alongside Polonia, Mother Sweden, Britannia, Helvetia, and others (see Edmondson 2003). The homeland embodied in a mother figure is linked to the myth of Mother Moist Earth (*Mat' Syra Zemlia*), the Great Goddess, who gives life, growth and nurture, but also takes life back, burying the dead within herself. By contrast, the state represents the fatherly principle. Consequently, the rule of tsarist Russia was imagined as 'Father Tsar' (*Car'-batiushka*) marrying 'Mother Russia' – a marriage repeatedly performed as such in the seventeenth and eighteenth centuries (see Edmondson 2003, 54; Hellberg-Hirn 1998, 111–135).

Nira Yuval-Davis (1997) has demonstrated that the categories of nation and gender are closely intertwined; she speaks of *gendered nation* and *nationed gender*. According to her, women not only function as the national community's biological reproducers but also as "symbolic border guards" (Yuval-Davis 1997, 37). One aspect of this function is the allegorical representation of the nation as woman or mother, aside from the female roles of the reproducer of culture, who preserves and passes on tradition, and of the bearer of the community's honour.

In view of such widespread and deeply engrained notions, it is not surprising that there is almost no room in literature for female protagonists' longing for lost homes; they rather fulfil the task of embodying that very home. Homesickness, thus, is the male role in the story.

The homecoming motif is closely connected to a biblical tale: the parable of the prodigal son (*bludnyi syn*) (Luke 15:11–32). The son has sinned against the father but shows repentance and is welcomed by the father with open arms upon his return. In the discourse about the sons' duty towards the Russian homeland, this Christian subtext was always

---

5   Exceptions are young maidens such as, e.g., *Suomi-neito*, who at the end of the nineteenth century came to replace a mother figure as the personification of Finland, as well as the *Kosovka devojka*, known from Serbian iconography and epics (see Edmondson 2003, 58).

present – in prerevolutionary and in atheist Soviet culture alike (see Sandomirskaia 2001, 59). He who leaves home commits an act of betrayal; return, thus, appears as the confession of a guilt (Sandomirskaia 2001, 70). However, the homeland lovingly forgives those who repent, and welcomes them back into the fold.

The return narrative of Russian emigration recurrently evokes this Christian compound of sin, penitence, and forgiveness. Interestingly, however, it is not the father who meets and embraces the prodigal son but the mother, or a woman or mother figure that personifies the motherland. As cases in point, I have selected for analysis four texts from Russian émigré literature: poems by first-wave poets Viacheslav Lebedev and Nikolai Turoverov and a novella by third-wave writer Efraim Sevela.

3. The prodigal son's 'evening return'

The poem *Vechernee vozvrashchenie* (Evening return), which Viacheslav Lebedev published in 1928, stands out due to two intertextual references to biblical texts: the Book of Ecclesiastes (1:4–7) with its verse about the wind that returns on its circuits and the previously mentioned parable of the prodigal son.

The poem's male poetic persona shows certain parallels with the prodigal son of the Gospel of Luke: He is returning home from a foreign land – although only in his imagination, which projects the longed-for future homecoming – suppliant, pitiful, leaning on his walking stick. Recalling his "noisy years" ["шумные года"; line 12] is painful to him; they stand in stark contrast to the "quiet evening" ["И будет вечер тих"; line 9] of his return home (Lebedev 1994, 126). The homecomer's "timid" ["робко"; line 7] knocking on the door echoes the humbleness and penitence of the biblical prodigal son. However, in contrast to the Gospel's forgiving father, in Lebedev's text, it is the mother who has longingly been waiting all those years for her son to come home and now recognises him instantly, in spite of the pitiful state he is in. Her reaction is not full of anger but, just as that of the Bible's forgiving father, full of mercy.

Lebedev's returning son does not manage to recognise his mother in the aged, lined face of the woman who opens the door:

> О, как узнаю средь морщин
> Твои черты, что, помню, были...
> – Ты крикнешь, жалостное: –
> "Сын!"
> И я, растерянное: –
> "Ты ли?".

> Oh, how will I recognise amidst the wrinkles
> The features of your face that I remember...
> You will exclaim a piteous:
> "Son!"
> And me, a distraught:
> "Is it you?"

If we conceive of the mother as the personified motherland, the primal Christian scene evoked by the text reflects a *leitmotif* of literary return narratives: the question of how much the regained homeland will resemble the one which the émigré once left.

4. The émigré between mother and stepmother

In the poem "Osypaetsia sad zolotoi..." ("Leaves are falling in the golden garden...", 1939) by the first-wave 'Cossack' poet Nikolai Turoverov, a mother is waiting in vain for her son to come home. She represents the poem's lyrical 'you', which can be recognised as a parent in line 6 but as a mother only in line 10 (Turoverov 1939, 36). The text evokes images of autumn and approaching winter that are traditionally associated with the 'autumn of life' and, thus, with old age and the idea of death being near. Throughout this poem, coupled, masculine rhymes are used – a conspicuous exception to Turoverov's poetry collection *Stikhi* (Poems) from 1939 – which reinforces the impression of uniformity and monotony characterising the mother's later life. Her final days consist in waiting for the son's return:

> Ты все смотришь на листьев полет,
> Ты все веришь, что сын твой придет,
> Возвратится из странствий – и вот
> У твоих постучится ворот. (Turoverov 1939, 36; lines 5–8)

> You still look at the flying leaves,
> You still believe that your son will come,
> That he'll return from his wanderings and all of a sudden
> Will knock at your door.

The monotony of waiting and ageing is emphasised by the identical end rhyme in all of these four successive lines. The poem concludes with anticipating death: "Недалек твой последний покой" ["Your last resting place is near"] (line 12). This reminds of the common homecoming-through-death motif: However, in Turoverov's poem, it is the vainly waiting mother who dies. Her death makes the son's non-return definite.

Whereas in "Leaves are falling in the golden garden…", the homeland left behind is represented by the mother, in the poem "Zhizn' ne nachinaetsia snachala…" ("Life does not begin from scratch…", 1939), France, the country of exile, appears as a stepmother – just like in the well-known Russian saying "Родимая сторона – мать, чужая – мачеха" ["The homeland is a mother, the foreign land – a stepmother"] (Dal' 2000, 336). France is the poem's lyrical 'you', which is personified throughout the text. The lyrical 'I' refers to himself as "son of foreign origin" ["чужеродный сын"] (Turoverov 1939, 27; line 8). The stepmother has accepted this son, but she also has her own children ["родные дети"] (line 5). She cannot or does not want to replace the stepson's Mother Russia. This is revealed by the fact that she does not let him into her house; he is forced to dwell at the threshold: "Долго жил у твоего порога, / И еще, наверно, поживу" ["I've lived for a long time at your threshold, / And will be likely to do so for another while"] (lines 11–12).

Significantly, France is apostrophised as "my cheery stepmother" ["Мачеха веселая моя"] (line 16). Given the gloom of the poetic persona who is mourning his past and has lost all his hopes, this cheerfulness seems inappropriate. Herein, Turoverov's poem echoes Georgii Ivanov's famous verse from 1932 "Likovanie vechnoi, blazhennoi vesny…" ("The exaltation of eternal, blissful spring…"), in which the lyrical 'I' feels repelled by the joyous atmosphere that reigns in "repugnant Nice" ["постылая Ницца"] (Ivanov 1994, 586; line 9). Springlike stepmother France, thus, other than a real mother, always shows the wrong feelings: "Ты меня с улыбкой не встречала / И в слезах не будешь провожать" ["You did not meet me with a smile / And will not say goodbye to me in tears"] (Turoverov 1939, 27; lines 3–4). Therefore, she cannot assure her stepson of being unconditionally accepted and loved.

5. The émigré's return into his motherland's arms

In Efraim Sevela's novella *Stop the plane – I'm getting off!*, the first-person narrator Arkadii Rubinchik, an émigré on his way back 'home', reflects on what symbolises 'home' for an emigrant Russian. He resorts to numerous linguistic clichés which have also been listed by Irina Sandomirskaia in her analysis of the Soviet homeland discourse (see Sandomirskaia 2001, 53ff.).

Россия… Родина… Родимая сторонка…[6]

> Если верить книгам и кино, то русский человек, или вернее, советский человек, где-нибудь на чужбине, в ужасной тоске или на смертном ложе, в последний сознательный миг непременно увидит белые березки, качающиеся на ветру, и это ему напомнит обожаемую родину. (Sevela 1980, 142)

> Russia… Homeland… Motherland…
> If we believe what the books and the cinema say, a Russian man,

---

6   According to Sandomirskaia (2001, 51), *rodnaia storonka* 'motherland' is a keyword in the narrative of 'love of the homeland'.

or rather a Soviet man somewhere in a foreign land, feeling desperately homesick or lying on his deathbed, will, in his last conscious moment, inevitably see white birch trees swaying in the wind, and be reminded by them of his adored homeland.

For Rubinchik, however, the symbol of Russia is not a birch, but a real woman he has known:

> Для меня символ России был в другом [...]. Через ностальгическую муть пробивалось и возникало как образ Родины одно и то же видение: лицо парторга нашего треста обслуживания Капитолины Андреевны [...]. Добрейшая Капитолина Андреевна. Матушка-заступница, но и строго взыскущая с нерадивых. Бог московских парикмахеров. Вернее, богиня. Простая русская баба [...] женщина с большой "Ж". (Sevela 1980, 142–143)

> For me, Russia was symbolised by something else [...]. Through the nostalgic mist, one vision cut through and arose as the Motherland's image time and time again: the face of our [hairdressing] service company's local party organiser, Kapitolina Andreevna [...]. Most kind-hearted Kapitolina Andreevna. Mother of Mercy, but also most demanding towards those who failed. The God of Moscow hairdressers. Or rather, Goddess. An ordinary Russian *baba* [older woman] [...] a woman with a capital 'W'.

Kapitolina Andreevna is the person who has offered him the testimonial he needed in order to receive his exit permit. Her personal relationship with Rubinchik is not merely a motherly one. However, in her function as the homeland's allegory, the narrator lends her essential maternal qualities, not incidentally associating her with the image of the Mother of Mercy as the sinners' advocate (*matushka-zastupnitsa*). This image ironically refers to a conflation, common in Russian discourse, of pre-Christian (Mother Earth) with Christian concepts (Mother of God).[7]

---

7   See Edmondson 2003, 54; Hellberg-Hirn 1998, 116.

Kapitolina Andreevna's document will also help Rubinchik upon his return to the Soviet Union – this is what he, at least, believes. His former party organiser's testimonial appears to him now as a lifesaver and the woman herself as the longed-for homeland that will enclose him in its arms again:

> Словно знала, провидица, что я обратно запрошусь. [...] Берегись, диван! Гремите, пружины! Принимай в объятия, заступница моя! (Sevela 1980, 192)
>
> As if she knew, the clairvoyant, that I would beg to be allowed back home. [...] Watch out, divan! Creak, springs! Take me in your arms, my advocate [zastupnitsa]!

The common metaphor of the protagonist returning into the motherland's 'fold' (womb) is used here by Sevela not only in a figurative sense but taken quite literally, and thus stripped of its pathos.[8]

Yet, in Sevela's novella, the mother figure becomes a symbol of the homeland in yet another respect, namely, the "old mother" (*prestarelaia mama, staren'kaia mama*):

> Скажите мне, как вы относитесь к своей престарелой маме, и я скажу вам, кто вы — животное, скотина или человек.
> Итальянцы — люди. Там матери — почет и уважение. О, mamma mia! Так, кажется, поют в Неаполе. Грузины у нас на Кавказе — еще больше люди. У них мама — Бог. Ну, уж о евреях нечего и говорить. Они в этом смысле — сверхчеловеки. Потому что в настоящей еврейской семье мама — Бог, царь и воинский начальник. (Sevela 1980, 178)
>
> Tell me how you behave towards your old mother, and I will tell you who you are – a beast, a brute, or a man.

---

8   Klavdia Smola (2019, 243) has rightly stated that Sevela is one of those Jewish writers for whom "every nationally and ideologically motivated romanticisation becomes an object of deconstruction and is freed from its taboos".

Italians are men. They respect and revere their mothers. O, mamma mia! This is, it seems, what they sing in Naples. Our Georgians in the Caucasus are even more human. For them, the mother is God. Well, and about the Jews, there's nothing left to say. In this respect, they are supermen. For in a truly Jewish family, the mother is God, the tsar and commander-in-chief.

In Rubinchik's view, the importance the old mother has in a society reveals everything about this society's merit: "[…] по этому признаку я вам определю с точностью аптекарских весов, чего стоит та или иная нация, та или иная страна" ["on this basis, I will determine for you as accurately as an apothecary's scale a nation's or a country's worth"] (Sevela 1980, 178). Compared to Russia, America comes off badly in this regard. As the narrator contrasts habits "in America" (*v Amerike*) with those "in our country, Russia" (*u nas v Rossii*), it becomes clear why he does not feel he belongs to his receiving country, and why returning to the Soviet Union is the only option for him. It is no option for Rubinchik to live in a society in which older people are moved to nursing homes and left there to await their death:

> В Америке – богатейшей стране, где евреи далеко не самая бедная часть населения, у каждой семьи по два-три автомобиля, у большинства – собственные дома, и комнат в этих домах столько, что в Москве бы там поселили семей пять не меньше. Так в этой самой Америке родители, престарелые люди, – отрезанный ломоть, от них избавляются под любым предлогом без всякого зазрения совести. […] Старики живут в этих домах [для престарелых] без семейной ласки и внимания, хорошо оплаченные кандидаты в покойники, и все их мысли невольно гуляют вокруг одной и той же темы: кто следующий в этом доме отправится в мир иной. Они живут среди дряхлости и тлена, и страшней такой пытки не придумать даже людоедам. (Sevela 1980, 179)
>
> In America – a very rich country, where the Jews are by far not the poorest segment of the population and where every family has two

or three cars – the majority has their own houses and so many rooms in these houses that in Moscow at least five families would be accommodated in them. Well, in this same America, parents, older people, are cut off, they are disposed of [by their offspring] under any pretext, without the slightest twinge of remorse. [...] Older people live in these [nursing] homes without their families' embraces and care, well-paid men and women destined to die, and all their thoughts are inadvertently focused on this very topic: who will be the next in the nursing home to depart this world. They live surrounded by frailty and decay, and even cannibals couldn't think of a more terrible torture.

Certainly, Sevela makes the protagonist of his satirical text exaggerate, in accordance with the genre's conventions. However, the comparison of people who expect their old parents to endure such a dreary end of life with cannibals highlights how alienated the narrator feels from this culture, which he, apparently, cannot consider as civilised.

In Rubinchik's view, the standing that old people have in Russia is completely different:

У нас в России, где не только нет лишнего места для стариков, где в одной комнатке живут три поколения вместе: внуки, дети и дедушки с бабушками, вас бы посчитали извергом и самым последним человеком, если бы вы заикнулись о том, что, мол, не мешало бы избавиться от стариков.
Свою собственную маму, которая тебя взрастила, вскормила, выходила из самых жестоких болезней, спасала от голода, сама недоедая, телом прикрывала во время бомбежек, разве можно во имя своего комфорта лишить ее на склоне лет семейного тепла, внимания, радости жить с внучатами и молодеть, глядя на них? (Sevela 1980, 180)

In our country, Russia, where there is no spare room left for the elderly, where three generations – grandchildren, children and grandparents – live together in one room, you would be considered a monster and the very foulest of men, if you only hinted that it wouldn't perhaps be bad to get rid of old people.

> For can you really, for the sake of your personal comfort, deprive your own aged mother – who has brought you up, fed you, helped you out of most terrible illnesses, saved you from hunger by depraving herself of food, who sheltered you with her body during the bombings – of family warmth, care, the pleasure of living with her little grandchildren and becoming young again by watching them?

In this part of the novella, the ironic undertone present throughout the text has vanished; for the first time, the narrator appears not a cynical distant observer but a man (or son) with feelings. Arkadii Rubinchik is, indeed, homesick. He is longing for his motherland, which is personified in varying mother figures. Yet above of all, he is longing for a country to call his ideal home, in which old mothers are not left alone by their children but loved and cared for by family caregivers – a home country, to which sons, and prodigal sons like himself, always return, thus fulfilling their duty toward their mother, or motherland.

6. Conclusion

As the literary texts selected for this paper among many other comparable ones show, emigration generates specific notions of home and belonging. On the one hand, the involuntary departure and the impossibility – perceived or real – of returning entail a sense of irreversibility and self-estrangement, which manifest themselves as the feeling of growing older. On the other hand, this specific 'émigré-aged-by-exile' type embodies a gendered experience: The relationship of 'homeland' and 'émigré' is conceived of and described in familial terms, as the longing of a prodigal son for his mother.

Whereas female characters are assigned the role of embodying the home, the roles of representing mobility, displacement, and the longing for return are attributed to and experienced mainly by male protagonists and personae. This gender and kinship pattern can be observed in numerous works of émigré literature throughout the twentieth century, from texts of the first- to the third-wave of Russian emigration, and beyond.

As Eva Hausbacher has argued, voluntary migration – which does not prevent people from returning home at least temporarily – on the one side, and involuntary emigration, on the other, produce quite different literatures (Hausbacher 2009, 10–12). While Russian émigré literature has targeted Russian-speaking audiences and dwelled on retrospection and memory, migration literature is oriented towards the writer's receiving countries, uses the latter's languages and is, thus, transnational and transcultural in nature. In what way these basic differences affect the age and gender of homesickness as represented in migration literature opens up spaces for further investigation.

Works Cited

Baak, Joost van. The House in Russian Literature: A Mythopoetic Exploration. Amsterdam: Rodopi, 2009.

Bal'mont, Konstantin. "Bez rusla." Stozvuchnye pesni. Sochineniia (izbrannye stikhi i proza). Jaroslavl': Verkh.-Volzh. kn. izd-vo, 1990. http://az.lib.ru/b/balxmont_k_d/text_0320.shtml [13.03.2021].

Campbell, Joseph. The Hero with a Thousand Faces. 2nd edition. Princeton, N.J.: Princeton UP, 1968.

Camus, Albert. Le Malentendu. Édition présentée, établie et annotée par Pierre-Louis Rey. Paris: Gallimard, 1995.

Dal', Vladimir. Poslovitsy i pogovorki russkogo naroda. Moscow: Eksmo, 2000.

Edmondson, Linda. "Putting Mother Russia in a European Context." Art, Nation and Gender: Ethnic Landscapes, Myths and Mother-Figures. Eds. Tricia Cusack and Síghle Bhreathnach-Lynch. London: Routledge, 2003. 53–64.

Florescu, Catalin Dorian. Der kurze Weg nach Hause. Zurich: Pendo, 2002.

Gramshammer-Hohl, Dagmar. "Altern und Exil in der russischen Emigrationsliteratur." Unterwegs-Sein. Figurationen von Mobilität im

Osten Europas. Eds. Andrea Zink and Sonja Koroliov. Innsbruck: University of Innsbruck, 2015. 255–266.

Gramshammer-Hohl, Dagmar. "Exile, Return and 'the Relative Brevity of Our Life': Aging in Slavic Homecoming Narratives." Aging in Slavic Literatures: Essays in Literary Gerontology. Ed. Dagmar Gramshammer-Hohl. Bielefeld: transcript, 2017. 185–201.

Gramshammer-Hohl, Dagmar. "Sehnsucht nach Rückkehr, Heimkehr im Tod. Die Nostalgie des Exils als Erzählung vom Ende." Wiener Slawistischer Almanach 82 (2019) (Special issue: Nostalgie. Ein literarisches und kulturelles Sehnsuchtsmodell. Eds. Anja Burghardt, Aage Hansen-Löve, and Brigitte Obermayr). 349–364.

Grübel, Rainer. "Lev Šestovs Philosophie des existentiellen Bruchs. Das Eigene und das Fremde im Exil." Exklusion. Chronotopoi der Ausgrenzung in der russischen und polnischen Literatur des 20. Jahrhunderts. Eds. Wolfgang Stephan Kissel and Franziska Thun-Hohenstein. Munich: Sagner, 2006. 57–88.

Hausbacher, Eva. Poetik der Migration: Transnationale Schreibweisen in der zeitgenössischen russischen Literatur. Tübingen: Stauffenburg, 2009.

Hellberg-Hirn, Elena. Soil and Soul: The Symbolic World of Russianness. Aldershot: Ashgate, 1998.

Ivanov, Georgii. Sobranie sochinenii v 3-kh tomakh. Vol. 1: Stikhotvoreniia. Moscow: Soglasie, 1994.

Lebedev, Viacheslav. "Vechernee vozvrashchenie." "My zhili togda na planete drugoi...": Antologiia poezii russkogo zarubezh'ia 1920–1990 (Pervaia i vtoraia volna). V 4-kh knigakh. Kniga 2-ia. Ed. Evgenii Vitkovskii. Moscow: Moskovskii rabochii, 1994. 126.

Manea, Norman. The Hooligan's Return: A Memoir. New York: Farrar, Straus and Giroux, 2003.

Neubauer, John. "Exile: Home of the Twentieth Century." The Exile and Return of Writers from East-Central Europe: A Compendium. Eds. John Neubauer and Borbala Zsuzsanna Török. Berlin: De Gruyter, 2009. 4–103.

Podchinenov, Aleksei, and Tat'iana Snigireva. "Homo revertens v russkoi literature." Rossica Olomucensia 50.2 (2011): 161–169.

Pushkin, Aleksandr. "Stantsionnyi smotritel'." Sochineniia v 3-kh tomakh. Vol. 3. Moscow: Khudozhestvennaia literatura, 1986. 75–84.

Sandomirskaia, Irina. Kniga o Rodine. Opyt analiza diskursivnykh praktik. Vienna: Ges. zur Förderung slawistischer Studien, 2001.

Schmid, Wolf. Elemente der Narratologie. Berlin: De Gruyter, 2014.

Sevela, Efraim. Ostanovite samolet – ia slezu! Munich: FYMCA-Press, 1980.

Smola, Klavdia. Wiedererfindung der Tradition. Russisch-jüdische Literatur der Gegenwart. Vienna: Böhlau, 2019.

Turoverov, Nikolai. Stikhi. Besançon: Tipografiia N. A. Kovalevskogo, 1939.

Yuval-Davis, Nira. Gender & Nation. London: Sage, 1997.

Ageing as Emasculation?
Rethinking the Father Image in Ang Lee's "Father Trilogy"

Yumin Zhang

1. Introduction

The father image has attracted significant interest among film scholars in a rich body of research on Ang Lee's works. Due to Ang Lee's Chinese heritage, scholars always consider the father image in his movies as a symbol of Chinese patriarchy. Therefore, the ageing and physically deteriorating father image is interpreted as Lee's intention to shatter the symbolic father in Chinese culture, despite his occasional sympathy and respect towards the Chinese father (Yu 2004; Fu 2006; Chen 2006; Sun 2007). My paper draws on an interdisciplinary methodology from ageing, gender, and postcolonial studies to reexamine the Chinese father image.

Age scholars have long argued that ageing "affects us all, and affects us all differently" (Lynne Segal 2013, 13). And it seems that most gendered studies of ageing have centered on women while ageing males have seldom been portrayed or discussed. This has contributed to the cultural "invisibility" of older men and, even more, "the inverse correlation" between masculinity and ageing (Saxton and Cole 2012, 98). The study of ageing masculinity thus remains largely unexplored. As feminist scholar Lynne Segal reminds us, "the scholarly material available for describing men's experiences of ageing remains more limited, far sparser for men than for women" (2013, 83).

My paper sets out to investigate the representation of the ageing Chinese father image in Ang Lee's "Father Knows Best" Trilogy: *Pushing Hands* (1991), *The Wedding Banquet* (1993), and *Eat Drink Man Woman* (1994). These three films demonstrate Lee's portrayal of the ageing fathers' experiences in transcultural spaces, in which generation gaps and cultural conflicts are intertwined. Lee's depiction of the Chinese father images demonstrates different forms of ageing masculinities in and between cultures, exploring the complex intersections among age, masculinity, and ethnicity. More specifically, by representing Master Chu in the *wen-wu* model in *Pushing Hands*, Lee dismantles the stereotypes of emasculated Chinese men in American mainstream culture and introduces a different perspective on perceptions of Chinese masculinities. By discussing the conflicts between Wai-tung's homosexuality and Mr. Gao's Confucian fatherhood in *The Wedding Banquet*, Lee explores both the suppression and wisdom of Confucianism, reflecting the positive values of Chinese ethics and traditions in defining flexible masculinities. By depicting Chef Chu's caring work and sexuality in *Eat Drink Man Woman*, Lee discusses the father's pursuit of a new life in his old age, dealing with issues of ageing, sexuality, and values of care in constructing masculinities. In other words, Lee's portrayal of the ageing Chinese fathers demonstrates that men's ageing experiences are anything but monolithic, and men's ageing is inflected by the particularities of race, culture, and sexuality respectively.

2. Master Chu in *Pushing Hands*: the *wen-wu* father[1]

Pushing Hands is Lee's first screenplay. It was first released in Taiwan in 1992 and later received a U.S. release after the success of *The Wedding Banquet*. *Pushing Hands* tells the story of a traditional Chinese father trapped by great changes in American society. A retired Chinese Tai Chi

---

1   This part relies on one chapter of my doctoral dissertation "Masculinities in Transcultural Spaces — Negotiations of Masculinities in Ang Lee's Films". https://edoc.hu-berlin.de/handle/18452/19713.

master, Mr. Chu (Sihung Lung), emigrates from Beijing to live with his son Alex (Bo Z. Wang), American daughter-in-law Martha (Deb Snyder), and grandson Jeremy (Haan Lee) in New York. The cultural differences cause misunderstandings and emotional conflicts among all the family members. Alex arranges a matchmaking picnic between Mr. Chu and Mrs. Chang (Wang Lai) to be absolved from his filial obligations. Feeling humiliated, Mr. Chu leaves home and washes dishes in a Chinese restaurant. Offended by his ruthless Chinese boss, Master Chu defeats the gangsters by turning their strength against them. Following his arrest, Mr. Chu's reputation as a Tai Chi master increases, and he later teaches Tai Chi to both Chinese and American residents in Chinatown. The film ends with Master Chu's accidental encounter with Mrs. Chang and hints at a possible union between them.

Portrayed as the "Yellow peril" and bachelor "Chinamen", Chinese men have long been depicted as "vile, womanly, cowardly and cunning" in American popular discourse (Pon 2000, 142). Such stereotypes are products of colonial and Orientalist discourse, resulting from American/Eurocentric writings. Analysing Ang Lee, Dariotis and Fung assert, "he presents his audience with alternative cultural histories that attempt to challenge the hegemonic views of the 'West'" (1997, 192). Following their line, I argue that Lee's depiction of Master Chu is culturally specific, providing an alternative understanding of masculinity in the *wen-wu* paradigm.

Kam Louie develops a *wen-wu* dyad to capture the Chinese masculine ideal over time in a broad spectrum, extending to contemporary China. According to Louie, "*wen* is generally understood to refer to those genteel, refined qualities associated with the literary and artistic pursuits of the classical scholars" (2002, 14). *Wu*, however, is a concept that embodies "attributes of physical strength and military prowess," as well as "the wisdom to know when and when not to deploy it" in the *wu* philosophy (2002, 14). "All ambitious males strive for both *wen* and *wu*", and those who achieve both are the great ones" (2002, 17).

Mr. Chu incarnates the traditional masculine ideal in terms of both *wen-wu* attributes. The opening shot of the film introduces him as a Tai Chi master: the camera casts an extreme close-up of hands pushing in the air, and then moves to a facial close-up of an old Chinese man. Fluid and dramatic camera movements portray his gestures with a diversity of shots, depicting Tai Chi visually as an emancipating, leisurely activity. Master Chu's physical prowess in Tai Chi is further displayed in the Chinese restaurant scene. After leaving his son's house, Master Chu finds a job as a dishwasher in a Chinese restaurant. The Chinese boss treats him disrespectfully, impatiently forcing him to leave the kitchen. Humiliated by his rudeness, Master Chu refuses to go. He stands rooted in place, summoning energy from Tai Chi, and resists the efforts of the Chinese gangsters to remove him. Whitney Crothers Dilley remarks that the father's "heroic action" requires "a distracting cultural shift" for the Western audience, which may be confused about Master Chu's "warding off the employer who has fired him and ordered him to leave the premises" (2007, 56). From the perspective of Chinese *wen-wu* masculinity, this fighting scene is a marvelous display of Master Chu's *wu* virility, which demonstrates not only physical strength but also the *wu* virtue. In Chinese culture, *wu* centers on but is not restricted to, martial and military force. *Wu* also embodies seven virtues: "suppressed violence, gathered in arms, protected what was great, established merit, gave peace to the people, harmonized the masses, and propagate wealth" (Louie and Edwards 1994, 142), which together means "the degree of military authority sufficient to make further engagement unnecessary" (142). In this sense, *wu* masculinity contains the Confucian notion of benevolence [仁] and self-restraints [忍] in deploying physical strength. The fighting scene embodies this *wu* philosophy. Master Chu behaves quite humbly and remains calm towards his ruthless boss until he is infuriated by his insulting words. Master Chu still remains calm and confident in the fight, displaying a Confucian concept of masculine honor in terms of benevolence and tolerance. Compared to the young gangster's bluff manners, he pushes them over leisurely with self-discipline and elegance. Such a scene may be read as a metaphor for Master Chu's remasculinization, symbolically transforming him from an emasculated Chinese man to a virile hero.

Master Chu strikes a balance of *wen-wu* attributes. Besides his prowess in Tai Chi, Mr. Chu exhibits other refined cultural practices such as writing calligraphy, reading poems, and playing chess. The camera casts several meaningful shots of the scroll on the wall and captures detailed moments of his practicing calligraphy, demonstrating his refined cultural taste in *wen*. Therefore, Lee's representation of Master Chu in *wen-wu* attributes provides an alternative interpretation to understand Chinese manhood, and thus dismantles the Orientalist stereotypes of Chinese men as emasculated.

Although Master Chu's masculinity is asserted in such a *wen-wu* model, his manliness is inevitably diminishing in the ageing process. The camera casts shots of Master Chu spending most of his time watching television at home. He takes a walk outside but then gets lost in the city. His *wen-wu* masculinity is also dwarfed in relation to his son Alex, who embodies the transformed *wen* man.

(01:12:15)
Mrs. Chang: "Mr. Chu, your Kung Fu is so powerful. How do you manage to have such elegant calligraphy?"[2]
Mr. Chu: "I am ashamed to talk about it. My grandfather was a scholar in the Qing Dynasty. My father was one of the Nation Founders, who is in charge of the Nationalist government. My son has a Ph.D. in computer science. In a family of scholars for generations, there is worthless me. I have practiced Tai Chi for life, but still cannot overcome the (pathetic) fate and circumstances."

This conversation demonstrates that Master Chu not only feels inferior to his ancestors, but also considers that his *wen* attributes in cultural refinements are inferior to his son's *wen* masculinity established through his middle-class profession and economic success. In *Theorising Chinese Masculinity* (2002), Kam Louie goes beyond pre-modern China, exploring the transformation of the *wen-wu* paradigm in the late twentieth century. He observes that the positive image of *wen* men in the new era is grounded in material success under Western influences. The

---

2   The English subtitles here are not accurate. Mrs. Chang points out critically that Mr. Chu's calligraphy skill is not as powerful as his Kung Fung and Mr. Chu's answer implies his inadequacy in *wen* attributes.

capitalist ethos reduces the values of certain attributes in traditional *wen* masculinity. Cultural tastes in calligraphy or music are rendered as less important whereas material success becomes a significant benchmark in the measurement of masculinity. Master Chu's self-perception demonstrates such a change in *wen*, destabilizing his traditional *wen-wu* masculinity.

Furthermore, the film underlines the deteriorating health of Master Chu, depicting an emotional image of the ageing father in the prison scene.

> (01:35:44)
> **Alex**: "Dad, we have bought a new house. It is much bigger than the old one."
> **Mr. Chu**: "What for?"
> **Alex**: "I am here to take you home."
> **Mr. Chu**: "Home? Whose home?"
> **Alex**: "Mine is yours."
> **Mr. Chu**: "Forget it. I see clearly now. The only thing that matters is that you have a happy life. If you want to show some filial respect, rent me an apartment in Chinatown. Let me peacefully pass my days and discipline my spirit. In your free time, bring the boy to see me. By this way, when we get together, there will be some good feelings."
> **Alex**: "Dad, all these years, I have studied and worked so hard to build a family in order that one day I could bring you the States, so you could have some good days in your life."
> (Alex bursts out into crying in the arms of Mr. Chu)

Film techniques are meaningfully employed to evoke emotional resonance and sympathy for the old Chinese father. The camera shows the father sitting in the prison from a high angle shot from the perspective of Alex, who stands in front of him, towering over him, thus marking the relationship dynamics of the vulnerable father and the powerful son. Then Alex bends down to Master Chu, and the camera moves closer to show Alex's head bowing lower to his father. The frozen shots keep Master Chu's profile in the dark, avoiding exposing his face, indicating his repression of emotions. Low and somber music played on the traditional

Chinese instruments er-hu portrays the inner pain and bitterness of the old father, whose face is not cast in light until Alex ends the conversation by bursting into tears in the arms of his father. The close-up of the father's withered face highlights his aging and his deteriorating health. Finally, the camera takes a long shot of the father hugging the son in the prison, demonstrating the ultimate reconciliation.

Besides the film techniques employed to stimulate understanding for the ageing father, the conversation also demonstrates Master Chu's self-adaption for the sake of his son in American culture. When Alex tells Master Chu to take him "home", the father asks whose "home" it is. It demonstrates the conflicts between two cultures. According the Confucian culture, "while his parents are alive, a son should not dare to consider his wealth his own or hold it for his own use only" [父母在, 不敢有其身, 不敢私其财].³ Such statements demonstrate the dominant position of father in the family over the son, who is expected to prioritize the needs of the father, providing him with material wellbeing in his old age. However, Master Chu has realized that American culture emphasizes personal boundaries and values self-reliance. He cannot take his son's home as his own. Alex's reply "mine is yours" indicates his regrets and adherence to the Confucian culture. But Master Chu finally choose to live alone. His choice is more an active self-sacrifice for his son according to Chinese culture than a forced acceptance of American cultural values. Master Chu prioritizes the happiness of Alex over his personal desire to live together with his son. In this way, Lee highlights the kindness, love and full devotion of the Chinese father to his son. Lee in this way maintains the self-esteem of the father and restores his image as a respectable father according to Chinese tradition.

In summary, portraying Master Chu as the *wen-wu* masculine ideal, Ang Lee challenges the assumption of Chinese men as emasculated. Despite of being destabilized in the transforming process of *wen-wu* attributes and ageing, Master Chu's masculinity is finally restored as a

---

3   This statement is from *The Book of Rites* (The Li Ki). Legge, James. Trans. *The Sacred books of the East*, Vol. 27–28. Ed. Max Müller. Oxford: Clarendon Press, 1923.

consequence of his adherence to Chinese traditions and self-adaption to American culture.

3. Mr. Gao in *The Wedding Banquet*: The Confucian father[4]

In the film *The Wedding Banquet*, a Chinese son Wai-tung Gao (Winston Chao) and his lover Simon (Mitchell Lichtenstein) are living in Manhattan. To stop his parents from pushing him to marry, he takes Simon's suggestion of a sham marriage with Wei-wei (May Chin), who is an artist from Shanghai and faced with deportation from the U.S. since she has outstayed her visa. Wei-wei moves into the basement and everything is supposed to be fine until Wai-tung's parents, Mr. and Mrs. Gao (Sihung Lung and Ah-Leh Gua), decide to make the trip from Taiwan to attend the wedding and meet their daughter-in-law. Wai-tung's plan for a small and uncomplicated civil ceremony at City Hall is thwarted when Mr. Gao's former driver offers his restaurant for a big traditional Chinese wedding banquet. Forced to drink excessively during the banquet, Wai-tung is seduced by Wei-wei and impregnates her. Ultimately, Wai-tung reveals his homosexual secret to his mother but wishes to keep it from his father. However, Mr. Gao sees through it early and shares his secret with Simon, whom he accepts as a kind of "son-in-law". Wei-wei finally decides to keep the baby and asks Wai-tung and Simon to be its fathers. The film ends with Mr. and Mrs. Gao's departure for Taiwan, and the whole family is left in the moment of pain, relief, and ambivalent emotions.

Mr. Gao is introduced as a retired military general to the audience at the beginning of the film through the voice of Mrs. Gao. Later, when he arrives in the apartment, the camera shots show his Chinese calligraphy scrolls, emphasizing his cultural attainments. As both a military general

---

4   This part relies on one chapter of my doctoral dissertation "Masculinities in Transcultural Spaces — Negotiations of Masculinities in Ang Lee's Films". https://edoc.hu-berlin.de/handle/18452/19713.

with *wu* power and a calligrapher with *wen* virtue, Mr. Gao conforms to the ideal Chinese masculinity. Moreover, the film portrays Mr. Gao as an ageing father full of wisdom, challenging the inverse correlation between masculinity and ageing in Western culture. In Chinese traditions, the old group represent experience, wisdom, order and authority, playing the role of moral governor. "The old is wise" is a deeply rooted idea. In ancient China, the elder people even could be elevated to high ranks, for the stage of old age is regarded as a natural progression towards maturation and wisdom. For example, in Tang dynasty, men in their 80s could be taken as county magistrate, in their 90s as county sima, and 100s as county governor (Xiao 2001, 87). This demonstrates a positive attitude towards ageing and a tradition of respecting the elderly. Therefore, the ageing father is considered as "a veritable hero in his son's eyes, in order that he may command, and maybe worthy to command his admiration and reverence" (Dawson, 154). Fathers in this sense are governors of Confucian moral and social criteria, "ever-watchful and loving guardian, happy in his son's well-doing and grieved, rather wroth, at his misdoings (154). In *The Wedding Banquet*, Mr. Gao is portrayed as such a Confucian father, emphasizing status hierarchy, social propriety and formality in the father-son relationship. He delivers a speech for the significance of the union at the wedding.

> (00:51:56)
> **Mr. Gao**: Wai-tung, Wei-wei, you two grew up differently. But fate unites the two of you here so far from home. It's something you should treasure. If differences arise... opinions... habits... you must work to resolve them. Always be thoughtful of (sic) each other. That's the key to a successful marriage.

Although this speech comes across as an inappropriate platitude in its comic context of the sham marriage between Wei-wei and Wai-tung, it sounds also like an insightful suggestion for establishing a harmonious and mutually beneficial partnership. Actually Mr. Gao follows his own words to "treasure" the family and be "thoughtful" of all the family members. Although no one tells him about Wai-tung's homosexuality, he "hears, understands and learns" and finally accepts Simon as another son: "Wai-tung is my son, and you are my son also". Shortly before his departure, the father, a typical Chinese male who makes little physical contact, holds Simon's hand tightly to bid farewell and thanks him, acknowledging him as a member of the Gao family. It demonstrates that the Confucian fatherhood does not mean a lack of love and intimacy, or psychological distance. The articulation of the soft and sentimental emotions of the old father cannot always be confined by the 'strict father' persona. Mr. Gao is portrayed far from a strict and stern father in the film. He hugs Wai-tung to express his parental love, recalling his memory when the son was a kid. He washes the dishes, an activity he regards as 'feminine' to show his comradeship with Simon: "Simon cooked, I'll wash". He leaves Wai-tung and Wei-wei a free choice whether to have the baby, though he expects a child to continue the family lineage. Lee's portrayal of Mr. Gao challenges certain stereotypes of the Chinese father with a stubborn adherence to outworn rules and ideas, indicating Lee's nostalgia for traditional Chinese fatherhood with aspect of wisdom, benevolence and love.

Moreover, Mr. Gao's masculinity is further constructed in the Confucian fatherhood in tackling conflicts between Wai-tung's homosexuality and the filial obligations, maintaining a harmony in family relations. In Confucianism, the discontinuing of a family name due to the lack of an heir is considered as the biggest offense against the ideal of filial piety, which is the most important determinant in defining manhood[5]. Fathers and sons are both governed by filial piety and "failure to do so would render himself an unfilial son in the eyes of his ancestor" (Ho 2013, 228). Wai-tung's homosexuality is the obstacle to fulfilling the filial obligations to both himself and his father Mr. Gao by discontinuing the familial lineage. The film centers around the issue of homosexuality, focusing on how Mr. Gao's fatherhood is maintained in the father-son conflict.

---

5   According to Bret Hinsch, the elevation of filial piety to a preeminent masculine ideal marks a radical distinction between manhood in China and the west (2013:7).

Firstly, the harmonious bonds are cemented by mutual secrets kept between Mr. Gao and Wai-tung. Wai-tung keeps his secret of homosexuality to maintain Mr. Gao's authoritative power and knowledge. When Wai-tung is challenged by Simon for his obedience to his parents, "look at yourself – your parents send you a form in the mail and you practically pee in your pants. You know, you are an adult – as a matter of fact, you're practically middle-aged." Wai-tung responds: "you're right, it's kind of stupid, all these likes, but I'm used to it". Simon cannot understand Wai-tung's lack of autonomy as a middle-aged man. In many cultures, particularly in the Western culture, manhood originally means departure from boyhood to adulthood, the need for asserting independence from the parents. A true man is mature, not only physically and financially, but also emotionally and in relationships. Nevertheless, a Chinese man always remains a child in relation to his parents. In contrast to asserting individual independence aggressively, he proves his maturity by suppressing his own desire for demonstrating a manly strength of will (Hinsch 2013, 8). Therefore, Wai-tung's obedience to his father not only indicates his maturity and manliness in self-restraint and filial piety, but it significantly demonstrates his great respect towards his father Mr. Gao.

Secondly, Mr. Gao does not exert authoritative demands on Wai-tung, but rather makes the mother Mrs. Gao the translator, and thus avoids the direct conflict between them. The film literally begins with the mother's voice on tape translating and speaking for the father, giving voice to his wish that Wai-tung would marry and procreate. Even when they arrive in the United States, the mother continues to act as the bearer of Chinese customs, while the father remains mostly silent. When Mrs. Gao is finally forced to recognize Wai-tung's homosexuality, she insists that Mr. Gao should not be told. "It would kill him", she says, sobbing quietly. It is true that his father has had a series of strokes, but her concern for his health masks the systemic role of secrecy as a bond in a patriarchal structure of authority. For the father to know things that are inconvenient or inappropriate casts doubt on his disciplinary parental role and threatens his authority. The greater his power is, the greater the prohibition on any challenge to it. Therefore, the mother becomes the bearer of guilt and a secret that, on the one hand, has made her role more significant; yet on the other hand, her agency and identity are completely disintegrated by the overwhelming importance of the connection between father and son (Dariotis and Fung 1997, 203).

But as it turns out, Mr. Gao has found out the "secret" his wife and son have tried to keep from him. Just before the Gaos depart, he gives Simon a birthday present, an envelope full of money, and reveals that he speaks English and has been aware of his son's homosexual relationship for a long time.

> (01:35:45)
> **Mr. Gao**: "Happy birthday, Simon."
> **Simon**: "Mr. Gao? You speak English?"
> **Mr.Gao**: "Please. Happy birthday."
> **Simon**: "My birthday. Even I forgot. Then you know, you've known..."
> **Mr. Gao**: "I watch, I hear, I learn. Wei-tong is my son. So you're my son, also."
> **Simon**: "Why, you...thank you."
> **Mr. Gao:** "Thank you."
> **Simon**: "When Wei-tong..."
> **Mr. Gao**: "No. Not Wei-tong, not Mother, not Wei-wei shall know. Our secret."
> **Simon**: "Why?"
> **Mr. Gao**: "For the family."
> "If I didn't let them lie, I'd never have gotten my grandchild" (in Chinese).
> **Simon**: "I don't understand."
> **Mr. Gao**: "I don't understand."

Mr. Gao here reveals (though not to Simon) that the cunning is necessary to ensure a familial continuity. In concealing his knowledge, Mr. Gao successfully maintains his authority as a proper father and surmounts the 'obstacle' of Wai-tung's homosexuality. Most significantly, as Fran Martin states, his (Mr. Gao's) power increases through the surprising but welcome revelation that such an initially distant "traditional, familial" and "Chinese" authority in fact contains within it what is effectively a familiar, liberal 'tolerance' of homosexuality (2003, 159). Consequently,

Mr. Gao's epistemological privilege over his son not only reconsolidates his authority, but also constructs a plausible image of reconciliation and harmony between father and son.

Thirdly, Lee's emotional portrayal of the ageing father further stimulates sympathy and concern from the son to maintain Mr. Gao's fatherhood. The beginning of the film reveals the poor physical health of the father through Mrs. Gao, rendering his long expectation for a grandchild understandable. Later, the father is found in a death-like doze in the room. The camera shows the father dozing on the sofa, using a high angle shot from the perspective of Wai-tung, who stands in front in low angle shots, visually foregrounding the contrast between the vulnerable father and the powerful son. Suspecting that he may be dead, Wai-tung comes close and bends down to check his breath. The camera takes a close-up of the father's withered face and then moves to the son, demonstrating Wai-tung's dilemma between his filial obligations to his ageing father and his individual freedom. The father turns to be rather weak each time when the father-son relation is on the edge. Finally, it is also due to the physical weakness of the father (he has a stoke) that Wai-tung agrees to keep the secret from him, thus avoiding to explicitly challenge the father's authoritative position.

In conclusion, Lee's sensitive portrayal of the father-son relationship exhibits a complicated picture of Mr. Gao as a paragon of Confucian fatherhood. Lee exposes the father's oppression of the son's male subjectivity, but meanwhile advocates Chinese tradition in the reconciliation of the father and the son. Despite of displaying an ageing and physically deteriorating father image, Lee underlines the father's wisdom in solving family conflicts, evoking understanding, awe and respect towards Mr. Gao. In this way, Lee also reflects on the positive cultural heritage in reconsidering the inverse correlations between ageing and masculinities.

4. Chef Chu in *Eat Drink Man Woman*: The caring and sexual father

Different from *Pushing Hands* and *The Wedding Banquet*, which focus on the father-son relationship, *Eat Drink Man Woman* tells the story of the father Chef Chu (Sihung Lung) and his three daughters: Jia-zhen (Kuei-Mei Yang), Jia-qian (Chien-lien Wu) and Jia-ning (Yu-wen Wang). Chef Chu is a retired master of Chinese cuisine in Taiwan. His wife has died many years ago and he has raised the daughters alone. Chef Chu regularly makes a sumptuous dinner for the big family get-together on Sunday evening, but the family table always becomes a battlefield for generational conflicts with an ending on bad terms. As his friend Chef Wen (Shui Wang) passes away, the youngest daughter Jia-ning and the eldest daughter Jia-zhen also move out of the house respectively, leaving Chef Chu alone. He decides to sell the house and start a new life with Jin-rong (Sylvia Chang) and her daughter Shan-shan. When he declares the love relationship at the dinner table, the whole family is shocked. All his daughters disagree to such a marriage between their ageing father and a young woman. In the end, the daughters accept the father's marriage with Jin-rong, with whom Chef Chu is expecting another child. The film ends with the second daughter Jia-qian's cooking for the reunion with the ageing father in the old house.

Lee's portrayal of Chef Chu demonstrates a refiguring of masculine identity in which age, values of care and emotional connections are intertwined. It focuses on the ageing father's experience of tenderness and complicated emotions, rather than simply portraying his sexuality in mechanical, phallocentric and ageist ways. The film opens with Chef Chu's marvelous culinary arts, exhibiting a domestic masculinity. The camera casts many close-ups of Chef Chu's cooking details, intercutting these with the daughters' reluctance in going back home, establishing him as the dominant family head. Although the three daughters are tired of the Sunday supper ritual, they dare not disobey their father. In the dinner scenes, the camera keeps casting characters in separate shots, indicating the alienation of them. The film depicts six dinner scenes, and the first four center on the daughters' escape from the family dominated by the father. In the first scene, the second daughter Jia-qian declares that she intends to invest in real estates and will move out. Her decision is a big blow for Chef Chu. Beautiful, independent and successful, Jia-qian works as an executive in an international corporation. Her resemblance with her mother indicates Chef Chu has preference toward her. At the dinner table, Jia-qian is critical of the taste of the soup, only to be impatiently interrupted and stopped by Chef Chu, asserting his unchallenged authority. When Jia-qian questions whether it is because of Chef Chu's deteriorating taste buds, he angrily disputes: "my taste buds are extremely good." Then the camera casts Chef Chu's receiving of the call from the restaurant, where he takes an authoritative position and can solve any unexpected problems in the kitchen. But it soon becomes clear that Chef Chu has lost his taste sensibility, relying on his friend Chef Wen for cooking. In the following dinner scenes, the obedient youngest daughter Jia-ning unexpectedly tells the family that she is pregnant. The eldest daughter Jia-zhen cannot wait for the end of the dinner to introduce her boyfriend. The camera casts long and distant shots of Chef Chu standing in front of the house, looking at the daughters' leaving, indicating his no longer being the family head.

Chef Chu's taste sensibility is a metaphor for his masculinity. As the daughters are leaving home respectively, Chef Chu is losing his sense of taste. When his friend Chef Wen passes away, he asks Jia-qian to change his tea to water, acknowledging that he cannot taste the difference. It indicates that Chef Chu has lost his masculine identity based upon domination. However, at the end of the film, when Chef Chu starts a new life with Jin-rong and reconciles with his daughters, he regains his taste sensibility. It can be interpreted as a recasting of caring masculinity.

The concept of caring masculinities has been put forward by K. Elliott in 2015. She proposes that "caring masculinities are masculine identities that reject domination and its associated traits, and embrace values of care such as positive emotion, interdependence, and relationality" (1). Elliot points out that the concept is not "a homogenizing character description of the 'new man'", but rather intends to "open up debate and discussion around the concept of care in men's lives" (2). Elliot identifies two main characteristics as the core of caring masculinities. The first is the rejection of domination. Because domination leads to inequality in a relationship, caring masculinities argue for an absence of domination in traditional masculinities to embrace gender equality. The second characteristic is recasting traditional masculine norms into affective, relational, interdependent and care-oriented qualities. For example, "respect" is not "fear" of the patriarch's authority but is coupled with "love". "Responsibility" can mean looking after a young life rather than being a breadwinner. Caring masculinities can therefore enrich men's lives emotionally, psychologically, and physically. In a word, caring masculinities can be recognized as "positive, enriching masculine identities", yielding new meanings for men (Elliot 2015, 15).

Chef Chu's masculinity is firstly reconstructed through his giving-up of domination in the father-daughter relations. After the death of his wife, Chef Chu takes the responsibility of bringing up the daughters. His caring work has left sweet memories for the daughters. Jiaqian has ever emotionally recalled her childhood with Chef Chu. However, as the daughters grow up and become independent, Chef Chu's caring work without boundaries seems to be oppressive, resulting in the daughters' rebellion and their escape from home. Chef Chu's later retreat from the daughters' lives not only brings a thawing in the father-daughter relationship but also recasts him from a dominant father to caring one. Hooks argues that "[r]ather than assuming males are born with the will to aggress, the culture would assume that males are born with the inherent will to connect" (2004, 117). Hooks' ideal of a connected, peaceful culture suggests that masculine identities do not have to include the practice of domination. With an absence of domination, Chef Chu further develops a caring masculinity in relation to his "new" daughter Shan-shan. Shan-shan is the daughter of Jin-rong, who later marries Chef Chu. Divorced and busy with her work, Jin-rong has no more time to take good care of Shan-shan. Chef Chu is much concerned with the little girl in kindergarten, preparing lunch boxes for her every day. Shan-shan exhibits her lunch boxes with great pride in front of all her classmates, which renders Chef Chu a "celebrity" in class. According to Niall Hanlon, "[c]aring was believed to offer common rewards, including feeling loved and respected for doing it, experiencing emotional intimacy and feelings of self-esteem, respect, and competence" (2012,137). In taking care of Shanshan, Chef Chu excludes domination, embraces the affective and emotional qualities of care and regains his self-esteem as a caring father.

Moreover, Ang Lee portrays a late love relationship between Jin-rong and Chef Chu, exploring the personal desires and sexuality of the ageing father. Chef Chu remains single half of his life in order to bring up his daughters and thinks little of himself. It is not until the end of the film that Lee declares that it is time for fathers to think what is best for himself. The film demonstrates the ageing father's loneliness and sexuality many times. After Chef Chu has solved the problem in the kitchen, the camera casts an emotional conversation between him and his old friend Chef Wen.

> *(0:23:01)*
> **Chef Chu**: I cannot cook any more. The tongue is getting worse. It depends on your face every time while I am cooking now.
> **Chef Wen**: No, it is all right. It's all about the chef who feels good. Cooking does not depend on your tongue. You are like a deaf man in a foreign country, Beethoven. The so-called good music is not in the ear, the good taste is not in your mouth. As for good women, I don't know where I can get.
> **Chef Chu**: You are drunk again.
> (They put arms on each other's shoulder, walking out of the kitchen)
> **Chef Chu**: Food and sex are what men and women desire. It is hard not to think about it. But I've been busy all my life only for it? It is annoying to think of it. Good taste (of food and sex), who has tasted it?

Such a conversation demonstrates the two ageing men's loneliness and desires. Chef Wen is the only one who understands and comforts Chef Chu. It is after Chef Wen's death that he determines to start a new life, pursuing the "good taste" of life. The camera casts several shots of his jogging in the park, figuring out healthy recipes, emphasizing his reconstruction of masculinity. When Jia-qian worries about her father's physical condition when seeing him in the hospital, Chef Chu is busy doing a pre-marriage checkup. At the end of the film, the camera casts shots of Chef Chu's intimacy with pregnant Jin-rong. He regains his taste sensibility and reconciles with the daughter Jia-qian in the old house for the last dinner. Such an ending indicates Lee's support and encouragement for Chef Chu's pursuit of his personal life, demonstrating Lee's care and concern for the ageing fathers in his "Father Trilogy".

In summary, Lee's portrayal of Chef Chu reconsiders the ageing father's experience in family responsibility and individual pursuits, recasting him from a dominating father to a caring one. Chef Chu's emotional vulnerability and his individual pursuits of sexuality for a new life in his old age demonstrate that more concerns should be advocated to the ageing men and their masculinities should not be overlooked or confined to certain gender norms.

5. Conclusion

This study has concentrated on the Chinese American filmmaker Ang Lee's "Father Trilogy" in order to analyse the ageing father image. These three films were directed in the early 1990s, in which China has transformed socially, culturally and economically, facing the ambiguities of entering the global arena. Lee's "Father Trilogy" illustrates some complex and profound changes in this period. Lee's representation of the ageing fathers concerns the conflicting encounter between China and the global world, questioning Western gender norms as universal, and reflecting Chinese cultural heritage in defining masculinities. However, Lee has never advocated a simplistic and essentialist fashioning of Chinese tradition. He instead explores a complex, profound and diversified transformation in masculinities through the ageing father images. For example, Mr. Chu's final withdrawal to Chinatown is not a sheer restoration of the Chinese *wen-wu* masculine ideal but also an adaption of his masculine identity. Lee's affirmation of the Confucian fatherhood in Mr. Gao is not a simplistic flaunt of the Confucian tradition but rather demonstrates a rethinking of the positive values of Confucianism in solving crisis and maintaining harmony for a family. Chef Chu's recasting of the caring masculinity demonstrate the practice of establishing new masculinities devoid of domination.

In this sense, Lee's depiction of the father images demonstrates the interactions between Chinese and Western cultures, pre-modern and contemporary world. In such a communicative arena, Lee advocates a flexible understanding of masculinities, which is more practice-based rather than an essentialist notion of certain cultures. In this sense, Lee's "Father Trilogy" portrays not just the variety but also the ambiguities that define men's gendered experiences of ageing.

Works Cited

[Chen, Xihe], 陈犀禾.[A comparative analysis of the Father Images in Ang Lee and Yimou Zhang's Films]. 台湾：国立交通大学出版社, 2006, 李安电影讨论会.

Dariotis, Wei Ming, and Eileen Fung. "Breaking the Soy Sauce Jar: Diaspora and Displacement in the Films of Ang Lee." *Transnational Chinese Cinemas: Identity, Nationhood, Gender*. Ed. Sheldon Hsiao-peng Lu. Honolulu: University of Hawai'i Press, 1997. 187–220.

Dawson, Miles Menander. *The Ethics of Confucius*. New York and London: The Knickerbocker Press, 1915.

Dilley, Whitney Crothers. *The cinema of Ang Lee: the other side of the screen*. London: Wallflower Press, 2007.

Eat Drink Man Woman. Dir. Ang Lee. Perf. Sihung Lung, Chien-lien Wu, Kuei-Mei Yang, Yu-wen Wang and Sylvia Chang. 1994, Good Machine.

Eliott, K. Caring masculinities: Theorizing an emerging concept. *Men and Masculinities*, 19 (2015): 240–259. http://dx.doi.org/10.1177/1097184x15577203.

[Fu, Rong], 付蓉. 从"恋父情结"解析李安电影中的文化内涵 [An analysis of the cultural connotation from the "Electra Complex" in Ang Lee's Films]. 电影评介 (2006): 8–9.

Hanlon, Niall. *Masculinities, care and equality: Identity and nurture in men's lives*. Basingstoke: Palgrave Macmillan, 2012.

Hinsch, Bred. *Masculinities in Chinese History.* Lanham, Maryland: Rowman & Littlefield publishers, Inc., 2013.

Ho, D.Y.F. "Fatherhood in Chinese Culture." *Father's Role: Cross Cultural Perspectives.* Ed. M. E. Lamb. Florence, KY: Routledge, 2013. 227–45.

Hooks, bell. *The will to change: Men, masculinity, and love.* New York, NY: Atria Books, 2004.

Legge, James. Trans. *The Book of Rites* (The Li Ki). *The sacred books of the East,* Vol. 27–28. Ed. Max Müller. Oxford: Clarendon Press, 1923.

Louie, Kam. *Theorising Chinese Masculinity: Society and gender in China.* Cambridge: Cambridge University Press, 2002.

Louie, Kam, and Louise Edwards. "Chinese Masculinity: Theorizing Wen and Wu." *East Asian History* 8 (1994): 135–48.

Martin, Fran. *Situating Sexualities: Queer Representation in Taiwanese Fiction, Film, and Public Culture.* Hong Kong: Hong Kong University Press, 2003.

Pushing Hands. Dir. Ang Lee. Perf. Sihuang Luang, Lau Wang, Bo Z. Wang Deb Snyder, and Haan Lee. 1992, Taiwan.

Pon, Gordon. "The Art of War or The Wedding Banquet? Asian Canadians, Masculinity, and Antiracism Education." *Canadian Journal of Education* 25.2 (2000): 139–151.

Saxon, Benjamin, and Thomas R. Cole. "No country for Old Men: A Search for Masculinity in Later Life." *International Journal of Ageing and Later Life* 7.2 (2012): 97–116.

Segal, Lynne. *Out of Time: The Pleasures and the Perils of Ageing.* London: Verso, 2013.

[Sun, Weichuan] ,孙慰川.试论李安<家庭三部曲>的叙事主体及美学特征 [The Narrative Subject and Aesthetic Features in Ang Lee's Trilogy]. 南京师范大学学报1 2007): 150–155.

Song, Geng, and Derek Hird. *Men and Masculinities in Contemporary China.* Leiden: Brill, 2014.

The Wedding Banquet. Dir. Ang Lee. Perf. Sihung Lung, May Chin, Winston Chao and Mitchell Lichtenstein. 1993. The Samuel Goldwyn Company. Taiwan and United States.

[Xiao, qunzhong], 肖群忠.孝与中国文化 [Filial Piety and Chinese Culture]. 人民出版社, 2001.

[Yu, Qunfang], 喻群芳. 李安电影中的恋父情结 [The "Electra Complex" in Ang Lee's Films]. 当代电影 5 (2004): 115–117.

Acknowledgements

This paper is supported by "the Fundamental Research Funds for the Central Universities", Zhongnan University of Economics and Law (103–31512210316, YB202138).

A Journey in Reverse
Myths of a Foreign Father in Aris Fioretos' Halva solen

Katharina Fürholzer

1. Introduction: intercultural generations through the ages

Implicitly oscillating between a fictional novel and a factual (auto)biography, *Halva solen* (2012; [Half the sun])[1] by Aris Fioretos – a Swedish writer of Austrian and Greek origin – presents the reader with an intergenerational migration story of a son confronted with the death of his father, a Greek physician who had immigrated to Sweden in the 1940s in the shadow of the Greek Civil War. Despite the emotional closeness between the son and the father (who are never called by their names but only described by their degree of kinship), the paternal (hi)stories of migration and (neurodegenerative) illness have caused a certain distance between parent and child. In his attempt to resolve the – almost mythical – foreignness surrounding his father, the son eventually embarks on an inner journey to reconstruct his parent's life. In the course of his biographical search, he traces his father's roots and routes in reverse order: beginning with the end of life, ending with the life's beginning.

While also touching on matters of care and relationality, matters of kinship, especially male first-degree blood relationships, are thus of par-

---

1 So far, *Halva solen* has not been translated to English. Unless stated otherwise, all English translations in this paper are mine.

ticular importance in Fioretos' book. By focussing on the lineal generational bond between a first-generation immigrant and a son who calls the father's outland his country of birth, *Halva solen* provides the reader with a story in which ties of kinship are contrasted with cultural ties. While studies on kinship used to be particularly anchored in anthropological studies, current research on present-day issues of migration in transnational contexts has recently become highly aware of the importance of this concept as well (see Andrikopoulos and Duyvendak 2020, 301–302). In this regard, the phenomena of mobility and kinship show certain analogies: on the one hand, "they both relate to power inequalities. The dynamics of kinship and the dynamics of mobility are products of power imbalances as well as the result of people's efforts to counteract these inequalities" (Andrikopoulos and Duyvendak 2020, 302). Additionally, kinship entails in itself a certain chronotopic mobility – as Janet Carsten argues, "kinship imaginaries encompass both past- and future-oriented visions. The capacity to think about and imagine past ancestors or to dream of future descendants, to travel forwards and backwards in time, is a fundamental property of kinship as it is of the human imagination more generally" (Carsten 2020, 331–332).

Based on a close reading of Fioretos' *Halva solen*, the aim of this paper is thus to understand in what way and with what (rhetorical and narratological) techniques the narrated stories of geriatric disease and migration-bound interculturalism lead to a juxtaposition of closeness and mythical foreignness. As I would argue in this regard, this mythical foreignness surrounding the father until the end of the story eventually opens the book up to other (migration) stories. While first ignoring the book's potential (auto)biographical ties, the second part of this paper will therefore also take an interest in matters of genre; in this regard, I will look at reader responses to Fioretos' work and the ethical implications of reading, interpreting, and biographical framing in the context of intercultural kinship.

2. Symptoms of alienation

In Fioretos' intercultural father-son narration, what is home to the one is alien to the other: while the father, the first-generation immigrant, was born in a country unfamiliar to the son, the son, the second-generation immigrant, was born in Sweden, a country that would remain foreign to the father until the end of his life. Due to this similarity of the unfamiliar within the verbatim familiar, the death of the father not only confronts the son with the loss of a parent who, until the end, had remained to some extent a mystery to him but also threatens to cut the fragile ties between the son's biographical identity and the chronotope of the father's past and origin. The son is thus left behind with an array of questions: who was his father, who and what shaped his early childhood days, his youth, his time before and after the migration? In what way were his biography, his longings and dreams, his doing and thinking, influenced by the Greek society and culture of that time? What was it like to lead a life shaken by war? How does it feel to bid farewell to this life and the people within it and leave a home country that has become foreign to find a new home in a foreign country? The son's questions remain unanswered, his possibilities to reach an understanding are limited; the father's country of birth, his environment, the Greek society and culture, the political and military circumstances of that time, the daily confrontation with the looming war, so much of the father's life remain literally outlandish to the son – his attempts to reconstruct the missing parts of his father's biography are faced with a chronotopic void filled with myths instead of facts.

That the narrated parent-child relationship is marked by cultural foreignness and distance is already insinuated in the very beginning of *Halva solen*, when the son learns about his parent's death via a phone call he receives from his mother while being abroad ("The son is sitting in a park café abroad when the mobile rings.", Fioretos 2012, 9). Being geographically separated, communication is only possible with the aid of auxiliary devices – spatial distance goes hand in hand with social distance. This depiction already corresponds to two primary dimensions of transitional families, namely the juxtaposition of spatial dispersion (i.e., having members of the family spread out across several nation-states) and relational interdependency (i.e., maintaining a sense of bonding despite long distance) (cf. Wall and Bolzman 2013, 61). The absence of specific details on the son's exact whereabouts, which are not revealed to the reader throughout the book, evokes the question as to what or who makes a country 'foreign:' are the son's current whereabouts (only) foreign to himself or (also) to his family? Is he staying in Greece, the father's home but a foreign country for the son, or in Austria, the native country of his mother, who, like his father, had been an immigrant to the son's country of origin, or in Sweden, his homeland and country of birth, that has remained foreign to the parents despite their thirty years of living there?[2] Or are his current whereabouts foreign to all of them because neither the son nor his parent(s) have a biographical relation to this place?

By denying any affirmative information, *Halva solen* emphasizes the subjectivity of terms such as 'abroad' or 'foreign,' while at the same time presenting the reader with the paradoxical dichotomy of the foreign in the familiar and the familiar in the foreign that may shape even the closest of kin relationships. In this context, foreignness is, however, not necessarily connoted in a negative way, as can be seen by one of the son's early memories of his father:

> the father walks like a metronome – matter-of-factly and steadily, with an unreal regularity in the movements, which causes others to take a step aside. An invisible force forms around him that makes men nod and women smile.
> Earlier, the son considered these reactions to be symptoms of the Dr Zhivago Syndrome. After all, strangers did not know who the father was. But the hat and the beard he wore at times made him look not familiar but nonetheless famous. For safety's sake, they greeted him. The summit of unjustified fame was reached in the Vienna of the

---

2   On several occasions, the decades the father had spent in Sweden are referred to as his time 'abroad,' cf. e.g. "During the years abroad, I've slept with my home village under the pillow – flat like a pebble, velvety like a cheek." (Fioretos 2012, 51; see exemplarily also 21, 78, 103, 105).

seventies. One day, the parents visited a museum in which Bruno Kreisky also happened to be. Perhaps the Austrian chancellor was opening an exhibition. When he spotted the father, he marched right across the hall and shook his hand enthusiastically. (Fioretos 2012, 66)

In the son's memory, the father's 'different' appearance usually did not cause hostile reactions such as (xenophobic) suspiciousness, but was met with curious respect. The positive associations linked to the father's otherness are further stressed by his comparison with Dr Zhivago, through which the father becomes characterized as a man who strives for the good and morally right, a man associated with idealism and humanism, a man who is even some kind of hero – a hero, however, who is not radiant and victorious but a tragic figure.[3]

The portrayal of the father as a tragic hero surrounded by an aura of foreignness is intensified by his medical (hi)story, as he is not only paraplegic after an accidental fall, but also suffers from Parkinson's disease and dementia. Thus, the father's life is marked by neurodegenerative diseases which lead to (self-)alienation. Accordingly, while the obscurity of the father's beginnings is owed to his migrational background, the obscurity of his end of life is an effect of his illnesses. The more the diseases affect his consciousness and personality, the more increases the distance to his surroundings. People around him are no longer able to understand his world view but need to rely on assumptions and speculations. For the son, the brutality of this pathological estrangement seems like the result of a hostile takeover:

> First came Colonel Parkinson, then General Dementia. Both sent their troops, which infiltrated the brain and slowly but surely turned off the nervous system. Despite his trembling and confusion, the

---

3   The comparison with Boris Pasternak's famous protagonist seems fitting on various levels, as both Yuri Zhivago and the father in Fioretos' narration are shown as physicians and poets standing in (inner) resistance to the political and military regimes of his home country (in *Doctor Zhivago* with regard to the Russian Revolution, in *Halva solen* with regard to the Greek Civil War).

father himself remained intact, albeit suppressed and eventually confined. When they talked to each other, it was unthinkable not to assume that he was still living somewhere behind the frontline, as self-evident and unexpected as ever. Yet the father was never besieged. (Fioretos 2012, 71)

From the son's perspective, Parkinson's and dementia are depicted as personified evils, as powerful and ruthless forces chasing and eventually managing to get hold of their victim. In this regard, the war metaphors[4] do not only serve as abstract proxies deployed to fathom the horrors of a life marked by neurodegenerative disease but seem to refer to one of the key moments of the father's biography. After all, it was the threat to become attacked by enemy 'troops' trying to 'infiltrate,' 'suppress,' and 'co^$nfine' their opponents that was crucial in his decision to leave his home country during the Greek Civil War. As a result, the father's pathographical and biographical (hi)stories are linked by the specific recourse to war metaphors, a link that is further strengthened by the narrator's figurative concatenation of the father's dementia with the realm of snow and ice:

> The ice palace in Doctor Zhivago is a symbol of frozen time. Maybe also of forgetting. Beneath the blanket of snow in his inside rests the past – untouched objects, vanished connections. Existence is congealed. A hasty movement and the meublement would powder. In recent years, the son has been thinking about whether this is what it looks like in his father's brain. He, who once was the world champion in delivering improvised speeches, can now hardly form a cohesive sentence. Already after a few words, he loses his train of thought, talks about something else, or falls silent. The thoughts crumble when touched. [...] The son asks himself: is the father held captive in an ice palace? Or is he the palace? (Fioretos 2012, 69)

---

4   See Susan Sontag (1978) for an extensive analysis of the use of war metaphors in the context of illness.

According to the narrator's metaphorical narrowing of neurodegenerative deterioration with the semantic field of winter, Parkinson's disease and dementia have put a bitter end to the once warm, light days of the father's 'summer' of life when his consciousness was still bright and intact. Now, in older age, the father's life has turned into a harsh and cold winter,[5] and the once impressive Zhivago-like figure has fallen into symptomatic oblivion, is no longer healthy and strong, but fragile and vulnerable. In fact, his vulnerability is so great that the slightest commotion might herald his final demise ("A hasty movement and the meublement would powder."). By metaphorically comparing the alienating effects of the illness with an abandoned house, the text calls to mind Homi Bhabha's notion of the "unhomely," this

> estranging sense of the relocation of the home and the world in an unhallowed place. To be unhomed is not to be homeless, nor can the "unhomely" be easily accommodated in that familiar division of social life into the private and the public sphere. [...] In that displacement the border between home and world becomes confused; and, uncannily, the private and the public become part of each other, forcing upon us a vision that is as divided as it is disorienting. (Bhabha 1992, 141)

In the metaphorical language of Fioretos' text, the father's innermost being has been invaded by an illness that has crept with icy cold into the once protective shelter of body and mind, has estranged it, alienated it, has left what once was familiar in 'unhomely' state, that unhomely in fact that this uncanny state is even noticed by those surrounding the father. With regard to the father's story of migration, this symbolic play with coldness and warmth, with darkness and light also allows to be read in a chronotopic manner: on the one side, there is Greece, the geographic epitome of sun and warmth, a place of the past, alive in memory only, and on the other side Sweden, land of snow and ice, home to a presence

---

5   Cf. also: "Perhaps he lived in the last chapter of his life in a world in which words and memories swirled around like flakes in a snow globe, without direction and gravity." (Fioretos 2012, 69–70).

marked by the threat that these memories, this past may fade away bit by bit until they have become forgotten. Hence, in the course of dementia's increasing obfuscation of time-bound lines of demarcation, the question arises at what point the remembered Greek past will appear more real to the father than the Swedish present. However, despite the severity of the threat the father's diseases pose to his consciousness and personality, the son begins to doubt that they are powerful enough to actually defeat the foundations of his father's being: "But does this mean that he [i. e. the father] is less himself than he used to be? The son still wonders what he would have learned about who one could be. Thinks: the nemesis is the lack of understanding." (Fioretos 2012, 71–72)

3. Fatherhood in retrospect

In light of the puzzle his father means to him, the son eventually embarks on an inner journey to reconstruct his parent's life. Through loose memories and anecdotes, cascades of questions that in times span several pages, and a conglomeration of "theses on a foreign father," the son compiles a biographical puzzle which in its fragmented form almost seems like an aesthetic tribute to the father's pathologically meandering state of mind. But his possibilities to do so are, naturally, limited, as ever since the father's illness and death, anything the son might want to ask is inevitably turned into a rhetorical question that only evokes a plethora of follow-up questions. In *Halva solen*, the conversational void caused by the father's terminal illness (hi)story is, however, revoked by a literary stratagem, as the narration is regularly interspersed with drama-like sequences consisting of staged dialogues between father and son that allow them to reunite, at least on a fictive level, and to try out possible answers to the son's concerns:

> A SON: Where did you love to be most in your life?
> THE DIED: Hard to say. Perhaps out and about.
> A SON: You mean on the move?
> THE DIED: M-hm. On the road. On my bare feet. (Fioretos 2012, 131)

Disrupting the natural flow of prose, the dramatic form changes the impression of reading a factual biography and instead lets the story appear as a work of fiction. Given the specifics of the intercultural parent-child relationship, the alienating effect evoked by the use of common paratextual attributes such as stage directions or role descriptions, as well as the fact that one of the dialogue partners is already dead, seems like a foreshadowing answer to the father's emanating foreignness. The confusion the playlets evoke is further increased by the awkward term "the Died," an infantilized appellation of the father derived from a quotation of his six-year-old granddaughter ("Grandpa, he is died." [sic] Fioretos 2012, 9). While the reference to children's language implicitly suggests that the son still views the deceased from the (restricted) perspective of a child, he eventually realizes that he might only be able to understand the father when he turns to a phase of the parent's life unrelated to himself:

> A SON: It's dragging on, but I intend to work my way back. Each new tableau will be a step – a year, a breath of air – back to the time before you became Dad. The ending will be the beginning. This is a song in reverse.
> THE DIED: What is that supposed to be good for?
> A SON: Well, I want to save you, of course! Make you a person who is not DAD and hence cannot die as Dad. (Fioretos 2012, 49)

By exclusively using the definite article when addressing the deceased (cf. *"the* Died" vs. *"a* son"), the son's significance for the life of his father fades into the background: it is the father's (life) story that is to be told, and all others are only secondary characters in this regard. In philosophical discussions about life and life after death, about matters of identity in a life lived between different times and places, about memories between fact and fiction, the dramatic sequences thus indicate the son's attempt to gain a more holistic understanding of the deceased – the loss of the parent is counteracted by the gain of the person he may have been outside the restrictive exclusivity of fatherhood.

Confronted with his father's death, the son therefore turns to the father's (temporal) beginnings and (spatial) origins. In the form of a remembrance and narration in reverse, he advances ever further, ever deeper into the dark. Starting from the known and familiar, and moving on to what is foreign to him, the son heads off to explore distant places and forgotten times. This inner journey leads him from the death of the father to his illness and need for care, to the father's life in Sweden as an immigrant physician, and eventually to the birth of his son, all of which is supplemented by loose references to the father's days as a medical student, the time of emigration, and his youth back home in his Greek country of origin. Like a wanderer going back a path in search of something lost along the way, the son retraces the father's steps in the opposite direction, follows his routes, his deviations and detours, tracks down the times and places where he stayed and those he left. By gaining an increased understanding of the foreign in the familiar, the temporal and spatial distance between the son's present and the father's reconstructed past is eventually paralleled by a growing closeness between parent and child. The experience of a paradoxical simultaneity of foreignness and familiarity as well as of des- and re-orientation is also repeated on a metatextual level: by departing from familiar norms of diegetic time, the anachronic line of vision in Fioretos' father-son narration implicitly mirrors the rejection of norm(alitie)s that experiences of illness and migration can mean for those affected. In this regard, the constant pausing and stumbling evoked by the temporal flashbacks create a moment of alienation also for the reader, which gradually dissolves alongside the son's growing advance into the family's history.

However, the son eventually must acknowledge that no matter how successful his archaeological search, the mysterious darkness framing the father's life will never fully dispel. The opacity, incompleteness, and unreliability that surround this biographical search for the father are not least due to the general susceptibility of error inherent to (auto)biographical work: As Martina Wagner-Egelhaaf (2005) points out, memory is the anchor point of narrated memories, which makes the (auto)biographical stance of remembrance usually an uncritical and unreliable one: after all, what is stored in memory is subject to constant shifts in perspective and accent. As a result, the remembered past is not to be seen as consistent but as something that is continuously constructed and re-constructed (60–61). Hence, (auto)biographical memory usually alternates between reality, truth, and fiction, between "historical reality and [the] subjective position of the author," (2) which is why (auto)biographical work is inevitably prone to perspective (43–44). In Fioretos' book, this is accentuated by the son's clear awareness that both fact and fiction form the foundation of his biographical search:

> The father contains much that concerns the son. If he [i. e. the son] wants to narrate [i. e. the father's story] back to before the beginning of the world, this can by no means be done without the myths. And neither with the things the father preferred to remain silent about, which always created a void that had to be filled with assumptions. [...] both facts and phantasy are needed [...]. (Fioretos 2012, 16)[6]

The son's inclination to resort to the realm of myths and fantasy in order to obtain a holistic picture of his father even causes him to elevate the parent to a saint or hero instead of showing him as the normal human being he was. The son's concatenation of his biographical approach with the world of myths and legends is explicitly emphasized in the fictive dialogues he has with his father: "When I come to consider it, you make a good Ikaros – you distort me like a Cretan," (Fioretos 2012, 94) the father notes on one occasion and critically adds: "Do you want people to lose faith in me? I was a father made of ordinary timber (pine, not birch)." (Fioretos 2012, 94) Time and again, the father warns the son against blurring the lines between biographical framing and glorification as it would not do him justice but create an image that no longer has much to do with the truth: "You look at me as if you were inventing me. Don't do that," (Fioretos 2012, 97) he admonishes the son. "I don't know what you think you're doing, my son. But I don't recognize myself in these ... *legends*." (Fioretos 2012, 94 [original emphasis]) In Fioretos' kinship, commemorating the dead is thus eventually presented as tantamount to the

---

6   See also, e.g.: "Before the son leaves the red room [i. e. the funeral home], he thinks that the father also consisted of myths" Fioretos 2012, 15).

instruction to accept foreignness as an integral part of identity. As the father at one point notes: "The past consists of many doors. Not all of them can be opened." (Fioretos 2012, 164)

4. Perception and acceptance of foreignness

Aris Fioretos' book *Halva solen* bears obvious resemblance to the migrational background of its author, which is expressed from the very beginning as it is a photograph of Fioretos' father that is shown on the book's cover.[7] Although *Halva solen* is not assigned to a specific genre, neither textually nor paratextually, – the book is simply described as a form of 'prose' – Fioretos' intercultural father-son narration thus has been frequently interpreted as a non-fictional (auto)biography.[8] While (auto)fictional (life) stories are at least to some extent the result of invention and thereby embody the unknown and unfamiliar, *Halva solen* is this way instead associated with the realm of the author's famil(iarit)y. In consequence, the (auto)biographized approach cannot be separated from matters of ethics. After all, when reading a literary work as a form of biography, the question arises as to whether the persons represented in it are, to quote G. Thomas Couser (2004), "liable to exposure by someone with whom they are involved in an intimate or trust-based relationship but are unable to represent themselves in writing or to offer meaningful

---

7   Cf. the photo credits in Fioretos 2012, copyright page.
8   Cf. e.g.: "In aphorism-like form, Fioretos builds up intimate memories of his deceased father, reconstructed with attention to detail, each fragment a deliberation with what constitutes his/a Greek father." (Lüderitz 2012); "Aris Fioretos […] turns his dad into a person who is not a dad, not completely, and therefore cannot die as dad." (Andersson 2012); "The book is a portrait of the author's father" (Leijonhufvud 2012); "The book takes a rear-view perspective in telling of the writer's father, always with the open question of how much we can know about another human being." (Kollberg 2012). The translations of the quoted reviews by Andersson, Leijonhufvud, and Kollberg are retrieved from the author's website: http://arisfioretos.com/en/halva-solen-en/.

consent to their representation by someone else." (xii)[9] Would the father of Fioretos' story, for instance, really have agreed to being publicly represented by his son? Has his privacy, reputation, and personal integrity been accounted for in his public portrayal? Would the father approve of the specific way he is depicted? In light of the father's neurodegenerative diseases or the fact that he was already dead when the book was written and thus unable to consent to his general and specific portrayal, matters of vulnerability and liability become all the more urgent, as the closer the relationship between an author and the persons represented by him or her, and the stronger the degree of dependence between them, the higher the ethical responsibility (see Couser 2004, 19). While Couser explicitly refers to the person of the author in this context, his deliberations also seem to carry weight for readers. After all, to read means to interpret means to frame biographically: reading about another person's life is inevitably a form of interpretation, which implies making assumptions about the life story of the person concerned. Despite their apparent differences in form and effect, Aris Fioretos' literary representation of the father's life in *Halva solen* touches, therefore, as much (ethical) matters of – fictional or factual – biography as the narrated son's attempt to reconstruct his father's life as a reader's potential equation of the book's characters with the life of the writer Aris Fioretos.[10]

However, by continuously playing with the dichotomous concurrency of foreignness and famil(iarit)y both on the level of content and form, *Halva solen* ultimately circumvents matters of vulnerability and (author) responsibility. In this regard, it is not least the fact that the book is not (paratextually) assigned to an explicit genre that prohibits us from reading *Halva solen* as a biographical account. Further strengthened by the dramatic – and obviously fictive – sequences and the pseudonymizing character-descriptions the book thus creates an estranging effect

---

9   For ethical implications of biographical work see also Couser 2012, 79–107. For ethical dimensions of pathographical writing see Fürholzer 2019.

10 For an in depth-investigation of the ethical responsibilities of readers towards books, authors, readers, and society see in particular Booth 1988, especially 126–137.

which makes it almost impossible for the reader to clearly distinguish between (auto)fictionality and (auto)biography – and thus between the realms of foreignness and famil(iarit)y. As a result, Fioretos' father-son narration becomes surrounded with the notion of unfamiliarity and foreignness commonly associated with the semantic space of fiction. Consequently, the author Fioretos as well as his family blur with the (potentially fictionalized) world of characters, which does protect them at least from biographical interpretation.

This is additionally strengthened by the book's persistent eschewal of personal names in favour of terms of kinship: the son, the brother, the wife, the father. In the German translation of *Halva solen*, this connotation is taken even one step further by the added subtitle "Ein Buch über einen Vater" [A book on a father]: by using an indefinite article instead of a definite 'the' or possessive 'my father,' the translation works from its very beginnings with generalizing proxies that allow being filled with different stories and names. As a result of all this, Fioretos' book *Halva solen* is not restricted to one particular biography but becomes opened up for other (migration) stories as well. In a review of the book, one reader thus draws analogies to her own story: "I identify with the unrest that over and over overwhelmed him [i. e. the father in *Halva solen*], which caused the family to move every other year." (Xeniana 2013) Another reader implicitly declares the figure of the Greek immigrant that can be found in several of Fioretos' books a symbolic ambassador for the wave of first- and second-generation guest workers in the middle of the twentieth century: "As the 'guest worker child' of the 'baby boomer' generation, I've read the book also as an honouring homage to the life of my father, who was born in Asia Minor in 1924 and died in Germany in 2003." (Werdelis 2013) Reminded of his own family history, he thus explicitly dedicates his review to the "memory of my father."

While *Halva solen* thus also opens up to the readers' own stories, its complex play with means of estrangement – starting from the (interwoven) topoi of geriatric disease and migration-bound transitions and the associated juxtaposition of closeness and distance, of familiarity and foreignness, through to the recourse to myths and phantasy, the merger of fact and fiction, and a correlating ambiguity of genre – never ceases to underline the general unfathomability of another person's life we may even encounter when trying to comprehend those next of kin.[11] The intertwined concurrence of the dichotomous poles of foreignness and familiarity that seems inherent to intergenerational migration stories such as *Halva solen* may challenge both their characters and their readers in this regard: after all, the son's ultimate insight that his father will always retain a certain degree of mythical otherness that the child may never fully grasp can also be understood as not only an ethical but also an ontological imperative for the book's readers. By emphasizing the mythical as the alpha and omega of the life told, *Halva solen* implicitly points to the fundamental ontology of human existence: there is no human being who will not remain at least to some degree a mystery to others, just as humans cannot fully grasp the *conditio humana* in itself. The ancient attempt of humankind to understand the origins of our existence – the riddle of human evolution both in the phylo- and ontogenetic sense, the singularity of individual humanization bound to the randomness with which egg and sperm meet each other, the miracle of birth and life – are ultimately as unanswerable as its counterpart, the unfathomability of dying and death, the possibility of a post-mortal existence, the overwhelming metaphysics of the afterlife. Those who do not shy away from the metaphysics of the beginning and ending of individual life and life in general inevitably will enter the realm of myths. Conjecture and phantasy will shape their search, fictionality will blur with reality, facticity will remain a wish, a dys- or utopia that will define the possibilities of what can and what cannot be said and understood. As Fioretos' book implicitly suggests, accepting foreignness in others can thus not least be understood as a token of respect for the (even mythical) unfathomability of both individual identity and the human condition.

---

11   By oscillating between the factual and the fictional – which, in the context of the book, seems like a consistent metaleptic mirror of the unfathomable ambiguity of the father's identity –, *Halva solen* not least reminds of Frank Zipfel's (2009) statement that (auto)fictional texts may level a "general (post)modern criticism against the concept of a homogeneous, coherent, autonomous, self-conscious and self-transparent subject" (307).

Works Cited

Andersson, Tim. "Fioretos kan väcka en död." [Fioretos can wake a dead person.] *Arbetarbladet* (12 March 2012). https://www.arbetarbladet.s e/artikel/fioretos-kan-vacka-en-dod (23 July 2021).

Andrikopoulos, Apostolos, and Jan Willem Duyvendak. "Migration, mobility and the dynamics of kinship: New barriers, new assemblages." *Ethnography* 21.3 (2020): 299–318.

Bhabha, Homi. "The World and the Home." *Social Text* 31/32 (1992): 141–153.

Booth, Wayne C. *The Company We Keep: An Ethics of Fiction*. Berkeley, Los Angeles and London: University of California Press, 1988.

Carsten, Janet. "Imagining and living new worlds: The dynamics of kinship in contexts of mobility and migration." *Ethnography* 21.3 (2020): 319–334.

Couser, G. Thomas. *Memoir: An Introduction*. New York: Oxford University Press, 2012.

Couser, G. Thomas. *Vulnerable Subjects: Ethics and Life Writing*. Cornell: Cornell University Press, 2004.

Fioretos, Aris. *Halva solen* [Half the sun]. E-Book. Stockholm: Norstedts, 2012.

Fürholzer, Katharina. *Das Ethos des Pathographen. Literatur- und medizinethische Dimensionen von Krankenbiographien* [Ethics of pathography. Ethical dimensions of illness biographies from the viewpoint of medical humanities]. Heidelberg: Winter, 2019.

Kollberg, Ingvar. "En blivande klassiker." [A future classic.] *Upsala Nya Tidning* (12 March 2012). https://unt.se/kultur/litteratur/en-blivande -klassiker-1690517.aspx (23 July 2021).

Leijonhufvud, Åke. "Halva solen lyser klart." [Half the sun is shining bright.] *Sydsvenskan* (12 March 2012). https://www.sydsvenskan.se/ 2012-03-12/halva-solen-lyser-klart (23 July 2021).

Lüderitz, Cathrin. [Review of the German translation of Aris Fioretos's *Halva solen*]. *goodreads.com* (22 March 2020). https://www.goodreads .com/book/show/14059593-halva-solen (23 July 2021).

Sontag, Susan. *Illness as Metaphor*. New York: Straus and Giroux, 1978.

Wagner-Egelhaaf, Martina. *Autobiografie* [Autobiography]. 2. ed. Stuttgart: Metzler, 2005.

Wall, Karin, and Claudio Bolzman. "Mapping the New Plurality of Transnational Families: A Life course perspective." *Transnational Families, Migration and the Circulation of Care: Understanding Mobility and Absence in Family Life*. Ed. Loretta Baldassar and Laura Merla. New York: Routledge, 2014. 61–77.

Werdelis, Stefan. "In memory of my father." [Review of the German translation of Aris Fioretos's *Den siste greken*]. *Amazon.de* (26. April 2013). https://www.amazon.de/letzte-Grieche-Roman-Aris-Fioretos/dp/3423143118/ref=sr_1_1?__mk_de_DE=ÅMÅŽÕÑ&dchild=1&keywords=der+letzte+Grieche&qid=1614873338&sr=8-1 (23 July 2021).

Xeniana. "A homage on a father." [Review of the German translation of Aris Fioretos's *Halva solen*]. *Amazon.de* (29. April 2013). https://www.amazon.de/Die-halbe-Sonne-einen-Vater/product-reviews/3446241213/ref=cm_cr_dp_d_show_all_btm?ie=UTF8&reviewerType=all_reviews (23 July 2021).

Zipfel, Frank. "Autofiktion: Zwischen den Grenzen von Faktualität, Fiktionalität und Literarität?" [Autofiction: Between the Borders of Factuality, Fictionality and Literacy?]. *Grenzen der Literatur: Zu Begriff und Phänomen des Literarischen* [Borders of Literature: On the Term and Phenomenon of Literariness]. Ed. Simone Winko, Fotis Jannidis and Gerhard Lauer. Berlin and New York: De Gruyter, 2009, 285–314.

Queer Kinship
Masculinity, Age and the Closet in the Windrush Generation in Bernardine Evaristo's *Mr Loverman* (2013)

Kristina Weber

1. Introduction

Since Anglo-Nigerian author Bernardine Evaristo's novel *Girl, Woman, Other* won the Booker Prize, jointly with Margaret Atwood, in 2019, the author and her work have received much critical and popular attention. While this novel takes the representation of diverse black woman characters as its subject matter, its direct predecessor *Mr Loverman* (2013a), Evaristo's seventh novel, focusses on the story of an old gay man and the themes of masculinity, homophobia and self-realisation. Evaristo wrote the novel as part of her doctorate in Creative Writing at Goldsmiths, University of London. In the theoretical part of her thesis, which discusses the representation of black men in British fiction, she states, "I had never encountered this mix of age, race and homosexuality in British fiction" that characterises her protagonist (Evaristo 2013b, 352). In fact, it is easier to find black British texts on older queer *women* than on men, if only slightly, and only when using a broad definition of the term 'older'.[1] Thus,

---

1   In *Girl, Woman, Other*, the queer women Bummi and Amma are at least middle-aged. In the queer black British anthology *Sista!* (2018), edited by Phyll Opoku Gyimah et al., there are a few non-fiction pieces by and about old(er) queer black women (Mason-John; Rose; Cole-Wilson; Ekine; and Beadle and Beadle-

the novel's representation of this intersectional and marginalised set of identities – one that is influenced by masculinity and age – is a trailblazing one.

The novel follows seventy-four-year-old Antiguan immigrant Barrington "Barry" Walker who has been married to a woman, Carmel Walker née Miller, for fifty years. He is the father of two adult children, Donna and Maxine, and grandfather to Daniel. He is, however, leading a double life since he has been having a much longer, secret relationship with a man, Morris de la Roux, for sixty years. The plot is centred on Barrington's slowly coming to terms with openly expressing his queer identity, and then coming out to his community. The inner conflict around these themes is closely connected to the normative expectations that his social environment associates with masculinity and age. The narrator-protagonist has internalised these expectations to such a degree that they negatively impact his potential of developing meaningful kinship ties. Barrington discloses his non-conformity in the climax of what can be called a coming-out plot,[2] thereby rejecting the unattainable standards for his performance of masculinity. In the novel's second half, he and Morris look forward to a happier rest of their lives where they can openly acknowledge each other as family and are part of a larger (black) queer community. The relationships to biological and legal

---

Blair, all 2018). Its equivalent anthology on black gay men, *Black and Gay in the UK* (Gordon and Beadle-Blair 2014), however – whose explicit intention is to fill a gap of representation in the British literary landscape – does not include any representation of old men, and barely any of middle age (if the 46-year-old protagonist of "Retrograde" by Donovan E F J Morris [2014] is to count as such). Caroline Koegler (2020, 5) points out how its dedication to "boys, girls, and girlboys" unnecessarily constricts the collection to young age.

2   The novel plays with this conventional plotline of queer stories by giving it to an old black man instead of a white teenager. A recent, very popular example of the latter trend is Becky Albertalli's young adult novel *Simon vs. the Homo Sapiens Agenda* (2015) with its accompanying blockbuster movie, *Love Simon* (Berlanti 2018), which falls neatly into this formula. By tapping into this tradition and subverting it, the particular set of marginalised identities of *Mr Loverman*'s protagonist is highlighted.

family[3] are re-negotiated and the chosen, alternative kinship ties that get a chance to develop through Barrington's character growth receive a higher standing. Thus, *Mr Loverman* contributes to a positive exploration of the possible kin relations of old gay black British men. Meanwhile, the novel simultaneously perpetuates normative ideas around these identity positions. The protagonist's high sex drive challenges the de-sexualisation of old age, while promoting both gay hypersexuality and the normative pressures around 'successful aging'. Further, since the coming out functions as such a turning point in his outlook on life – and his position within kin networks – it frames his closeted life as tragic, worthless and lost. Throughout this chapter, I will investigate how Barrington's kinship formations are entangled with these discourses.

2. Masculinity in Intersection with Age, Queerness and Migration

2.1 The Windrush generation

Having migrated to Great Britain in the early 1960s, the main characters Morris, Barrington and Carmel are clearly positioned as part of what is now called the 'Windrush generation,' the first large-scale wave of (mostly) Caribbean immigrants to arrive in Great Britain as labourers from 1948 to the early 1970s. This background is laid out in the novel in Barrington's clothing style, the Caribbean community around his wife's church friends, and the history of discrimination in the job and housing markets.[4] As Caroline Koegler (2020) and Lucinda Newns (2020) have both pointed out recently, placing a gay character within this specific history is groundbreaking. It redefines the established images of "hypermasculine heterosexuality" (Newns 2020, 142) that have been

---

[3] These include spouses and their family members (legal kin), as well as one's own children, parents and siblings (biological kin).

[4] See, for instance, the collection of accounts from members of this generation in Grant (2019), who attest to such circumstances.

attached to male immigrants of this generation, not least due to such portrayals in novels like Sam Selvon's *The Lonely Londoners* (1956), which is now considered a black British classic.

The Caribbean is furthermore notorious for its homophobic attitudes, ones that have been recognised by several scholars to be a relic of colonial anti-sodomy laws (see e.g. Gaskins 2013, 430). This cultural climate at large, not just the Windrush generation, produces distinctly hegemonic expectations for a masculine gender expression. The concept of 'hegemonic masculinity' was introduced by Raewyn Connell in 1995, who suggests that masculinities exist in the plural, rather than as one monolithic expression, and that some realisations of masculinity – by young, white, heterosexual men – are privileged over others. Those men who do not occupy these spaces are stigmatised as deviant and effeminate (Connell 2005 [1995]). The Caribbean context, then, produces a very rigid image of an ideal masculinity that queer men cannot live up to.

2.2 Failure to meet society's normative expectations of masculinity

This context leads to Barrington's difficult relationship with these expectations. The main character constructs himself as highly masculine by explicitly referring to traditional (one might say old-fashioned) masculine ideals, and actively modifying his behaviour to meet them. He is the patriarch in his home who rejects doing any domestic work, hates feeling and expressing emotions, always dresses in a three-piece suit, and thinks gender nonconforming people are ridiculous. Yet, due to his queerness, there are parts of his gender expression that are considered feminine or flamboyant: His partner Morris jokingly describes him as "So bloody-minded, so individualistic, so clothes-conscious and what some might call a 'colourful personality', at least when they being [sic][5]

---

5   The narration and dialogue are occasionally rendered in Caribbean dialect. Due to its frequency, I will not continue to mark such deviations from Standard English.

polite" (Evaristo 2013a, 101). His clothes-consciousness and individualism point to a feminine inscription of his gender, and the "colourful personality" directly denotes flamboyance. The final phrase of this quote indicates that Barrington's gender expression is non-normative enough for others to point it out and judge him for it since the 'impolite' phrases one might find are most likely femmephobic slurs.[6] Although Morris's specific utterance here falls under teasing and banter, it gives clear hints at Barrington's gender expression that does not comply with the intensely masculine ideals he and his surroundings hold for him. His autodiegetic and unreliable narration does not pick up on his deviance, however. This signifies the protagonist's dissociation and denial of the difference between his gendered reality and his idealised view of himself.

The negotiation between his queerness and the normative expectations for masculine gender expression that he has grown up with dominates much of the novel's discourse and the protagonist's outlook on life. At one point, Barrington connects the perpetrators of a violent homophobic attack he endured in London in the 1970s with the attitudes that were common in Antigua: "They was the same kind of boys who bullied any boy back home who wasn't manly enough, who wore too-bright shirts, who was a bit soft in his manner, who needed straightening out" (Evaristo 2013a, 122). The cultural contexts of Antigua and Great Britain thus both police gender expression, as men and boys who do not successfully perform a very specific – and, arguably, toxically confined – branch of masculinity are outcast and punished. It is repeatedly made plain to Barrington that gay men cannot meet the heterosexual norms of hegemonic masculinity, which makes him even more determined to try, and it forces him to hide a significant part of his life and personality for over seventy years.

Whenever Barrington falls short of the masculine norm, chiefly through his queerness, he experiences self-hate, a feeling that has

---

6   Femmephobia, sissyphobia and similar terms describe the latent stigmatisation of feminine gender expression in (cisgender) men, even within gay circles (see Brightwell 2018, 15–16).

been described as internalised homophobia (cf. Allen and Olleson 1999, 33–34). As teenagers and young men, he and Morris had hoped they could 'cure' themselves of their orientation, which they are forced into experiencing as pathology through their homophobic surroundings. In the narrative present, the protagonist fearfully imagines a day when he is shunned as a "HOMO" or "*Buggerer of men*" (Evaristo 2013a, 132, 134) in the streets of London if he ever admits his relationship and orientation to others. The usage of slurs, especially the latter variant that is specific to Caribbean dialect, shows the impact of homophobia from both of his life contexts. Barrington struggles strongly with society's unattainable expectations of masculinity, and his internalisation of them, which leads to conflict and inner turmoil. As I will show below, this fear and self-hate negatively influence his kinship ties.

2.3 Non-normative male ageing

Another aspect that influences Barrington's experience of his masculinity is his age. From the very beginning, the characters' old age is part of their self-image and the narrator's cynical banter. Most often, allusions to old age underline the story's comic tone:

> So there we was in the dancehall amid all of those sweaty, horny youngsters (relatively speaking) swivelling their hips effortlessly. And there was I trying to move my hips in a similar hula-hoop fashion, except these days it feels more like opening a rusty tin of soup with an old-fashioned tin opener. (Evaristo 2013a, 2)

The two men are noticeably older and their lives, for which they sometimes express nostalgia, have changed because of it. However, they do not excessively mourn that fact or succumb to lethargy as a result. They rather continue with adapted versions of their former activities. As Stephan Karschay and Joanna Rostek have pointed out, instead of treating old age "as a problem-ridden and negatively connoted stage of life", as novels frequently do, *Mr Loverman* adopts a "positive stance [...] on the issue of (male) aging" (2016, 132).

Their qualification in parentheses is apt, since the novel's positivity towards ageing does not extend to Barrington's forty-year-old daughter, Maxine. She receives the most age-related comic treatment, where she sometimes becomes a stereotyped character. Maxine is childish, uses exaggerated youth slang such as *"whatevs"* or *"Totes* amazeballs" (Evaristo 2013a, 91, 100), dresses like a teenager, and her profession in the fashion industry has her pretend she is "twenty-nine for eleven years already" (Evaristo 2013a, 96). It thus seems like there are few positive or optimistic aspects to this character's advancing age. This diverging portrayal corresponds to what Susan Sontag (1972) has termed the 'double standard of aging'. In the essay, she identifies "childish, immature, weak" behaviour as being "cherished as typically 'feminine'" (Sontag 1972, 38), which represents Maxine's character and stigmatises female ageing. The male characters' ageing process is either negligible, positive, or leads to the final, liberatory coming out, while this female figure stagnates in trying to remain forever young.[7]

The connection between the portrayal of the male characters' old age and their masculinity is especially visible in Barrington's sex life. He and Morris have always barely been able to keep their hands off each other, and Barrington reports having had many casual, anonymous sexual encounters in London's back-alleys over the years. This characterisation corresponds to hegemonically masculine ideals of virility and sexual prowess, while simultaneously perpetuating the stereotype of promiscuous gay men. It even connects these revolutionary queer characters to the mentality of Selvon's (1956) womanising protagonists (), the mere difference being the gender at which they direct their overt sexual advances.[8] Yet, the stigmatised expectation for *men in old age* is that they become desexualised and celibate, and thus lose part of their

---

7   Barrington's wife Carmel negates some of the stereotypes and stigmas that Sontag (1972, 31) criticises around female ageing, most notably by entering a relationship with another man as soon as she is separated from Barrington (Evaristo 2013a, 279), which challenges the idea of older women being "sexually ineligible much earlier than men" (Sontag 1972, 31).

8   Evaristo (2013b, 362) herself admits to this connection in her doctoral thesis.

perceived masculinity. For these septuagenarians, however, sex retains a central role in their relationship, for example since they prefer giving sexual services to the other over actually communicating about their conflicts (Evaristo 2013a, 242). This characterisation is further entangled in the pressures around 'successful aging': "the idea that a person *needs* to be sexy and have sex in order to attain optimal health, vitality, and a 'successful' ageing process" (Przybylo 2021, 181) is as problematic as the automatic desexualisation of old age. The novel thus treads a thin line between creating farcically hypermasculine (and thus hypersexual) characters, and revolutionary representations of old, gay, black British life.

The narrative also diegetically addresses the normative assumption towards old men with regard to sexuality. Before the protagonist's formative coming-out moment that initiates his changed outlook on gender norms, he largely only imagines young men's bodies as possessing 'manly', and thus desirable, attributes. He describes his memory of a young Morris as "a perfect specimen of manhood", and admires how much his young grandson's "masculine" physique resembles what he used to look like himself (Evaristo 2013a, 115, 171). After his coming out, he suddenly asserts how attractive Morris's older body is to him: "Don't care how buff you is, I still want you" (Evaristo 2013a, 244). He can now express his emotions more openly and lets go of some of those expectations of what can be considered 'manly.' These altered attitudes towards others' attractiveness translate to a gradually changing view on his self-worth.

If we think of age in terms of generation and upbringing, rather than only the number of years or the biological components of an ageing body, then a further impact on the internalised expectations of masculinity, and by extension the closet and social isolation, can be observed. For most of their lives, the characters have lacked any positive role models that could have given them hope that being openly queer may not exclusively lead to problems, isolation and violence (see de Vries 2010, 152). There are brief mentions of Quentin Crisp, the queer trailblazing dandy-like figure of the 1930s, whom Morris is inspired by, but Barrington rejects identifying with him due to the flamboyance and femininity he expresses (Evaristo 2013a, 137–138). The cultural and historical settings, as well as the identity positions of the queer characters, impact their attachment to masculinity and the life strategy of secrecy.

3. Queer and old age kinship

3.1 The kin concept of chosen families

In a society that desexualises old men, i.e. assumes that they are both undesirable and have no desire themselves (see Przybylo 2021, 184), Barrington and Morris are able to navigate being closeted more easily now than as young men who were seemingly (and inexplicably, to a normative society) uninterested in sex. Thus, Morris argues that they do not need to hide in their old age as carefully as they did before. When Barrington shows reluctance to moving in together and consequently outing themselves as being romantically involved, Morris says:

> As for discretion, [...] there'll be no gossip, Barry. You think folk be whispering, *Oh, look at those two horny studs goin' at it behind closed doors?* No, man. They be saying, *Oh, look at those two sweet* OAP [old age pensioner] *gentlemen keeping each other company and changing each other's bedpans.* (Evaristo 2013a, 44)

The two lovers, who are almost as sexually active now as they have always been, would never be suspected as such due to the expectations of desexualisation, and the kinship and caregiving roles that older adults often take up in each other's lives.

This directly leads to the status of fictive kin or chosen families for the protagonist. The former gerontological concept is equivalent in its usage and real-life functions to the queer studies' terms 'chosen family' or 'family of choice,' which were first articulated by Kath Weston (1997 [1991]). As many recent empirical studies from the emerging field of Queer Gerontology have shown (see Ramirez-Valles 2017), such kinship bonds, which very frequently include caregiving roles, are especially relevant to the intersectional experience of LGBTQ+ elders.[9] Factors such as rejection from biological families, possible lack of children, or discrimination in care facilities lead to an accelerated reliance upon non-biologically related caregivers and alternative kinship ties for this social group. Their precariousness means that other people who are not related to them, by law or birth, and who would not be part of traditional or biological kinship ties, provide much needed support, comfort, familial connections and companionship (see Smith and Muraco 2019, 162).

3.2 Alternative kinship in *Mr Loverman*

Although the caregiving aspect is not explicitly mentioned again in the novel, the concept of chosen family at large gains increasing significance. Next to his self-image and confidence that would be negatively affected by being openly queer, Barrington mostly fears that isolation and the loss of kinship ties would result from such a step: "I don't like being an outsider" (Evaristo 2013a, 159). All the community groups that offer themselves to Barrington over the first half of the novel are negatively impacted by homophobia, internalised or otherwise, and by his caution around being outed as queer. Ironically, exactly his fear of losing kinship ties prevents him from developing them in the first place. He was never romantically interested in his wife, Carmel, and even learns to strongly dislike her over the course of their insincere marriage, so this traditionally legal kin does not provide support and companionship. Yet, he does not ask her for a divorce since her role as what has been colloquially termed his 'beard'[10] helps to keep him safe and his orientation undetected. This also means, though, that they are trapped in what both

---

[9] Studies that specifically focus on the caregiving aspect include, for instance, Heaphy et al. (2004), Muraco and Frederiksen-Goldsen (2011), Croghan et al. (2014), or Knauer (2016). Most of such studies only focus on US-American and white participants.

[10] A gay person (usually a man) is described as having a 'beard' when they enter a relationship with someone from the 'opposite' gender, purely in order to appear heterosexual to others. This is frequently done without the knowledge of the partner, who believes that they are a genuine couple.

metaphorically describe as a 'prison' of a marriage (Evaristo 2013a, 106, 140, 236).

Moreover, the looming threat of his family members' anticipated reactions to his queerness negatively impacts all contact between them. Barrington dreads the upheaval and alienation that his coming out must lead to:

> I realize I might never sit down to a meal with my wife and daughters ever again. Our fragile nuclear family is about to explode. What parental price will I have to pay? I have no doubt that from wifey and Donna's point of view, I will go from head of the family to dead in the family. (Evaristo 2013a, 90)

He is invested in his biological and legal kinship ties and is afraid that being open about his queerness will eradicate them. His fear furthermore leads to a lack of deeper friendships, as he cuts ties with his hippie friend Peaceman as soon as he hints to Barrington that it would be safe to come out to him. The reproduction of homophobic discourse by Carmel's close Antiguan friends, which goes back to the presence of Caribbean homophobia, means that he also does not get on with them. Before his coming out, the only truly sincere and affirmative relationship he has is with Morris, his significant other and best friend.

Barrington and Morris are strongly committed to each other, know their partner better than anybody else, and want to spend the rest of their lives together. Yet, they must still learn throughout the novel to be the family that the other needs. His fear of isolation and estrangement from his biological family means that Barrington has disappointed and hurt Morris when he backed out from divorcing Carmel in the 1980s. Since his own divorce at that time, Morris has been living alone, and he admits to his partner how lonely and cut-off he has felt ever since. Morris's character represents the gay elder who is isolated from most kinship ties and is on track to spending the rest of his life secluded, largely unsupported and alone. When Barrington finally does want them to move in together in 2010, Morris rejects him at first due to his own fears of upheaval and change after thirty years of living as a bachelor. This is one instance where the rhetorical effects of old age are not humoristic, as Morris asserts that it is useless to start their shared life now, when there is so little of it left. He says, "[W]e [are] nearer to death than to life" and claims he has given up on finding happiness and fulfilment (Evaristo 2013a, 44). At many other points, Barrington also looks back on his life and mournfully regrets how much of it he has spent hiding his true self.

The representation of their old age functions here to emotionally underline the tragedy of their lives in the metaphorical closet. This negative framing of queerness in old age, and especially of coming out at a mature point in life, is a common one, as seen for instance in the photography series *Not Another Second* by The Watermark in New York City. Each of the exhibits, which have been published in a coffee table book (Newby 2021), lists how many years the senior LGBTQ+ person has 'lost' due to having lived a closeted double life. Barrington is similarly portrayed as having lost those sixty years. Both queer characters in the novel have poor mental health and a bleak outlook on life due to their lifelong secret, which Jill Wilkens has also identified as a common occurrence for old LGBTQ+ people (2015, 91). The longer queer people remain isolated in the closet, the harder it gets for them to identify with their lives. Moreover, this can inhibit their formation and maintenance of sincere, supportive kinship ties. However, this fatalistic view in *Mr Loverman* and the photography series remains the dominant parameter in the identity construction of queer elders. It is doing them a disservice if the majority of their lives is written off as useless, tragic and 'lost,' only because they had to prioritise their immediate safety. Doubtlessly, the act of coming out and being able to show one's authentic self can be life-changing and affirmative, and being forced to do the opposite is often detrimental, yet its centrality and necessity in queer narratives should be questioned.

This discourse can be analysed in two directions. For one, it echoes what age studies scholars have discussed using concepts like the 'life review' and other processes of identity formation through narrative strategies such as reminiscence.[11] Coined by psychiatrist Robert N. But-

---

11 See the literature review by Gerben J. Westerhof, Nicole Alea, and Susan Bluck (2020).

ler (1963), the life review describes the psychological process of recalling one's life in old age and working through past conflicts to arrive at a coherent view of the personal past. For Barrington, this look back on his life is rather reflected in depression and despair, in accordance with what Butler (1963, 68) calls the "severe form" of the life review. Barrington's narrative of his life is judged as nearly completely negative due to his time in the metaphorical closet. Secondly, it prioritises sexual orientation, especially of the openly announced kind, over all other identities and life events. Barrington's relationship with his queerness structures the plot, his kinship ties, and his life narrative. This privileging of sexual identity echoes some form of identity politics that must not remain unquestioned.

Nevertheless, for Barrington's story, coming out functions as a watershed moment that not only changes his outlook, but also lastingly influences his kinship ties. After the climactic turning point of coming out to his family (Evaristo 2013a, 196–197), he reconnects with Morris and they take up their former physical and emotional intimacy again. The conflicts and tensions that have arisen over the years due to their anxiety about being unmasked as a couple can be left behind and the two men now assume the public role of each other's life partner. This is symbolised most succinctly through Morris's move into Barrington's family home.[12] His grandson, Daniel, has stopped visiting after the coming out, Barrington's daughters moved out long ago, and Carmel moves back to Antigua after divorcing her husband. Morris now physically and symbolically fills the empty space that the protagonist's legal and biological kin have left. This conclusion to the novel's overarching conflicts lends itself to a reading of Morris as not merely his romantic partner, but specifically as Barrington's chosen family, in favour of his socially accepted, heteronormative legal kin. They break through old rooms and literally re-assemble the make-up of Barrington's family home to suit their tastes and needs. Joseph Ronan (2021, 637–638) has analysed that "[traditional] family and queerness are opposed" in the novel, and in the end, they

---

12 See Koegler's essay (2020) on the significance of homemaking and the family home for Barrington's life as a queer immigrant.

form a "reshaped family" instead. The constant reiteration of the rejection of same-sex relationships by (most of) their surroundings, and the fact that such legal advancements as marriage equality did not happen until a year after the novel's publication, let alone its setting, make their kinship bond a clearly non-traditional and revolutionary one.

Many of Barrington's other relationships can also become more sincere once he is less invested in obsessively performing heteronormative masculinity. His younger daughter, Maxine, is the first person with whom he has a positive coming-out experience (Evaristo 2013a, 218–221) and she becomes a reliant supporter of his new life, which he is grateful for (Evaristo 2013a, 271). Brian Heaphy and others (2004) define chosen family as a construction that can include and *redefine* the relationship with selected biological family members. Barrington's connection to Maxine becomes even more sincere and life-affirming once he can display his whole self to his favourite daughter. His 'choice' of close family does not include Donna, his eldest daughter whom he never got along with well and who sides with her mother over Barrington in her parents' conflict. Daniel is only included in his family construction a year after the coming out, when the young man apologises for his discriminatory initial reaction. It is significant that they never come out to Morris's homophobic sons and even free up a separate space in the house to present as his 'bachelor pad' if need be (Evaristo 2013a, 295). This fraught familial relationship lingeringly inhibits the two men's full self-realisation and the restructuring of their gender identities and social connections. It leaves a bittersweet aftertaste to readers, while also counteracting the otherwise utopian 'happily ever after' of their second chance at life. This qualifies the so-far unquestioned privileging of 'being out' criticised above since they are better off, and have a happier life, because they *do not* come out to those young men. For old queer people, it is necessary to *choose* how one's family is constituted and to redefine what the connection must mean for them, and not all bio-legal kin can be included to the same extent. The construction of 'kin' does not require a blood connection, and conversely, purely biological relations do not suffice for being, or remaining, someone's kin. The dynamic concept offers space for rejecting another set of rigid social norms, next to those of masculinity, and for finding the right form of companionship, family and support. *Mr Loverman* contributes to positive (re)imaginings of how gay members of the Windrush generation can forge connections with others in their old age.

The last community or kinship group in the novel, next to the non-normative, familial partnership with Morris, and the re-negotiation of biological kin, is that of other queer people, which proves to be one of the biggest, and to the protagonist most unexpected, positive influences. The concept of a 'queer community' and designated spaces such as gay clubs or pride parades are well-researched, and studies in Queer Gerontology name it as one of the biggest alternative kinship groups for old queer people.[13] In the novel, the earliest example happens in the 1970s, long before his official coming out, with Merle, a teenaged friend of Donna's who has been disowned by her Montserratian parents due to her queerness. Barrington is inspired by her resilience and feels ashamed that he is not as brave as she is in living her queerness openly and enduring the backlash from her community. He ends up providing her with housing and other resources to fill her lack of kinship ties. Furthermore, they have a silent understanding about Barrington's relationship with Morris, whereby he appreciates that he does not need to be on his guard and can be himself around her, and he thinks of her using the fond pet name "Little Merley" (Evaristo 2013a, 132–133) way into her own adulthood when she is a parent herself. She can fall back on Barrington's care and support (financial as well as ideological) over the years and he takes up a father position in her life. Merle fills the understanding and supportive daughter role long before his biological daughters are trusted to react to, and asked to accept, their father's true self. In her character, the necessity of having chosen, instead of solely bio-legal kin becomes tangible through the established familial role she fulfils for Barry (and he for her), instead of either of their traditional

---

13 The most salient example of the impact of this family dynamic is the era of the AIDS crisis with its peak in the 1980s, where ill, socially ostracised people heavily relied on support from the LGBTQ+ community. See, for instance, Brian de Vries (2010, 153) or Brian Heaphy (2007, 204).

'folks.' She further embodies an alternative to the imagined 'fix-all' quality of coming out: her understanding and offer of kinship exist before and in opposition to the imagined necessity of a grand announcement.

After Barrington's coming out, Maxine introduces Morris and her father to her friend group of young gay men, the most typical queer community in the novel. At first, the couple find themselves overwhelmed by the queer subcultural space in Soho (nicknamed 'Gay-ho'). Barrington does not initially thrive as much in this environment as the more open-minded Morris does. This is due to his confrontational character, which he ascribes to his age ("I really do feel like a grumpy ole man today", Evaristo 2013a, 259), and implicitly to his self-consciousness around bold gender non-conformity. A further influence is the marginalised position they occupy in this traditionally youth-centred space – it takes visiting a bar explicitly conceived for "the older gay clientele" for them not to feel completely out of place. Therein, they are still the only *black* older queer men (Evaristo 2013a, 248) – even within queer spaces, and hence the queer community, they are on the margins. This self-consciously points to how unusual the representation of this set of intersecting identities is, and what challenges the group of old black queer people faces regarding the forging of community ties.

Despite his initial resistance, Barrington goes from being in awe at holding his lover's hand in public for the first time, which he feels emboldened to do in the company of other queer people (Evaristo 2013a, 247), to eagerly consuming (black) queer literature provided by Lola, a black PhD-student researching pre-colonial African homosexuality.[14] The couple becomes entrenched in queer life and culture, and they open themselves up to the queer community. This contact is what Barrington credits as the main factor in "com[ing] to terms with what I been fearing and hiding all my life" (Evaristo 2013a, 274), i.e. opening himself up to society's scrutiny of his gender through exhibiting his queerness, and leads to the novel's happy end. He receives the resources and support he needs to connect with his identity and overcome his now unfounded

---

14   See Newns (2020, 153–154) on the significance of Lola's presence for decolonising this queer space and opening it up to the protagonists' belonging.

fear of social isolation. Instead of making Barrington an outsider, as he feared for sixty years, his openness and his rejection of hegemonic masculinity allow him to become a social 'insider' for the first time in his life. Realising that there is a community of accepting people waiting, he can now conceive of living authentically in the world.

4. Conclusion

The protagonist's overemphasis on and eventual negotiation of masculinity, the threat of homophobia, and the realisation that he has been living an unhappy double life for too long trigger a radical reshaping of his outlook on life, his home space, and consequently his family ties. Letting go of his masculine and heteronormative expectations for himself and others, which he developed out of his cultural and historical contexts, enables Barrington to admit to his sexuality and live life more openly. By having him adopt a larger kin network and redefine the relationship with his traditional, biological family, *Mr Loverman* envisions the possibility of a positive old black gay life in contemporary Britain that is entrenched in black and/or queer community. The novel follows the assumption that (family) relationships are essential to one's well-being, especially in old age. Opening up the Windrush generation's queer population to the possibility of fulfilling community widens the narrow confines for this group. Nevertheless, the fatalist view of the 'lost years' of a long life in the closet prevails. While the novel creates a fictional environment that reveals the structural nature of the characters' problems, its suggestion that coming out is the all-round solution needs to be challenged.

Works Cited

Albertalli, Becky. *Simon vs. the Homo Sapiens Agenda*. New York: Harper Collins, 2015.

Allen, David J., and Terry Oleson. "Shame and Internalized Homophobia in Gay Men." *Journal of Homosexuality* 37.3 (1999): 33–43.

Beadle, Monica, and Rikki Beadle-Blair. "Monica Beadle in Conversation with Rikki Beadle-Blair." *Sista! An Anthology of Writing by and about Same Gender Loving Women of African/Caribbean Descent with a UK Connection.* Ed. Phyll Opoku-Gyimah, Rikki Beadle-Blair, and John R. Gordon. London: Team Angelica, 2018. 133–147.

Brightwell, Laura. "The Exclusionary Effects of Queer Anti-Normativity on Feminine-Identified Queers." *Feral Feminisms: Queer Feminine Affinities* 7 (Spring 2018): 15–24. https://feralfeminisms.com/exclusionary-queer-anti-normativity/. (Accessed 29 May 2019).

Butler, Robert N. "The Life Review: An Interpretation of Reminiscence in the Aged." *Psychiatry* 26.1 (1967): 65–76.

Cole-Wilson, Olivette. "Reflections (of an Older Black Lesbian)." *Sista! An Anthology of Writing by and about Same Gender Loving Women of African/Caribbean Descent with a UK Connection.* Ed. Phyll Opoku-Gyimah, Rikki Beadle-Blair, and John R. Gordon. London: Team Angelica, 2018. 233.

Connell, Raewyn. *Masculinities.* Second Edition. Cambridge: Polity, 2005 [1995].

Croghan, Catherine F., Rajean P. Moone, and Andrea M. Olson. "Friends, Family, and Caregiving among Midlife and Older Lesbian, Gay, Bisexual, and Transgender Adults." *Journal of Homosexuality* 61 (2014): 79–102.

Ekine, Sokari. "Love in the Age [of] Evolution." *Sista! An Anthology of Writing by and about Same Gender Loving Women of African/Caribbean Descent with a UK Connection.* Ed. Phyll Opoku-Gyimah, Rikki Beadle-Blair, and John R. Gordon. London: Team Angelica, 2018. 237–241.

Evaristo, Bernardine. *Mr Loverman.* London: Hamish Hamilton, 2013a.

Evaristo, Bernardine. *Mr Loverman and the Men in Black British Fiction: The Representation of Black Men in Black British Fiction.* Doctoral Thesis, Goldsmiths, University of London, 2013b. http://research.gold.ac.uk/id/eprint/9545. (Accessed 25 May 2019).

Evaristo, Bernardine. *Girl, Woman, Other.* London: Hamish Hamilton, 2019.

Gaskins, Joseph, Jr. "'Buggery' and the Commonwealth Caribbean: A Comparative Examination of the Bahamas, Jamaica, and Trinidad and Tobago." *Human Rights, Sexual Orientation and Gender Identity in the Commonwealth*. Ed. Corinne Lennox, and Matthew Waites. London: School of Advanced Study, University of London, 2013. 429–454.

Gordon, John R., and Rikki Beadle-Blair, eds. *Black and Gay in the UK: An Anthology*. London: Team Angelica, 2014.

Grant, Colin. *Homecoming: Voices of the Windrush Generation*. London: Jonathan Cape, 2019.

Heaphy, Brian. "Sexualities, Gender and Ageing: Resources and Social Change." *Current Sociology* 55.2 (March 2007): 193–210.

Heaphy, Brian, Andre K. T. Yip, and Debbie Thompson. "Ageing in a Non-Heterosexual Context." *Ageing & Society* 24 (2004): 881–902.

Karschay, Stephan, and Joanna Rostek. "'Man haf fe do wha man haf fe do': Humour and Identity (Re)Formation in Bernardine Evaristo's *Mr Loverman*." *Anglistik: International Journal of English Studies* 27.1 (March 2016): 125–136.

Knauer, Nancy J. "LGBT Older Adults, Chosen Family, and Caregiving." *Journal of Law and Religion* 31.2 (2016): 150–168.

Koegler, Caroline. "Queer Home-Making and Black Britain: Claiming, Ageing, Living." *International Journal of Postcolonial Studies* 22.7 (2020): 879–896.

Love, Simon. Dir. Greg Berlanti. Fox 2000 Pictures, 2018.

Mason-John, Valerie. "Those Were the Daze." *Sista! An Anthology of Writing by and about Same Gender Loving Women of African/Caribbean Descent with a UK Connection*. Ed. Opoku-Gyimah, Phyll, Rikki Beadle-Blair, and John R. Gordon. London: Team Angelica, 2018. 111–114.

Morris, Donovan E F J. "Retrograde." *Black and Gay in the UK: An Anthology*. Ed. Gordon, John R., and Rikki Beadle-Blair. London: Team Angelica, 2014. 251–260.

Muraco, Anna, and Karen Frederiksen-Goldsen. "'That's What Friends Do': Informal Caregiving for Chronically Ill Midlife and Older Lesbian, Gay, and Bisexual Adults." *Journal of Social and Personal Relationships* 28.8 (December 2011): 1073–1092.

Newby, Ines. *Not Another Second: LGBT+ Seniors Share Their Stories*. Tucson: Watermark Retirement Communities, 2021.

Newns, Lucinda. *Domestic Intersections in Contemporary Migration Fiction: Homing the Metropole*. New York: Routledge, 2020.

Opoku-Gyimah, Phyll, Rikki Beadle-Blair, and John R. Gordon, eds. *Sista! An Anthology of Writing by and about Same Gender Loving Women of African/Caribbean Descent with a UK Connection*. London: Team Angelica, 2018.

Przybylo, Ela. "Ageing Asexually: Exploring Desexualisation and Ageing Intimacies." *Sex and Diversity in Later Life: Critical Perspectives*. Ed. Trish Hafford-Letchfield, Paul Simpson, and Paul Reynolds. Bristol: Policy Press, 2021. 181–198.

Ramirez-Valles, Jesus. "Queer Gerontology." *Critical Gerontology*. (04 January 2017). https://criticalgerontology.com/queer-gerontology/. (Accessed 08 March 2021).

Ronan, Joseph. "LGBT Fiction." *The Wiley Blackwell Companion to Contemporary British and Irish Literature*. Ed. Richard Bradford. Vol. II. Chichester: John Wiley & Sons, 2021. 631–642.

Rose, Kayza. "When is the Right Time?" *Sista! An Anthology of Writing by and about Same Gender Loving Women of African/Caribbean Descent with a UK Connection*. Ed. Phyll Opoku-Gyimah, Rikki Beadle-Blair, and John R. Gordon. London: Team Angelica, 2018. 231–232.

Smith, Christine, and Joel A. Muraco. "Together, Forever? Relationships." *Living Out Loud: An Introduction to LGBTQ History, Society, and Culture*. Ed. Murphy, Michael J., and Brytton Bjorngaard. New York: Routledge, 2019. 143–172.

Sontag, Susan. "The Double Standard of Aging." *Saturday Review of the Society* 23 (September 1972): 29–38.

de Vries, Brian. "The Value and Meaning of Friendship in Later Life." *A Guide to Humanistic Studies in Aging*. Ed. Thomas R. Cole, Ruth E. Ray, and Robert Kastenbaum. Baltimore: Johns Hopkins University Press, 2010. 141–162.

Westerhof, Gerben J., Nicole Alea, and Susan Bluck. "Narrative and Identity: The Importance of Our Personal Past in Later Life." *The Cambridge Handbook of Cognitive Aging: A Life Course Perspective*. Ed. Ayanna

K. Thomas, and Angela Gutchess. Cambridge: Cambridge University Press, 2020. 383–389.

Weston, Kath. *Families We Choose: Lesbians, Gays, Kinship.* New York: Columbia University Press, 1997 [1991].

Wilkens, Jill. "Loneliness and Belongingness in Older Lesbians: The Role of Social Groups as 'Community'." *Journal of Lesbian Studies* 19.1 (2015): 90–101.

Formen männlicher Identität in Spielfilmen von Ines Tanović

Renate Hansen-Kokoruš

Vorbemerkungen

Nach dem Fall des Sozialismus in Osteuropa, dem Zerfall Jugoslawiens in den frühen 90ern und besonders dem Ende des Kriegs in Bosnien und der Herzegowina im Jahr 1996 wandelten sich in den neuen Ländern des Übergangs, deren politische und ökonomische Systeme tiefgreifende Veränderungen durchgemacht hatten, auch die Geschlechterverhältnisse fundamental. Als Ergebnis von Arbeitsplatzverlust und der zunehmenden Schwierigkeit von Männern, unter den prekären Verhältnissen ausreichend für ihre Familien zu sorgen, gerieten die Vorstellungen von Männlichkeit in eine Krise und wurden mit Schwäche konnotiert. Während im Sozialismus Frauenemanzipation und Gleichheit der Geschlechter politisch verbürgt waren,[1] führten die neoliberalen Wirtschaftssysteme zu einer großen Zahl von Arbeitslosen oder Menschen in prekären Arbeitsverhältnissen und zu sozialer Unsicherheit, was deutlich mehr Frauen als Männer traf. In Beruf und Familie wurden Lebensmodelle von Männlichkeit und Weiblichkeit aus der Zeit vor dem 2. Weltkrieg restituiert, mit traditionellen Rollenverteilungen von Männern (Arbeit, Geld, Familienoberhaupt)

---

1   Gegen Ende der 80er Jahre erhielt darin auch die Familie einen höheren Stellenwert.

und Frauen (Kinderbetreuung, Privatheit, Haushalt, vgl. Luleva 2008). Nationalistische Parteien und religiöse Einrichtungen propagierten in ihren Programmen solche Vorstellungen der Retraditionalisierung und einer hegemonialen Maskulinität, ja sogar von Hypermaskulinität, und ebneten diesen Rückschritten in der gesellschaftlichen und politischen Praxis den Weg. Frauenemanzipation wurde zum Attribut sozialistischer Ideologie erklärt (vgl. Luleva 2019).

Es ist wenig überraschend, dass sich Diskussionen um geänderte Geschlechterrelationen und Männlichkeit auch in zeitgenössischen Filmen aus dem Raum der postjugoslawischen Staaten finden. So zeigt der Nachkriegsfilm, v.a. in Produktionen des selbstviktimisierenden oder des selbstbalkanisierenden Typus (vgl. dazu Pavičić 2011) nicht selten Vertreter balkanisch-stereotypisierter »toxischer Männlichkeit« – martialische Kriegshelden, Machos und Vergewaltiger, die nicht nur gegenüber der anderen Kriegspartei, sondern auch dem weiblichen Geschlecht permanent ihre Stärke und Überlegenheit unter Beweis stellen müssen. Sie ziehen sich durch die Spielfilme der »Region«, wie die Nachfolgestaaten Jugoslawiens auch zusammengefasst werden, vor allem bei der Behandlung von Kriegsthemen.[2] Diesem Bild des gewaltbereiten und gewalttätigen Mannes, das sich auch von vielen Männlichkeitsimagologien im jugoslawischen Film geradezu diametral abhebt,[3] stehen Darstellungen gegenüber, die, nicht zuletzt als Folge

---

2 Eindrückliche Beispiele liefern der finstere Film *Cabaret Balkan* (*Bure baruta*) von G. Paskaljević (1998) und der Antikriegsfilm *Pretty Village, Pretty Flame* (*Lepa sela lepo gore*) von S. Dragojević (1996). Neben vielen anderen kritisieren *The Tour* (*Turneja*) von G. Marković (2008) oder *Esmas Geheimnis* (*Grbavica*) von J. Zbanić (2006) z.B. Gewalt verherrlichende Männlichkeitsbilder, die zudem ideologisch u.a. durch den Ethnonationalismus besetzt sind, und setzen dem solche entgegen, die sich nicht nur hinsichtlich ihrer Geschlechteridentität unterscheiden, sondern sie auch ideologisch und kulturell hinterfragen. Die Soziologin Blagojević, die sich unter Rückgriff auf D. Gilmore mehrfach mit Misogynie auseinandergesetzt hat, hebt die Universalität und den strukturellen Charakter dieses Phänomens – nicht nur in der serbischen Gesellschaft und Kunstproduktion – hervor. (Vgl. Blagojević 2005a; Blagojević 2005b)

3 Der Kriegsheld ist im jugoslawischen Film stark mit dem Partisanenmythos verbunden und als Verteidiger gegen die nationalsozialistischen Invasoren und

des Kriegs, männliche Identität in Frage stellen oder erschüttern.[4] Während also die veränderten Weltmodelle in den Figurenhorizonten und Geschlechterbeziehungen der Kriegs- und Nachkriegszeit im postjugoslawischen Film der letzten beiden Jahrzehnte eine wichtige Rolle spielten und dabei Kriegsthemen aufgearbeitet wurden, stehen unterschiedliche Generationsorientierungen und -einstellungen in der gegenwärtigen Gesellschaft deutlich weniger im Fokus.

Gerade den Generationsaspekt hebt Ines Tanović mit ihren beiden Spielfilmen *Our Everyday life* (*Naša svakodnena priča*, 2015) und *The Son* (*Sin*, 2019) hervor, die in Alltag, Familie und Privatheit Generationskonflikte und unterschiedliche Lebensorientierungen thematisieren. Was ihre Filme besonders für den Zusammenhang von Männlichkeitsbildern und Alter interessant macht, ist der familiäre und generationsmäßige Zusammenhang, der außer in diesen beiden Filmen auch in ihrer Episode an der bosnisch-kroatisch-mazedonisch-serbisch-slowenischen Spielfilmserie *Some Other Stories* (*Neke druge priče*, 2010) realisiert wird.[5]

---

    national definierte faschistische Aggressoren profiliert. Daraus leitet sich seine positive Darstellung ab, die in der kollektiven Erinnerung für das ideologische jugoslawische Selbstverständnis eine zentrale Rolle einnahm. Vgl. dazu den Sammelband von Jakiša 2015, insbesondere die Beiträge von Vervaet zur fiktionalen Schaffung des Partisanenmythos (71–89), Jakiša zur Themeneinführung (9–28) und Petrović zum Soldatenfoto als Popkultur (137–156). Darüber hinaus existiert eine Vielzahl filmischer Männerbilder, die bislang nicht unter diesem Gesichtspunkt, sondern unter anderen Aspekten oder in Einzelanalysen untersucht wurden.

4 PTBS dürfte im Film *Zwischen uns das Paradies* (*Na putu*, J. Žbanić, 2010) der Grund für die Labilität von Amar und sein Abdriften in den religiösen Fanatismus sein, während *Men don't cry* (A. Drljević, 2017) das Thema erstmals mit einer ganzen Gruppe von Kriegsveteranen in Therapie zentral behandelt. Neben den psychischen Folgen werden mehrfach auch die körperlichen als sichtbarstes Zeichen einer kompletten Traumatisierung behandelt; vgl. dazu auch den in Pula preisgekrönten Film *No One's Son* (*Ničiji sin*, A. Ostojić, 2008).

5 Dieser Episodenfilm von fünf Regisseurinnen behandelt das Thema Schwangerschaft unter verschiedensten Aspekten. Nach Tanović' Angaben bildet in ihrer Episode, die gegen Kriegsende spielt, Haris, Ende Zwanzig und im Kampf um seine Existenz (Tanović 3), den Ausgangspunkt der Generationendarstellung.

Die Regisseurin spricht anlässlich ihres letzten Films auch klar von Kontinuität der Fabel, wenn sie sagt: »I have unconsciously allways followed the same character and the same family« (Tanović 3), was sie in einem weiteren Interview bestätigt.[6] Beide Filme behandeln mit ihren männlichen Protagonisten also nicht nur Männlichkeitsbilder, sondern beleuchten sie im Entwicklungs- und Alterungsprozess. Die Einblendung von Generationskonflikten erlaubt eine Verbindung von individuellen und kollektiven Werten sowie eine weitere Differenzierung der unterschiedlichen Lebensorientierungen. Im scheinbar Privaten des Einzelnen treten so auch gesellschaftliche, soziale, ökonomische, politische und kulturelle Entwicklungen zutage. »Männlichkeit konstituiert sich«, wie Luleva (2008: 197) unter Bezug auf Connell zutreffend feststellt, »durch eine doppelte Relation: in Bezug auf Weiblichkeit und in Bezug auf andere Männlichkeiten.« Dieser theoretischen Einsicht folgt der vorliegende Beitrag angesichts der hier zentralen unterschiedlichen männlichen Generationsorientierungen in den Filmen nur bedingt und bezieht Weiblichkeitsbilder nur zur Erläuterung der Modelle von Männlichkeit ein. Im Rahmen einer umfassenderen Studie wäre das jedoch zu ergänzen. Bevor im Folgenden die Männlichkeitsbilder genauer untersucht und dazu in einem weiteren Schritt Rückkehrmotiv und Raumsemantik einbezogen werden, werden die beiden Filme kurz vorgestellt.

Die Filme Our Everyday Life und The Son

Our Everyday Life kreist um eine vierköpfige im Sarajevo der Nachkriegszeit: Ein älteres Ehepaar – die Mutter Rentnerin, der Vater wird gerade aus seiner privatisierten Firma entlassen, was er zunächst verheimlicht – muss wieder zusammenrücken. Der arbeitslose Grafikdesigner Saša

---

Da in dieser Serie die weiblichen Figuren mit ihren Dilemmata im Vordergrund stehen, wird sie in die folgende Analyse nicht einbezogen.

6 »From the omnibus movie ›Some Other Stories‹, through ›Our Everyday Life‹, I actually deal with the same family.« (Tanović 2)

zieht nach seiner gescheiterten Ehe wieder bei den Eltern ein und muss sich jeden Tag Vorwürfe seines Vaters anhören. Seine Schwester Senada war im Krieg als Halbwüchsige nach Slowenien geschickt worden, von wo sie nun, hochschwanger, mit unsicherer persönlicher Perspektive und abgebrochenem Studium, ebenfalls heimkehrt. Als sich Sašas Auseinandersetzung mit dem Vater zuspitzt, bietet die Krebserkrankung der Mutter eine Möglichkeit zur Versöhnung. Für Saša eröffnet sich eine neue Lebensperspektive durch einen neuen Job und durch Lidija, eine ehemalige Schülerin seiner Mutter, die für kurze Zeit aus Texas zurückgekehrt ist und die er zum Bleiben bewegen kann. Auch im Zentrum von *The Son* steht eine vierköpfige Familie: Senad, ein Architekt in den 50ern, seine Frau Jasna, Gewerkschaftsvertreterin bei den kommunalen Verkehrsbetrieben, der knapp volljährige Adoptivsohn Arman und der ca. 13jährige gemeinsame Sohn Dado. Arman macht eine schwere Identitätskrise durch, als er erstmals eine Reise zu seiner leiblichen Mutter antritt, die einfach nicht erscheint. Seine Enttäuschung, Wut und Selbstzweifel lässt er an seinen Eltern und in der Schule aus, der Streit eskaliert auch in der Familie. Armans Schulabschluss ist gefährdet und die Mutter nimmt sogar eine dienstliche Beurlaubung in Kauf, um seine strafrechtliche Verfolgung zu vermeiden. Als Arman Dados gleichaltrige Peiniger zu russischem Roulette zwingt, flieht Dado in Panik und gerät in vermintes Gelände. Arman erkennt seinen Fehler und holt ihn heraus; beider Rückkehr am Vorabend von Armans Volljährigkeit zeichnet ein versöhnliches Ende.

Männlichkeitsbilder im Generationszusammenhang

Die Handlungen der beiden Filme, die um die Jahrtausendwende und zeitgenössisch zu verorten sind, hängen familiär zusammen, was schon die schauspielerische Besetzung unterstreicht: Die Eltern in *Our Everyday Life* werden in *The Son* als Großeltern von denselben Schauspielern dargestellt (Emir Hadžihafizbegović und Jasna Beri), ihr Sohn Saša bzw. Senad (*The Son*), da ca. 20 Jahre älter, von Uliks Fehmiu. Die Arbeit an einem großen Thema mit familiärem Zusammenhang ermöglicht es, die Figuren im Zusammenhang ihrer Generation zu beleuchten. Das verbindende Element jeder Generation ist das generationsprägende Ereignis, das ihr spezifisches Verhältnis dazu prägt, die Emotionen und Weltbilder der Generation. Die Fokussierung auf die unterschiedlichen Generationen und ihre Orientierungen erlaubt es, die kollektiven Veränderungen im historischen Wandel zu verstehen. Das zentrale, aber nicht verbalisierte prägende Ereignis der mittleren und älteren Generation ist der Krieg, allerdings mit ganz unterschiedlichen Akzenten. Während er für Sašas/Senads Generation durch die Teilnahme als Soldaten lebensbedrohlich und durch die späteren beruflichen Konsequenzen existenzbedrohend war, erlebt Muhameds Generation ihn als radikalen Bruch mit dem eigenen sozialistischen Weltbild und Lebensstil. Die jüngere Generation, ganz mit sich selbst beschäftigt, zeigt keine kritische Auseinandersetzung mit dem Krieg, dessen Folgen im Stadtbild noch weithin sichtbar sind und plötzlich massiv ihr Leben beeinflussen.

Die alte Generation: Vater und Großvater

Vater Muhamed, oft aus Sašas Perspektive in der Familie präsentiert, aber auch in der Firma und mit seinen Freunden, v.a. dem Friseur, ist eine Figur des Gestern, ein typischer Vertreter der älteren jugoslawischen prosozialistischen Mittelstandsgeneration, für die Bildung und Erwerbstätigkeit beider Partner selbstverständlich geworden war. Die »gemischte« internethnische Ehe mit Marija war in der Nachkriegszeit des sozialistischen Bosnien nicht nur ein erklärt antinationalistisches, sondern auch ein recht häufiges Phänomen, das im Nachkriegsland schon auf wesentlich geringere Popularität stieß. Den gesellschaftlichen Gleichberechtigungspostulaten der einstigen sozialistischen Gesellschaft steht Muhameds traditionelles patriarchalisches Rollenverständnis im privaten Bereich gegenüber, im Bild eines Familienoberhaupts und starken Mannes, der zu Hause das Leben bestimmt und für den traditionelle Rollenverteilungen wesentlich sind, was jedoch unzeitgemäß ist: Weder ist es für die Familienmitglieder maßgeblich, noch liegen die Lebensmodelle immer im Ermessen des Einzelnen. Dieses Familienbild hatte bereits im späten Sozialismus eine Aufwertung erfahren. Dass es sich dabei aber nicht um individuelle, sondern sozial und gesellschaftlich weithin akzeptierte Konzepte dominanter Männlichkeit handelt, zeigt die Unterordnung weiblicher Figuren (im Arbeitsprozess, als Kundschaft) in den Episoden aus dem Friseursalon. Wegen seiner hegemonialen Vorstellungen von Familie interessiert Muhamed vorrangig, ob die von ihm auch für andere entworfenen Lebensziele erreicht werden. Er ist keinesfalls gewillt, diese Situation, die er als Autoritätsverlust erlebt, hinzunehmen, gerät darüber in Konflikt zu allen Familienmitgliedern und manövriert sich zusehends in die Isolation. Muhamed, in dessen Wertesystem die Familie eine Selbstverständlichkeit darstellt, kann aber über sich und seine Probleme nicht mit der Familie reden, sondern nur mit seinen männlichen Freunden. Er fällt v.a. durch negative Emotionalität auf, in einer Bandbreite, die von Ignoranz und Sich-blind-Stellen über forsche Zurückweisung (z.B. anlässlich des über Skype gefeierten Geburtstags der Tochter) bis zu Aggressivität (gegenüber dem Sohn) reicht. Erst im Ernstfall, als seine Frau eine Krebs-Diagnose erhält, ist er fähig, emotionale Anteilnahme zu zeigen und den familiären Zusammenhalt zu suchen.

Muhameds weitere Lebensplanung wird durchkreuzt und verläuft anders als erwartet. Denn als die Firma gegen seinen Willen privatisiert wird, schickt man ihn, der am Ende seiner Berufslaufbahn steht, in Rente, was er als persönliches »Versagen« durchlebt. Mit vorgetäuschter Stärke sucht er seine Schwäche zu verbergen, denn er ist v.a. mit seinen eigenen Problemen beschäftigt. Er ist allgemein unzufrieden, mit seiner sozialen Lage, dem Autoritätsverlust in der Familie und einem gesellschaftlichen Umfeld, das sein bisheriges Weltbild in Frage stellt. Der Ausschluss aus dem Arbeitsprozess, über den er sich hauptsächlich definiert, bereitet ihm die größten Probleme. Verständnis findet er nur bei seiner Clique und Alterskohorte, die auch sein Grundproblem teilt, die fehlende berufliche und persönliche Anerkennung im neoliberalen postjugoslawischen Bosnien mit neuen, auf Profit und Einfluss fokussierten Eliten, was Muhamed als fatal empfindet. Denn garantierte Arbeit und das damit verbundene soziale Umfeld, wichtigste Faktoren für sein Selbstbild, sind unter den neuen Wirtschafts- und Gesellschaftsverhältnissen, in denen Arbeitsplatzabbau zum Programm gehört, keine vorrangigen Ziele mehr. Muhamed verzichtet aus Trotz und falschem Stolz, zum eigenen Nachteil und dem der Familie, sogar auf einen ihm zustehenden Firmenanteil. Für ihn und die Freunde sind bei der Arbeit gute persönliche Beziehungen zu Freunden und Kollegen sowie ihr Wohlbefinden wichtiger als gute Arbeitsleistung und hoher Verdienst – ein typisches Phänomen im jugoslawischen Sozialismus.

Als alter Mann und Großvater (in *The Son* ist er ca. Mitte 80) ist Muhamed nicht nur »zahm« geworden, sondern durch seine Demenz dem Zeitgeschehen und der Erinnerung entrückt. Nach dem Verlust der hegemonialen Rolle in der Familie (die eher seinem Selbstverständnis und Wertesystem entsprach als den realen Machtverhältnissen), ist auch sein Körper vom Verfall gezeichnet und seinem Willen entzogen. Der elementarste Autonomieverlust ist das deutlichste Merkmal des Alters, wie das Füttern und die Windeln zeigen. In ihm wird die These von der Weisheit des Alters widerlegt. Muhamed wird nurmehr im zusammengeschrumpften Radius der Familie gezeigt, wo er nicht mehr aktiv partizipiert und sich auch nicht mehr artikulieren kann. Vergessen sind die Auseinandersetzungen mit den Kindern, die ihn nun umsorgen, dafür hat er – wie auch seine Frau – einen engeren Draht zu Arman entwickelt, dem das Heim der Großeltern bei Konflikten im Elternhaus einen Rückzugsort bietet. Sein einstiger Freundeskreis wird mit jeder Todesnachricht immer kleiner. Dem Merkmal des krankhaften Verstummens wohnt Symbolkraft inne, denn es unterstreicht seine Unfähigkeit zur Äußerung von Wünschen und Bedürfnissen. Umgekehrt dient der demente Greis im Film als ikonisches Zeichen einer Geschichtsvergessenheit der Gesellschaft einerseits und der ideologischen Entwertung einer Generation andererseits, die sozialistische System nach dem 2. Weltkrieg aufgebaut hatte.

Die mittlere Generation: Sohn und Vater

Der Mittdreißiger Saša, Protagonist in *Our Everyday Life*, befindet sich in einem tiefen Dilemma: Nach früherer Selbstständigkeit (Ehe, Arbeit) begibt sich der arbeitslose Grafikdesigner notgedrungen, da arbeits- und wohnungslos, wieder in elterliche Abhängigkeit – übertrieben umsorgt von der Mutter und attackiert vom Vater. Er wird gegen seinen Willen wieder in die frühere Rolle als »Kind« zurückgedrängt. Die Trennung von Nina hat er noch nicht ganz verwunden, sucht aber zugleich vorsichtig nach einer neuen Partnerin. Wie sein Vater wirkt Saša zunächst verschlossen, spricht nicht von sich, ist aber im Gegensatz zu seinem Vater empathiefähig, einfühlsam und verständnisvoll – v.a. gegenüber weiblichen Personen. Für Hausarbeiten (z.B. Vorbereiten der Paprika zum Kochen von Ajvar), die sein Vater nur als »unmännlich« und typisch weiblich abtut, ist er sich nicht zu schade; er ist offen für andere Sichtweisen und hält keine fertigen Rezepte zur Problembewältigung bereit. Entscheidend für sein Männlichkeitsbild, das nicht auf strikten Oppositionsbeziehungen beruht, scheint die Abgrenzung gegenüber dem hegemonialen Männlichkeitsbild des Vaters zu sein.

Saša ist ebenso wie seine gemischt-ethnische Familie aufgrund fehlender religiöser Symbole oder Rituale als typischer Vertreter des multikulturellen atheistischen Zusammenlebens im Vorkriegsbosnien auszumachen, was auch seine Sozialisation bestimmt hat.[7] Die knappen, meist bildlichen Hinweise auf seine Vergangenheit zeigen ihn als Künstler der jüngeren Generation, deren Vorbilder den Olympischen Winterspielen 1984 ihr internationales grafisches Erkennungszeichen verliehen hatten, das im Film – wie in der Kultur der Stadt – als Zeichen der damaligen kulturellen Offenheit und internationalen Anerkennung fungiert. Diese Generation hatte sich auch von sozialistischen Autoritäten emanzipiert und orientierte sich an westlicher – auch jugoslawischer – Popkultur und Offenheit. Mit dem Konzertplakat für Božo Vrećo, einen queeren Folkloresänger, kann er der aktuellen Alternativkultur zugeordnet werden, die ethnonationalistische und geschlechterstereotype Ideologien hinterfragt. Wie sein Umgang mit den weiblichen Familienmitgliedern und Lidija, in die er sich verliebt, belegt, beurteilt er traditionelle Rollenbilder kritisch und grenzt sich in seiner Geschlechtsidentität nicht scharf ab.

---

7   Seine Generation ist, wie der Film andeutungsweise in Details zeigt, allerdings schon nach dem Titoismus groß geworden und ironisierte vor dem Kriegsausbruch die Staatsideologie mit ihrem Heldenpathos. Westliche und jugoslawische Kultur stellen in diesem Verständnis keinen Gegensatz dar.

Saša ist eine Figur des Heute und trotz ihrer Loyalität gegenüber dem multinationalen Bosnien (er ist Kriegsveteran) nicht rückwärtsgewandt, sentimental oder jugonostalgisch. Trotz der deprimierenden Lage im Land hat er es nicht wie seine Ex-Frau verlassen, sondern versucht wieder neu Fuß zu fassen. Sein Generationserlebnis, das im Film nur ikonisch visualisiert wird, ist der Krieg, der ihn zu Beginn seiner Berufs- und Lebensplanung aus der Bahn geworfen und körperlich wie seelisch gezeichnet hat. Saša ist die Negation eines Kriegshelden und vermutlich sogar kriegstraumatisiert[8]. Seine Lebensumstände stellen ein Abbild der desolaten bosnischen Nachkriegsgesellschaft dar, der Verarmung der gutbürgerlichen Schicht und der allgemeinen Depression; er gehört zu den ökonomischen und sozialen Verlierern des Kriegs. Der Vater hingegen wirft ihm mit Faulheit und Schmarotzertum individuelles Versagen vor, obwohl er selbst an den neuen gesellschaftlich-ökonomischen Verhältnissen gescheitert ist. Die Auseinandersetzungen mit dem Vater zeigen die Unterschiedlichkeit ihrer Wertesysteme, den Stellenwert von Arbeit und sozialer Sicherheit. Saša kann wie seine Generation darauf nicht mehr bauen, aber er nutzt die Krise auch als Chance. Zukunft ist für ihn allenfalls in kürzeren Intervallen planbar, keinesfalls für sein ganzes Leben. Anders als Vater Muhamed schaut er nicht in die Vergangenheit des sozialistischen Jugoslawien, auch der Krieg interessiert ihn nicht. Wie der Filmtitel zeigt, ist sein Leben ein Alltagskampf, um wieder auf eigene Beine zu kommen. Dem Vater macht er Ignoranz, Egoismus und ein patriarchalisches Lebensmodell zum Vorwurf, das männliche Rechte weiblichen Pflichten gegenüberstellt, obwohl Mutter Marija wie die meisten Frauen im sozialistischen Jugoslawien nicht nur als Lehrerin voll berufstätig war und »nebenher« Haushalt und Familie gemanagt, sondern auch für den familiären Zusammenhalt gesorgt hatte und weiter sorgt. Saša weist die gesellschaftliche Retraditionalisierung der Geschlechterverhältnisse zurück.

Offenheit hat sich auch Senad in *The Son* bewahrt, der als gealterter Saša in den Fünfzigern betrachtet werden kann und dem die berufliche

---

8 Darauf deutet seine passive und tendenziell depressive Haltung hin, ohne dass der Film explizit die Vergangenheit des Protagonisten ausleuchtet.

Selbstständigkeit gelungen ist. Er hat nun eine eigene Familie und ist Vater zweier adoleszenter Söhne, beide auf der Suche nach der eigenen Identität. Auch in dieser postjugoslawischen Familie sind beide Partner berufstätig, er freiberuflich und sie angestellt. Die Familie wird am Beispiel des renovierten bosnischen Hauses, der Gerichte usw. als stärker auf Privatheit orientiert, als traditionsbewusst und innovativ zugleich dargestellt, ohne altmodisch zu wirken.[9] Senads Verhältnis zur Familie unterscheidet sich stark von dem des Vaters im Vorgängerfilm, der v.a. alle sozialen und familiären Belange seiner Frau überlassen hatte, doch fällt auch er gelegentlich in alte Rollenmuster zurück. Senad hat als gereifter Sohn die eigenen Erfahrungen umgesetzt, begreift seine Vaterrolle anders als sein Vater, geht auf Frau und Söhne zu und sucht das Gespräch, um in den zahlreichen Konflikten v.a. mit Arman eine Lösung zu finden. Er versteht sich nicht als das dominante Familienoberhaupt, entscheidet gemeinsam mit seiner Frau und versucht, selbst wenn nicht immer erfolgreich, den Söhnen gegenüber Argumente anzuführen und Entscheidungen nachvollziehbar zu machen. Senad und seine Frau verbringen Zeit im jeweiligen Freundeskreis, wo beide über ihre Elternrolle sprechen und sie mit den anderen vergleichen. Sowohl bei den Männern als auch bei den Frauen zeigen die Peergroups die Ähnlichkeit der Probleme. Dennoch ist der familiäre Zusammenhalt stärker und die Probleme mit den Kindern werden kleingeredet, beschönigt, ja z.T. verneint, um den eigenen Erziehungserfolg nicht in Abrede zu stellen. Trotz Senads Bemühen um die beiden Söhne trachten diese, den elterlichen Einfluss so weit wie möglich zu umgehen. Senads Kombination aus Verständnis und Verpflichtung zur Verantwortung stößt beim Versuch der Söhne, die eigenen Interessen durchzusetzen, immer wieder auf Widerstand. Wie weit Väter und Söhne voneinander entfernt sind, zeigt der Selbstmord von Armans Freund, dessen Vater keine Ahnung von den diversen Plänen des Sohnes (u.a. sich dem IS anzuschließen) hatte. Senads Bemühungen um die Söhne – so suggeriert

---

9   Das steht im Unterschied zur Wohnung der Eltern in einem großen Wohnkomplex aus der sozialistischen Zeit, was das räumliche und symbolische Setting für deren Weltbild ausmacht.

es die Rückkehr in der Schlusssequenz – zeigt zwar auch Rückschläge, ist aber letztlich erfolgreich.

Adoleszenz: die Söhne

Die Generation der Jugendlichen, die den Übergang vom Jetzt in die Zukunft verkörpert, steht im Mittelpunkt des Films *The Son*: durch Arman, Dado und andere ihrer Alterskohorte. Ein die Generation prägendes historisches Ereignis ist hier noch nicht auszumachen, wohl aber der Hintergrund einer von Zerstörung gekennzeichneten Nachkriegsgesellschaft. Mit der Pubertät bilden Fragen der Identitätssuche den Fokus, was bei Arman durch die Adoption zusätzlich vertieft wird. Die Jugendlichen erproben unterschiedliche Männlichkeitsmuster wie Abenteurertum, den Machismo starker Kriegshelden, erträumte starke Männlichkeit im virtuellen Raum, zeigen aber auch scheues Zurückweichen vor Dominanz, machen erste Liebeserfahrungen. Besondere Bedeutung nehmen bei Arman weibliche Anerkennung und Sexualität ein, die er mit seiner Freundin gerade zu entdecken beginnt. Die Labilität seines Selbstbewusstseins zeigt sich in seiner Empfindlichkeit gegenüber jeder Art von Kritik. Der ältere Arman setzt sich rücksichtslos über Grenzen hinweg und brüskiert Lehrer und Eltern, die sich um Verständnis bemühen, schützt aber auch den jüngeren Bruder Dado. Aus gekränkter Selbstliebe erkennt er seine Adoptiveltern nicht als Autoritäten an.

Dado, dessen Leben stark vom Virtuellen (Videospielen) geprägt ist, sieht in ihm sein großes Vorbild, dem er zunehmend durch sein Verhalten und Imponiergehabe nacheifert, auch wenn er es im Gegensatz zu Arman vermeidet, durch Regelbrüche aufzufallen. Das macht den größten Unterschied zwischen beiden aus: Dado versucht durch Lügen und Opportunismus Konflikten mit den Eltern aus dem Weg zu gehen, während Arman sie nicht nur in Kauf nimmt, sondern geradezu provoziert. Mit dem russischen Roulette, zu dem Arman die Peiniger seines Bruders nötigt, geht Arman entschieden zu weit, denn Dado, in Vielem noch ein Kind, gerät dadurch in Panik und in Todesgefahr. In dieser Situation treffen das virtuelle Kampfspiel und die Wirklichkeit in drastischer Wei-se aufeinander und Dado erlebt erstmals mögliche reale Konsequenzen dessen, was er in seinen Videospielen ständig bedenkenlos erprobt.

Das Vertrauen in Armans scheinbar verschworene Peergroup erweist sich als trügerisch: Die halbstarken Freunde, auf die Waffen als Mittel der »Stärke« eine große Faszination ausüben, erkennen die Konsequenzen ihrer Handlungen nicht (z.B. das Kapern einer Straßenbahn, illegalen Waffenbesitz usw.).[10] Schlaglichtartig zeigt der Selbstmord von Armans Freund die potentiell gefährlichen Verirrungen der Adoleszenten. Der hatte sich selbst mit den engsten Freunden nie wirklich über sich ausgetauscht, und auch die Freunde hatten kein Gespräch mit ihm gesucht, obwohl er die Unterstützung des IS angekündigt hatte. Hinter Provokation und Phrasen, aber auch Radikalisierung und Gewaltbereitschaft zeigt sich die Brüchigkeit des jugendlich-pubertären Selbstbewusstseins. Armans Agieren ist als Suche nach Identität und Orientierung einerseits, aber auch als Zurückweisung bestehender Lebensmodelle der Eltern- und besonders der Vätergeneration zu begreifen, ohne dem zugleich eine positive Alternative und Ausgestaltung entgegensetzen zu können. Innerhalb dieser Generation werden verschiedene Generationseinheiten sichtbar, d.h. große Unterschiede hinsichtlich Bildung oder im Umgang mit Gewalt, v.a. im unkritischen Umgang mit latenter gesellschaftlicher Gewalt und Gewaltbereitschaft. Angesichts dessen wird mit Armans Rachefeldzug für den Bruder auch eine mögliche Verkehrung der Rollen, dass Opfer nämlich zu Tätern werden können, angedeutet.

---

10   Symbole der Selbstbestimmung dominieren über echte Interessen. Arman ist bereit, für ein »eigenes« Auto, mit dem er seiner Freundin imponieren kann, sehr viel zu opfern: Ohne Führerschein baut er mit dem Auto des Vaters einen Unfall und verkauft dessen Geschenk, ein neues Fahrrad, für ein Schrottauto. Waffen stehen bei den Jugendlichen sehr hoch im Kurs – als Attribute angeblicher männlicher Stärke, die sie selbst damit kaschieren – sowohl in Dados Ballerspielen als auch in scharfen Waffen, die sich Arman und Freunde besorgen und mit denen sie bedenkenlos um sich schießen.

Die Semantik der Rückkehr

In beiden Filmen kommt der Rückkehr eine wichtige Rolle für das Selbstbild zu. Saša kehrt unfreiwillig zurück, denn die Rückkehr ist mit dem Verlust der Selbstständigkeit verbunden und bedeutet den Rückfall in die erneute finanzielle Abhängigkeit von den Eltern. Für sein Selbstbewusstsein bedeutet das einen herben Rückschlag; der Vater begreift es als persönliches wie berufliches Versagen. Saša kämpft gegen diese Sicht an und bemüht sich um eine neue berufliche Perspektive mit einem Neustart in die erneute Unabhängigkeit. Tatsächlich ist diese Lage nicht persönlich verschuldet, sondern Ausdruck der wirtschaftlichen und gesellschaftlichen Misere im Nachkriegsbosnien, das durch hohe Arbeitslosigkeit und »brain drain« der gut ausgebildeten jungen Generation gekennzeichnet ist.

Auch Muhameds vorgezogener Ruhestand hat eine ungewollte Rückkehr in die Familie zur Folge, die nicht mit seiner Vorstellung von einem geruhsamen Lebensabend korelliert. Auch wenn er es sich nicht offen eingesteht, ist auch diese Rückkehr als Misserfolg konnotiert, offenbart sie doch zugleich den unwiederbringlichen Verlust einer einst patriarchalen Rolle in der Familie. Der Unterschied liegt darin, dass Saša die Situation für einen Neustart nutzt, während sie bei Muhamed eine Rückentwicklung einleitet, die in die Demenz mündet.

Rückkehrerinnen sind auch zwei weibliche Figuren in *Our Everyday Life*: Schwester Senada und Sašas spätere Partnerin Lidija. Bei Senada, die als Kind aus dem belagerten Sarajevo nach Slowenien kam und nun hochschwanger, ohne abgeschlossenes Studium und ohne ihren Partner in ihr Elternhaus zurückkehrt, scheint die Rückkehr nach Bosnien dem Scheitern ihres Lebensentwurfs gleichzukommen. Doch der Schein trügt in beiden Fällen: Senada trifft damit die Entscheidung über ihre eigene Zugehörigkeit und Identität sowie die des Kindes, keinesfalls über eine gescheiterte Vision.[11] Lidija, die in die USA emigiriert war – für viele

---

11 Da die Figur im zweiten Film nicht fortgeführt wird, bleiben viele Fragen zu ihrem Lebenskonzept offen. Ihre Entscheidung, unverheiratet das Kind großzuziehen, passt nicht in das traditionelle Familienbild ihres Vaters Muhamed. Ob

aus dem ehemaligen Jugoslawien geradezu der Inbegriff des beruflichen Erfolgs –, ist nur vorübergehend zur Wohnungsauflösung und Ausstellungsorganisation nach Sarajevo zurückgekehrt. Durch die Liebesbeziehung mit Saša, der ihr einen Sessel als Symbol der Sesshaftigkeit in Sarajevo schenkt, kann auch diese Spätheimkehrerin die alte Heimat, die ihr neue künstlerische Möglichkeiten bietet, akzeptieren. Gegenüber den Rückkehrmotiven der beiden Männer ist bei Senada und Lidija die Rückkehr vor allem emotional positiv besetzt und nicht rational oder ökonomisch bedingt.

In *The Son* finden sich zwei Motive der Rückkehr: die des sichtbaren Misserfolgs und die der glücklichen Heimkehr. Der Film beginnt mit Armans freudiger, erwartungsvoller Verabschiedung und seiner frustrierten Rückkehr. Die Enttäuschung über die nicht erschienene leibliche Mutter, die ihm das Kennenlernen und die damit verbundene biologisch-genealogische Identität verweigert, leitet eine ganze Serie von wütenden Provokationen Armans gegen seine Umwelt ein. Dem gegenüber liegt bei Dado, der in Panik vor seinem Bruder in ein Minenfeld im Wald geflohen war, eine lebensgefährliche Verirrung zugrunde. In der Lösung der Situation verbindet sich die glückliche Rettung (Dados) mit Armans Identitätssuche, da er nicht nur der Retter seines Bruders und Vorbild ist, somit erstmals eine positive Perspektive bietet, sondern mit seiner Heimkehr auch symbolisch einen positiven Ausgang seiner Identitätssuche signalisiert.

Symbolische Räume

Die Chronotopoi in den beiden Filmen verweisen auf Semantiken und Werte, die auch für die jeweiligen Männlichkeitsbilder von Relevanz sind und deshalb in diesem Zusammenhang in die Betrachtung mit einbezogen werden.

---

sie alleinerziehend sein wird und ihr slowenischer Partner sich der Verantwortung stellen wird, beantwortet der Film nicht. Möglich scheint sogar, dass sie sich – wie Armans Mutter – durch Freigabe des Kindes zur Adoption und Emigration ins Ausland jeder weiteren Verantwortung entzogen hat.

Der städtische Raum Sarajevos gibt, wie situierende und kontextualisierende Panoramaeinstellungen, aber auch bekannte Motive der Stadt erkennen lassen, beide Male den Handlungsrahmen ab. Der historische Bezug greift auf die Symbole der olympischen Winterspiele 1984 zurück, die im kollektiven Gedächtnis der Stadt bis heute einen hohen Stellenwert einnehmen und mit der multikulturellen und internationalen Weltoffenheit der Stadt identifiziert werden – eine Konnotation, auf die besonders bei Kriegsausbruch und in der Nachkriegszeit immer wieder verwiesen wurde. Der Mythos des einigenden Geists der olympischen Spiele wird durch Plakate bei Saša und in der Firma des Vaters beschworen, aber auch durch die jungen Figuren, u.a. Armans Freundin, als sie über die von serbischen Tuppen zerstörte Bob-Bahn auf dem Trebević laufen. Dieses Detail der verwüsteten Sportstätte ruft den barbarischen Beschuss der Stadt von eben diesen Positionen und den Missbrauch der olympischen Idee auf. Obwohl der Krieg fast nie explizit verbal erwähnt wird, ist er visuell präsent; diese Details machen deutlich, dass die Belagerung genau diesen Zusammenhalt der (ethnisch gemischten) Bevölkerung zerstören sollte. Jede Einblendung von Symbolen der Winterspiele, sei es das Maskottchen Vučko, Plakate oder einfach das spezifische Logo, das jedem in der Stadt bekannt ist, ruft die Konnotationen des Kriegs und der dreieinhalbjährigen Belagerung der Stadt auf den Plan.

Ebenso deutlich zeigt sich das in der Gondel der Drahtseilbahn. Diese Attraktion der Vorkriegszeit wurde bereits in den ersten Tagen des Kriegs zerstört und symbolträchtig 2018, am 6. April, dem Tag des Kriegsbeginns, wieder eröffnet. Die Seilbahn führt auf den Belagerungsberg Trebević, der wegen der Minen und der Erinnerungen an den Beschuss lange von der Bevölkerung der Stadt gemieden wurde. Wenn Armin und Dado mit seinen Peinigern und Verführern (sie hatten Dado mit Drogen versorgt) eine Gondel besteigen, die auf den Berg fährt, dann verdichtet sich die Bedeutung in diesem Chronotopos und eine Vorstellung von mit Gewalt und Stärke konnotierter Männlichkeit wird aufgerufen: Die nagelneue Gondel, der man ohne Hintergrundwissen diese Konnotation nicht anmerkt, fährt hoch ins wieder erschlossene Erholungsgebiet. Mit den Minen in den abgelegeneren Teilen wird noch immer der Krieg, mit der Erneuerung aber auch der Wiederaufbau der Stadt evoziert. Der enge Raum der Gondel, die zwischen Himmel und Erde, zwischen klar abgegrenzten Räumen verkehrt, bietet keinerlei Fluchtmöglichkeit. Arman nutzt genau diese Konstellation für das erzwungene russische Roulette, einen gewalttätigen Racheakt für die Misshandlung und Verführung des Bruders. Dieser Raum des Übergangs vom scheinbar friedlichen Miteinander zur tödlichen Bedrohung ruft die unterschwellig bewusste Kriegssituation wieder hervor: Dado ist im Minenfeld des nächtlichen Walds einer existentiellen Gefahr ausgeliefert. Für beide Brüder hat das nichts mit Abenteuer zu tun, sondern die potentiell todbringende Grenzerfahrung führt ihnen schlagartig den Ernst der Lage vor Augen.

Die Festung, allgemein Schutzort vor Kriegshandlungen oder Objekt von schwierigen Eroberungen, als Ruine aber auch Raum des Abenteuers und der Gefahr, fungiert als Geheimort für Armans Clique und ist als Ort ihrer Intimität nur Eingeweihten bekannt: Er dient ihnen für ungestörte Treffen, zum Rückzug, zur Erprobung von Verbotenem und Initiationsritualen. Dort wird Verbotenes praktiziert (Alkohol, Rauchen, illegale Schusswaffen) und es werden, abseits jeder Kontrolle durch Autoritätspersonen, Männlichkeitsriten erprobt. Mit der Festung verbunden ist die Vorstellung vom heroischen Mann, der durch Stärke erfolgreich bzw. siegreich ist. Der verlassene Raum, kärglich ausgestattet, ist selbst ein Ort der Grenzüberschreitung, der ausschließlich männlichen Freunden zugedacht ist und auch durch seine Lage oben auf einem Berg mit einer scharf abfallenden Felskante Gefahr signalisiert.[12]

Die Wohnungen haben die Bedeutung des privaten, intimen Raums, der zuverlässig Auskunft über die Figuren, ihren sozialen Status, Bildungsniveau (z.B. die Bibliothek der Familie) und ihre Werte gibt. Im Unterschied zur Festung in *The Son* beherbergen sie Familien. Im Fall von *Our Everyday Life* erfordert die beengte Wohnung angesichts der vielen Bewohner große Rücksichtnahme. Die Wohnräume der einzelnen Figuren sind nicht immer klar abgrenzbar und Überschreitungen der Grenzen des Privaten sind, wenn auch unterschiedlich motiviert, an der

---

12 Arman nutzt ihn auch als Liebesnest, womit er gegen die Regeln der Gruppe verstößt.

Tagesordnung – sei es von Seiten der Mutter oder des Vaters. Insofern liefert die kleine Wohnung in *Our Everyday Life* auch die Information über die äußerste Beschränktheit von Privatheit und Intimität. Anders als Saša verfügt Lidija über eine eigene, fast leere Wohnung, die sie mit niemandem teilen muss und nur für sich und ihre Kunstprojekte nutzen kann. Sašas Reaktion zeigt, dass für ihn eine solche Lebensform, die nach und nach ausgestaltet wird, seiner Vorstellung von Offenheit entspricht. Seine symbolische Geste, sie mit einem Sessel zum Dableiben zu bitten, zeigt sein deutliches Votum.

Zwar verfügt Armans Familie über ein Haus und mehr Platz als in *Our Everyday Life*, aber Arman teilt sich mit Dado ein Zimmer; es ist ein ständiger Raum der Konflikte. Als Konsequenz verlässt er bei Auseinandersetzungen das Haus und schafft sich mit den Freunden einen ungestörten Rückzugsraum. Betrachtet man das Haus als Ausdruck von Senads Lebenskonzept, dann bestätigt sich darin auch Sašas Vorstellung: als individuell ausgestalteter Raum, der gegenüber seinem Elternhaus viel mehr Freiheit und Unkonventionalität sowie kreative Modernität in einem grundsätzlich geschlossenen und abgeschotteten muslimischen Haus signalisiert.[13] Die Durchlässigkeit der Raumgestaltung korrespondiert mit der auch sonst gezeigten Offenheit dieser Figur, aber auch ihrem positiv begriffenen Traditionsbewusstsein.

Das Auto fungiert als Symbol der Selbstständigkeit und Selbstbestimmung, des imaginierten Erwachsenseins und der Mobilität – letzteres v.a. in dem Raum, der mit anderen Verkehrsmitteln kaum oder schlecht erschlossen werden kann (z.B. die Überwindung der Grenze zu Ost-Sarajevo oder zur Natur). Angesichts der alten Autos ist auch deutlich, dass es sich hierbei nicht um Statussymbole handelt. Wie das Kapern der alten und völlig demolierten Straßenbahn durch Arman und seine Freunde zeigt, verkörpern Fahren und Lenken Selbstbestimmung und Überwindung elterlicher Kontrolle. Das Auto ist für Arman auch ein Ort der Zuflucht und herbeigesehnter Verwirklichung. Auch bei Saša,

---

13 Dieser urbane Haustyp zeichnet sich durch einen von außen nicht sichtbaren, von der Familie genutzten Hof der Privatheit aus. Auch das sich daran anschließende Haus ist von außen nicht einsehbar.

der sich ein Auto leiht, wird das deutlich. Allein die Tatsache, dass er die Mutter darin fährt und einen neuen PC für sie transportiert, stellt in beider Augen einen Akt der neu gewonnenen Autonomie dar.

Schlussbemerkungen

Die zahlreichen Einzelbeobachtungen zu den Männlichkeitsbildern der drei in den Filmen dargestellten Generationen belegen ihre historische Situiertheit und Wandelbarkeit. Im Einzelnen lässt sich folgendes festhalten:

Muhamed, Vertreter des Gestern, des sozialistischen Jugoslawien, dessen Aufbau er ebenso erlebt hat wie seinen Zusammenbruch, den er v.a. ökonomisch am eigenen Leib erfährt, wünscht sich in der Familie klare, traditionelle Rollenverteilungen. Da er sich selbst über die Arbeit definiert, erwartet er das auch von seinen Kindern, die ihn aber nach seiner Vorstellung enttäuschen. Denn v.a. seinem Sohn gelingt es nicht, sich beruflich erfolgreich zu etablieren, und der Vater ist nicht bereit, ihn z.B. durch einen Firmenanteil weiter zu unterstützen, sogar um den Preis, selbst dabei leer auszugehen. Der renitente und verständnislose Vater, selbst in einer schwierigen Lage, widerlegt auch in der späteren Verkörperung als dementer Greis die These von der Weisheit des Alters. Zwar hat der Kranke und Hilfsbedürftige jede aktive Rolle eingebüßt, zeigt aber im hohen Alter mehr Emotionalität gegenüber seiner Familie.

Der Vertreter des Jetzt, Saša bzw. Senad, in Jugoslawien sozialisiert, aber schon Teil der Alternativkultur, steckt zunächst mitten im existentiellen Kampf um seine materielle, persönliche und geistige Selbstständigkeit, die ihm trotz der schwierigen neoliberalen postjugoslawischen Verhältnisse gelingt. Seine Rolle in der Familie gestaltet er nach wesentlich offeneren Vorstellungen als noch sein Vater. So nimmt er die Erziehungspflichten und andere Aufgaben gemeinsam mit seiner Frau wahr und versucht, die Söhne ohne Gewalt zu verantwortungsvollen Menschen zu erziehen, was ihm aufgrund der Komplexität der Situation allerdings nicht immer gelingt. Senad zeigt auch gelegentliche Rückfälle in männliche Stereotype: er delegiert Arbeiten oder betrinkt sich trotz seiner Diabeteserkrankung mit seinen Freunden beim Männergrillabend. Ihn zeichnet jedoch aus, dass er sein Handeln reflektiert und auch anderen gegenüber nachvollziehbar zu machen versucht, für seine Söhne ein Vorbild sein will.

Die Söhne Arman und Dado, die die Zukunft verkörpern, kennen nichts anderes als das neoliberale postjugoslawische Wirschaftssystem. Sie erproben die unterschiedlichsten Vorstellungen von Männlichkeit, vornehmlich aber solche, die diskussionslos und als Reaktion auf Verunsicherung die eigenen Interessen durchzusetzen suchen: durch Einsatz von Umgehungsstrategien (Dado) oder aggressive und kompromisslose Durchsetzung eigener Vorstellungen (Arman). Beide zeigen eine auffällige Vorliebe für waffenverliebte Demonstrationen von Stärke und Macht – Dado virtuell, Arman auch real. Dado ahmt den älteren Bruder und andere scheinbar starke Gleichaltrige nach; die Offenheit des Vaters setzt er mit Schwäche gleich. Arman erkennt die reale Gefahr der unreflektierten Imitation zumindest bei Dados beginnendem Drogenkonsum und reagiert entschieden, ein Moment, das seine einsetzende Reife und sein Verantwortungsbewusstsein beweist. Bei der Suche nach der eigenen Identität werden – das zeigt auch das Beispiel des toten Freunds und seines geplanten Fortgangs zum IS – auch gefährliche Wege eingeschlagen, die nicht rational beurteilt und mit Vertrauenspersonen besprochen werden. Die Zukunft dieser männlichen Generation (und mit ihr der Gesellschaft) lässt der Film zwar prinzipiell offen, aber er signalisiert eine versöhnliche Perspektive. Diese hängt – so seine Botschaft – in hohem Maße davon ab, inwiefern es den Eltern und anderen gelingt, dieser Generation durch die Vermittlung von Verantwortung und Empathie nahezubringen, dass sie selbst mit ihrem selbstreflektierten Verhalten und den von ihnen ausgeübten Rollen die Schlüssel zur Form ihres privaten und gesellschaftlichen Zusammenlebens in der Hand haben.

Bibliographie

Adriž, Iris, Vladimir Arsenijević, und Đorđe Matić (Hgg.). *Leksikon YU mitologije*. Zagreb: Konzor, 2000.

Apelt, Maja, und Cordula Dittmer. »›Under pressure‹ – Militärische Männlichkeiten im Zeichen Neuer Kriege und veränderter Geschlechterverhältnisse.« *Dimensionen der Kategorie Geschlecht: Der Fall Männlichkeit*. Hgg. Mechthild Bereswill, Michael Meuser, Sylka Scholz. Münster: Westfälisches Dampfboot, 2011. 68–83.

Bancroft, Claire. *Yugonostalgia: The Pain of the Present*. Independent Study Project (ISP) Collection. 787 (2009). https://digitalcollections.sit.edu/isp_collection/787. Accessed 03 Mar 2021.

Bereswill, Mechthild, Michael Meuser und Sylka Scholz. »Männlichkeit als Gegenstand der Geschlechterforschung.« *Dimensionen der Kategorie Geschlecht: Der Fall Männlichkeit*. Hgg. Mechthild Bereswill, Michael Meuser, Sylka Scholz. Münster: Westfälisches Dampfboot, 2011. 7–21.

Blagojević, Marina. »Mizoginija kao jedna moguća paradigma.« *Mapiranje mizoginije u Srbiji: diskursi i prakse* (II tom). Beograd: Asocijacija za žensku inicijativu, 2005a. 15–19.

Blagojević, Marina. »Mizoginija: kontekstualna i/ili univerzalna?« *Mapiranje mizoginije u Srbiji: diskursi i prakse* (II tom). Beograd: Asocijacija za žensku inicijativu, 2005b. 20–36.

Bogdal, Klaus-Michael. »Männerbilder. ›Geschlecht‹ als Kategorie der Literaturwissenschaft?« *Geschlechtertheorie – Geschlechterforschung: ein interdisziplinäres Kolloquium*. Hgg. Marion Heinz, Friederike Kuster. Bielefeld: Kleine, 1998. 189–218.

Dedić, Nikola. »Yugoslavia in Post-Yugoslav Artistic Practices: Or, Art as...« *Post-Yugoslav Constellations: Archive, Memory, and Trauma in Contemporary Bosnian, Croatian, and Serbian Literature and Culture*. Eds. Vlad Beronja, Stijn Vervaet. Berlin: de Gruyter, 2016. 169–190.

Goulding, Daniel. *Jugoslavensko filmsko iskustvo, 1945.-2001*. Trans. L. Bekavac. Zagreb: V.B.Z. 2004.

Helfferich, Cornelia. »Männlichkeit in sexuellen und familalen Beziehungen: Differenz, Dominanz und Gemeinschaftlichkeit.« *Dimensio-*

nen der Kategorie Geschlecht: Der Fall Männlichkeit. Hgg. Mechthild Bereswill, Michael Meuser, Sylka Scholz. Münster: Westfälisches Dampfboot, 2011. 206–222.

Jakiša, Miranda. *Partisans in Yugoslavia. Literature, Film and Vidual Culture.* Bielefeld: transcript, 2015.

Kersten-Pejanić, Roswitha (Ed.). *Doing gender – doing the Balkans: dynamics and persistence of gender relations in Yugoslavia and the Yugoslav successor states.* München: Sagner, 2012.

Luleva, Ana. »Caring Masculinities in der bulgarischen postsozialistischen Gesellschaft – eine Alternative zu patriarchalen Männlichkeiten?« *Caring Masculinities? Männlichkeiten in der Transformation kapitalistischer Wachstumsgesellschaften.* Hgg. Sylka Scholz, Andreas Heilmann. München: oekom, 2019. 121–132.

Luleva, Ana. »Krise der Männlichkeit und/oder die (Neu-)Erfindung des Patriarchats. Der Fall der bulgarischen postsozialistischen Transformation der Geschlechterverhältnisse.« *Postsozialistische Männlichkeiten in einer globalisierten Welt.* Hgg. Sylka Scholz, Weertje Willms. Berlin: LIT Verlag, 2008. 195–214.

Mannheim, Karl. »Das Problem der Generationen«. *Schriften zur Wirtschafts- und Kultursoziologie.* Wiesbaden: Verlag für Sozialwissenschaften, 2009. 121–166.

Pavičić, Pavica. *Postjugoslavenski film. Stil i ideologija.* Zagreb: Hrvatski filmski savez, 2011.

Tanović 1: https://azra.ba/intervju/155726/ines-tanovic-uoci-sff-a-od-oca-sam-naucila-sta-je-sreca/ Accessed 21 Jan 2021.

Tanović 2: https://variety.com/2019/film/global/ines-tanovic-on-her-sarajevo-opening-film-the-son-and-next-project-1203303820/ Accessed 21 Jan 2021.

Tanović 3: https://rm.coe.int/interview-with-ines-tanovic-web/16808e9903 Accessed 21 Jan 2021.

Filme

Svakidašnje priče [Everyday Life Stories]. Dir. Ines Tanović. Sarajevo Dokument, Studio May, Spiritus movens, 2015.
Sin [The Son]. Dir. Ines Tanović. Sarajevo Dokument, 2019.

Aging Behind Bars
Perspectives from Incarcerated Men in the United States

Andrea Zittlau

Introduction

Since the 1980s, commonly attributed to the "War on Drugs," the prison population in the United States has risen, making the country the one with the highest incarceration rate worldwide. While the U.S. comprises only five percent of the world's population, it houses 25 percent of the world's prison population (Hurley 2018, 27) with a total of 2.3 million people currently living behind bars. Apart from the number of people incarcerated, the United States is also leading the statistics of longest prison sentences in the world. Therefore, the number of people who will age behind bars continues to rise. Especially people with a life sentence will face the challenges of old age in an already challenging environment that is not equipped with facilities and attitudes of care. I understand care not only as an interest in the well-being of others but also as the structural and institutional means to facilitate care-work.

As over 90% of all people incarcerated in the United States are male and housed in all-male facilities, the aspect of masculinity plays a crucial role in discussions of aging behind bars. However, masculinity intersects with issues of class and race that are highly relevant in U.S. prisons. Publications of recent years, especially Michelle Alexander's *The New Jim Crow* (2012) or Bryan Stevenson's *Just Mercy* (2015) highlight the complicated role systemic racism plays in the process of mass incarceration in the United States. While I recognize the complicated grit of race, class, gender, and age, I will not be able to entangle these components satisfactorily in this article. Concerning the U.S. prison system, I highly recommend Marie Gottschalk's profound study *Caught* (2014), which succeeds in further complicating the identity constellations of prisoners within the structures of American politics.

Rather than providing a profound analysis of aging behind bars, I would like to use this article to present a diversity of voices on aging from incarcerated men in different correctional institutions in the United States. Due to my role as a creative writing teacher, I am able to facilitate conversations in prison environments and collect original voices that often remain unheard otherwise. Thus, I understand this paper as a forum for these voices and the material they provide for further discussion.

However, the voices of the men are, of course, already mediated and selected by me, as I also provide the transition and the context. The texts I include here were either part of creative writing assignments (and therefore conceptualized as fiction) or shared in personal correspondences. I did not edit the writing. All men gave me permission to include their thoughts here. I am grateful for their generous trust and apologize if my interpretation of their voices compromises the agenda they had in mind. Due to prison regulations, I am only able to use the writer's first name. As aging in prison, and aging in general, is not a smooth, clear and linear procedure, this text is likewise a collage that illustrates in its format the conflicting processes.

I divided the material in three different sections arranged by topics that reappeared in the writing or my research. The first section will introduce different portrayals of elderly men addressing care on a personal level. The second section will present a Senior Center in its creation process in the State Correctional Facility of the city of Chester. Here an institutional attempt for care will be discussed by also highlighting the perspective of one of the center's initiators who is an incarcerated man with a life sentence. The last section is devoted to self-care and health issues.

"I never did know his real name" – Perspectives on Aging and Dying in Prison

Frank was born in 1933 and is currently serving a life sentence in the State Correctional Institution of Phoenix, the largest maximum-security prison in Pennsylvania with a population of approximately 3.000 men. He is a writer, occasionally publishing poetry and short stories. In the following text Frank, himself elderly, describes an elderly inmate.

Home
by Frank

He was an old guy when I met him. I never did know his real name. Had an Indian nickname. Once in a while, I almost come up with it. It wasn't like Brave Warrior or Running Bear. He was called after one of the tribes—like, Apache. It's on the tip of my tongue. He was the only convict who could go and come when he wanted. You might see him anywhere. Him and his baggy pants. Carried an old cloth bag—wide and deep—something like what the fellas used on ice-trucks years ago. The guy had a bit of everything in his cell. If you lost a button, or knob off your TV or radio, he'd find you one. They said he didn't want to go home. Been in prison too long. Some forty years. They said the world had changed too much. I'd heard him say one time, "Go home? This is my home. . ." I don't know if he meant it. He collected stamps. We guys saved them for him. And on a rare occasion—when he wasn't in those baggy pants—he'd hold court on the radiator. Would have his yellowish-gray hair combed to the side. Wore it kind of long. He'd take a puff on his cigar, then smile like he owned the world. I guess a good cigar does that to a fella. When he got sick, he fought to stay out of the hospital. His ankles swelled up so he hardly could walk. The guys would pull him on a wagon to the medication line. He'd wave like an old bear in the circus. The guys kept up a good face. But we felt bad for the old-timer. I was off the cell-block when they carried him out. About a week later we got the news. I still think of that old-timer. But I never did know his real name.[1]

The shock of death with the realization that one does not know the name or not know the person who passed away is a very common theme in the writing by incarcerated men. It is particularly striking in Frank's piece, as he himself is an elderly person, surely struggling with health issues. The man in his autobiographical creative piece is a curiosity but also a source of pity. The story speaks of care as the other men assist him to receive his medication and support his decision to stay out of the prison hospital, as the hospital units are notorious for their lack of care and horrifying hygienic conditions. "Home" is as much a description of an old man in prison as it is an obituary to the man without a name. It honors the man who passed away, yet the description reveals that Frank hardly knew him. As such, it portrays the anonymity in prison.

A similar note was sent to me by Russell, currently serving a life sentence at a facility in Delaware which houses about 2.500 men. Russell has spent the past three decades behind bars with little hope for parole. In a personal correspondence (August 14th 2021), he writes about the aging process of a friend:

> I can vividly recall witnessing an older prisoner, who I'd befriended during the first few months of my sentence suddenly lose his sense of hope, and shortly afterwards rapid deterioration consumed his entire being. It was like watching a ripe fruit gradually rot. The spark his eyes once held had dimmed, and his robust physique steadily dwindled. He had transformed into a moldy raisin, and within a year, he was gone. If I had to guess, I'd place his age roughly around 70. But who could say for sure what exactly the catalyst was, that tipping point that led to my friend's precipitous decline and demise.
> Perhaps he grew weary of the many years of mistreatment he's received from an apathetic medical staff, who routinely left bedridden patients unattended for days, as they wallow in their soiled sheets.

---

1   With kind permission by Frank and Jayne Thompson who facilitated the creative writing workshop in 2013 in which this piece was written.

> On the other hand, perhaps it was the emergence of some latent psychological reaction stemming from those 23 hour a day stints in the sensory depriving isolation unit he'd endured for months as a younger man. [...] In addition ... my friend had to overcome losing a lower leg to diabetes. The strictly regulated movements and access to outdoor exercise, concomitant with malnutritious meals ... certainly took a deadly toll upon his health.
>
> As I reflect upon my friend's final moments, it occurred to me that he was dying alone in his isolated cell in the prison infirmary. All family support had dried up years ago. He received no visits or letters. I can still picture him sitting there in his wheelchair with those vacuous eyes, his drawn-in cheeks, and small sagging shoulders – with death knocking at the door. A cold chill ran through me as I pondered, 'Will that be me one day?'
>
> (Personal Correspondence, August 14, 2021)

Like Frank in his text "Home", Russell writes about a memory of his early years in prison. Coping with the verdict of a life sentence, the reality of aging behind bars manifests in an elderly convict who mirrors their own fate and whose physical condition – depending on medication and being in a wheelchair due to leg amputation – causes extreme anxiety. Russell looks for the causes of the fading mental and physical health of his friend. He refuses to accept these conditions to be due to aging only, pointing sharply to the conditions of incarceration. He looks for his friend's past, surely also in an attempt to rewrite his own future.

Russell is recalling his friend at an age that makes him painfully aware of his own fragility and health issues behind bars as Frank likewise writes his story when he is an elderly inmate himself. Interestingly, neither Frank nor Russel addresses their own mental and physical struggles. However, the tenderness of their writing, the careful crafting of the people they describe, reveal their care. Frank playfully compares the man to a circus bear, certainly in the sense of a likeable person, although the comparison also reduces the man to an object of entertainment. Except for the statement that the man calls prison his home, we do not get his perspective in the story. By not quite believing this statement, Frank reveals his own position: Home to him is not prison, and yet he has likewise spent the majority of his life behind bars and will likely die there. The story reveals the fact that Frank refuses to acknowledge this process as much as the longing for a life behind bars.

Russell uses a raisin to compare his friend to, a sweet fruit that changes shape as it dries. He goes back to his metaphor when he mentions the support that had dried up, the fruit therefore becomes an illustration of the physical as well as mental condition of his friend but it also represents the missing care and support system. The image of the unresponsive man sitting in his wheelchair reflects Russell's shock as he realizes the possibilities of his own condition rapidly changing for the worse. The lack of care by the hospital and prison staff is a fact, as Russell describes it, the lack of family care often a result of dysfunctional families to begin with or the consequences of long prison sentences in remote locations that make an active and lively relationship often additionally difficult.

Lack of care as a symptom of prison life is addressed by Terrance in my personal correspondence. Terrance is in his early forties and recently managed to overturn a decades-long prison sentence in SCI Phoenix, Pennsylvania. While still incarcerated, Terrance wrote:

> As I'm sitting here typing this letter, there is an old man dead on the tier beneath me, my neighbor, a block worker just came to the door and told my celly that old man Dave just died. I did not know old man Dave, nor did I know the other old man who died a few weeks ago from Covid. Old man Dave was sick, but he did not have Covid. It's sad because people die and nobody cares, nobody really wants to reflect on the depth of death by incarceration, which to me is double torture. [...] To be sick in prison is like being sick in the desert and no one is around to help – here, in prison, the only people who will help have no power to do anything.
> (Personal Correspondence March 23, 2021).

Terrance openly reflects on death and on the fact that death is a common companion of prison life. The person who died has a name in his writing, Dave, and by naming him "old man Dave" Terrance indicates that the man, though dying of sickness, was an elderly inmate who must have been known for his name to travel. Due to the omnipresence of death in prison "nobody cares". Terrance is concerned about the lack of care on an administrative level and acknowledges the resignation. It seems, according to Terrance, very frustrating to care as he generalizes and writes that those "who will help have no power to do anything" – while it remains unclear who "those" are.

None of these statements involve concrete descriptions of care (except Frank's mentioning of a group of inmates helping the man to get his medication when he was unable to do so himself), rather the fear of not being cared for as it is blamed on the prison system. All three perspectives vividly show the impersonal atmosphere of prison life where it is best to stick to yourself, be aware of the gossip but do everything to avoid becoming part of it.

"Mentors, Father Figures and Peace Makers" – Perspectives on the Senior Center Project

The previously presented perspectives lament the lack of professional, effective, institutional care in correctional facilities in the United States. However, the State Correctional Institution Chester, in Pennsylvania is about to change the lack of care for the elderly in the prison system by creating a Senior Center behind bars. The SCI Chester is an all-male medium security facility in the city of Chester in Pennsylvania and the temporary home of roughly 1.200 inmates. This is less than half compared to the population numbers in the facilities that Frank, Russell, and Terrance live in at the point of their writing. It is also important to highlight that the other prisons mentioned before are all maximum-security prisons housing also people on death row with a particularly high number of long-term inmates which is not the case for the SCI Chester. Therefore, it is the more interesting that the Senior Center, one of the first of its kind behind bars, emerges in Chester. It was scheduled to open in 2020, but then the Covid-19 pandemic hit. Nevertheless, the plans were finalized and only the opening (had to be) postponed.

In SCI Chester, the average age is 38. The facility was designed to provide men who are serving a shorter prison sentence and have a history of substance abuse with therapeutic and educational programming. However, a few men serving life are also accommodated there and at first glance, the topic of aging is especially relevant for those men since they will spend most of their lives behind bars and will pass away in prison. However, aging is also a relevant issue for offenders who return to prison, those having a long criminal history, and the group of first-time offenders older than 50 years. The Department of Corrections considers inmates 50 years or older 'elderly', and SCI Chester currently has more than 180 elderly inmates – approximately 18 percent of its population (*Correctional Newsfront* 2020). Nearly 25 percent of the overall U.S. prison population is 50 years or older (Hurley 2018, 17). In a report about conditions for the elderly in prisons in the U.S., Human Rights Watch focusses on populations 65 and older (Hurley 2018, 17).

The idea for the Senior Center at SCI Chester was born in 2019, when a team of older incarcerated men began planning the center as a place for friendly exchange and community space as well as a symbolic place of honor for themselves and their peers. I had the privilege of visiting the large room that will serve as the central meeting point for the center that is decorated with murals of people the men admire, like Angela Davis, and a cozy corner with red armchairs. While the grey brick walls and the floor still reminded the center's visitors of prison, the attempt to create a space that does not feel like prison was evident. After pandemic restrictions will be lifted, the center will serve as a community place and recreational activity area.

As one man explained to me, the people who will use this center "are mentors, father figures and peace makers" who feel very much "underappreciated by the Department of Corrections" (Personal Correspondence with Michael, January 4, 2021). The extended function of the Senior Center is already apparent here. As prisoners experience the loss of identity and material possessions, the loss of autonomy, occupational status, heterosexual relationships, and societal rejection (Coretta 2012, 126), the need to matter and be influential is understandable. As such, the center is also relevant as a place of privilege and thus marks the senior population in the prison (especially the long-term inmates) as occupying a desirable place within the complicated prison hierarchies. Michael's statement also reveals the clash of masculinity visions inside prison walls and stresses the mental needs for long-term inmates.

Prison masculinities have inspired a number of studies and books, particularly focusing on its intersectional quality in correctional facilities. Prisoners come overwhelmingly often from disadvantaged populations, were often unemployed previous to their prison term or in precarious economic and living situations, and have histories of substance abuse and comparatively little education (Jewkes 32, 2002). Within the framework of gendered norms, men in prison are already emasculated – lacking power and economic influence. Conclusively, masculinity in prisons is often described as "hypermasculinity," which is "an exaggerated form of key masculine conventions, particularly aggression, violent domination, and independence" (Coretta 2012, 126) that is practiced in order to compensate for the lack of gendered influence in society. While most men in prison come from populations that have established a certain habitus there is, in addition to the male performance they bring already with them to prison, a specific prison male performance that develops according to complex prison hierarchies that define status among the men by crime, length of the sentence, positions in the prison, and other factors (such as physical appearance, which is demonstrated by excessive workouts) (Jewkes 38, 2002).

Michael, who is referring to himself and other seniors at SCI Chester as "mentors, father figures and peace makers", is a 60-year-old man serving a life sentence. The need to assign himself power that has been taken from him is apparent in his statement, but it is also a status symbol for those serving life in a prison that mainly houses offenders with shorter sentences. Thus, 'lifers' will see men come and leave constantly and can only build longer relationships within their own group. As one of the initiators of the Senior Center and a spokesperson for the group that will meet there, Michael writes in a letter to me about his role in the prison:

> I've been incarcerated 37 years. Men like myself, who have spent decades behind bars have taken responsibility to maintain order

within institutions. Lifers, specifically, are the lifeblood between peers and the administration to maintain peace and order. We are mentors to the younger, hardheaded inmate population. We are the gatekeepers, facilitators and managers for every group, program and workshop that takes place within the institution. We introduce rookie officers to the prison environment by helping them transition safely and successfully through the prison environment. You hear incredible stories from Superintendents, staff and people who have made rank, about how inmates helped them with their careers and in some cases, their decision for advancement in the D.O.C. I saved an officer's life and prevented a riot and a gang war between whites and blacks and Crips and Bloods. I helped officers, especially young females, understand just how important being a Correctional Officer is to fulfilling life.
[...]
Lifers and long termers do a lot for the D.O.C., yet at the end of the day in the eyes of the system of justice, we're nothing but a number, a person that committed a crime and deserves to be locked up for decades. (Personal Correspondence, January 4, 2021)

In its *Correctional Newsfront* newsletter, the Pennsylvania Department of Corrections frames the Senior Center as "designed to provide inmates older than 50 years with senior-specific programming and treatment with inmates their own age," (2020) clearly stressing the therapeutic value and framing the center as part of the prison program for inmates. The newsletter also recognizes Michael's perspective, perhaps also as essential for attracting men to use the facility. Designed with the help of the gerontologist Ebony Johnson, the Senior Center seeks to serve as a quiet space with plants and fish but also as a place to do arts and crafts and other recreational activities for men older than 50, the newsletter writes (2020). Furthermore, the center seeks to prepare older inmates for reentry, addressing topics such as medical care and housing as well as employment, topics that will make Michael painfully aware of the fact that he will not be able to go home as many of the others will. The newsletter recognizes that "offering programs such as this can help encourage and motivate senior inmates, who can positively affect their younger peers and the DOC staff," (2020) confirming Michael's role description and acknowledging the immense emotional stress that accompanies a life sentence or any prison sentence, particularly in older age.

"I do not [...] have any health problems" – Perspectives on the Aging Body

Michael and the other initiators of the Senior Center are healthy men older than 50. They participate regularly in the educational and recreational programs that SCI Chester offers and have the mental strength and physical capacity to initiate and actively coordinate programming in the Senior Center according to their personal needs. After all, the Senior Center will depend on inmates and volunteers to function.

However, the center will not be able to provide care for those with special physical and mental needs. Besides urgent medical and physical needs for medication or such seemingly simple equipment as additional blankets and the necessity for accommodation for people with restricted mobility, Martha Hurley points out that elderly inmates are prone to violence and extortion in the general population due to their weaker physical conditions (2018, 19). This is certainly not framed by Michael and not part of the Senior Center's mission. Further issues that Hurley addresses are the need for caretakers when elderly prisoners need help getting dressed, eating and cleaning up after themselves (2018, 67), needs that remain unaddressed in my correspondences – also because men with special needs will be transferred to the prison hospital and no longer stay in the general population.

When I taught creative writing in Graterford in 2016, the largest maximum-security prison in Pennsylvania at the time with 3.500 men (the prison has been closed recently and replaced by Phoenix, a new facility of the same size), I met Billy who is in his late 60s. Incarcerated in his early twenties, Billy has a 60- to 90-year prison sentence and can expect parole at the earliest in his late seventies. I would like to include Billy's voice because it reveals the work that staying healthy takes in prison and therefore illustrates the harsh reality of those who have not been able to participate enough in prison programming and thus lack a voice within the prison. Those who cannot participate in meetings, who are physically and mentally not well enough to voice their needs, will inevitably be silenced inside a system that gives little voice even to those who are able enough to speak up. The threat of violence is very real.

A few years after teaching the prison class, I heard that Billy became severely ill. During our class, he always seemed a tough but tiny and fragile man, so I sent him a feel better card, also because I knew that Billy does not have family and receives neither letters nor visits. This is Billy's response:

> I received the "Feel Better" card from [...] you. Thank you for the card [...] and also for your concern for me. However, I am afraid someone has given you wrong information. I was never in the prison hospital or any other hospital. I was sick about 6 weeks ago, and missed a [...] class. I think it was just the basic winter cold. I just did not want to go to the [...] class and take the chance of others catching my cold. [...] I do not take any type of medication, or have any health problems. I'm 5"9', and weigh between 150 and 170 pounds, depending on how hard I am working out. In fact, I was the only prisoner in Graterford last year to take Senior Fitness class on Sunday evening, Wellness class on Monday evening, Yoga class on Tuesday afternoon, Sports Conditioning class on Wednesday evening, and Yoga class again on Thursday evening. All these exercise classes took place in the prison Field House, two twelve week sessions for each class and I took all of them.
> (Personal Correspondence, April 23, 2017)

First of all, I would like to acknowledge the amazing programs that Graterford had to offer at the time, concerning that there are senior fitness classes and opportunities designed for the elderly to stay fit and healthy (as far as this is possible inside the prison). However, on one occasion, Billy excused himself from the writing class in favor of 'conditioning' and on my way to the writing class, I saw the men running up and down the stairs of the prison's lecture hall, which turned out to be the activity called 'conditioning class'.

Billy's attempt to stay firm and fit comes from a fear of damaged health, a fear that is very real in prison. This returns me to the initial stories by Frank and Russell whose descriptions of elderly inmates reveal their anxieties about their own health. However, younger inmates, who clearly dominate the prison population, can often not relate to the difficult process of aging. In my personal correspondence with Terrance, he vividly addresses the health issues of his cellmate:

> Let me tell you what I'm dealing with (not complaining). I have a new cell mate, actually I'm on a new unit. My new cell mate is an older guy (62) with 38 years of prison time served on a life sentence. He has a lot of stuff which is understandable since he's been in prison almost as long as I've been alive. But he's a hoarder so a lot of his property is extra crap that he's collecting for a rainy day, and when you hold onto stuff in a small cell it becomes cluttered and difficult to clean. [...] My celly has no teeth, so he doesn't do any maintenance on his mouth, no gargling or brushing his tongue, so he has bad breath, and he farts all day, so either I'm smelling breath or fart, sometimes both. Could you imagine living in a room the size of a large closet, with another person, their clothes and shoes and food, and appliances, and their legal papers that can fill a trunk. All this is compounded by the fact that we are locked in here together for over 23 hours a day.
> (Personal Correspondence, March 23, 2021)

Terrance's perspective is particularly valuable. For one, he describes an elderly inmate with a set of health issues that Terrance has somehow adopted as they are problems that affect him, too. While Frank and Russell, whom I quoted in the beginning, both reflect on an elderly inmate once they are experiencing aging themselves, Terrance does not relate the health issues to complaints that might catch up with his own body. He seems to judge his cellmate's struggles as solvable problems. He could take care of his oral hygiene, the letter seems to suggest, supervise his diet better and part with most of his belongings. To Terrance, these problems are not part of old age, yet he shows compassion for the situation of his cellmate by stressing the fact of the long time spent in prison. While Frank almost admiringly recalls the fact that the old man he describes in his story has everything in his cell, to Terrance, his cellmate (who seems likewise well equipped) is a hoarder.

The relationship between cellmates is often very challenging, as they are all confined to a very small space most of the time. Movement in prison was restricted particularly harshly under Covid-19 regulations. The lack of privacy seems to make care work impossible. Again, the man does not have a name in Terrance's letter, and we do not learn anything about him apart from the aspects that directly affect Terrance's well-being. However, in the earlier quoted remark about "old man Dave", the information about the death was passed on to the man Terrance describes and not to him (he just overhears the news). This shows that the man who challenges Terrance's daily life is connected enough in prison to have news about the death of someone personally delivered.

The report Terrance gives of the daily living conditions also shows how life can indeed become challenging for older prison inmates. While Terrance was waiting to be paroled and practiced patience on many levels, other incarcerated men might not have tolerated the inconveniences of sharing their cell with someone who might affect their daily lives. What is perceived as challenging is certainly up to the individual perspectives, yet a glimpse into the prison life provided here with ego-documents shows that particularly health issues and old age may make men targets of scorn and, thus, easy victims of violent outbursts.

Conclusion

Aging in prison means aging in an environment that provides very limited possibilities of care. Apart from physical activities, the men lack mental challenges and receive food that is problematic in many ways. Additionally, the prison is a place with constant fear of punishment and violence by staff or other inmates. To have to depend on others in your daily routine makes you indeed fragile and likely to become a victim of violence in an already violent system. As such, Billy's workout obsession, which is shared by many men behind bars, is not only a demonstration of masculinity and physical power, it is also a hoped-for strategy to stay young in an institution in which being old (and dependent) can be unimaginably horrifying. The insistence of the men I quoted here of being mentally and physically able reveals their fear of inability because they live in the presence of those who they fear to become one day. The Senior Center at SCI Chester seeks to provide stability and a place of hope that creates a momentary vision of healthy aging within prison walls. As such, it contributes immensely to the mental sanity of its inmates, but time will show if its management will succeed in including those who may need special assistance.

I would like to conclude with a poem Billy wrote in a writing class for a small publication in zine format (2016). It is the most fitting end for this article because as it thinks about staying young, it connects the past with the future and blurs the lines between the prison and the world outside.

Staying Young

> Late at night, dark outside,
> suffering from insomnia, unable to sleep,
> he does push-ups, and paces,
> he is lean, hard, the consummate loner.
> So stiffened and composed the lines of his face,
> events could be dated by wrinkles he had acquired,
> made time itself appear old-fashioned.
> When he looks in the mirror, the enemy stares back,
> it's a frightening vision, a quiet steady look,
> a disarming smile, a face he doesn't know.
> You said you would save me from snare,
> falling for 90 years into a trap I dug myself.
> He is stuck in a never ending dark night bog.
> His story is not like a road one should follow,
> more like a house, you go inside and live in darkness,
> an altered life, viewed from bars, walls, and dark nights,

roaming in corridors that never led to freedom.
A dizzy variety of experiences, cultures, and men,
all these swept clean like a blackboard,
ignored, neglected, relegated to the darkness,
the human heap, slowly eroded.
All gone, the man that was,
the past restored, the process reversed,
staying young, really did exist,
only in thoughts and dreams,
preserving them in the darkness of sleep.

Works Cited

Alexander, Michelle. The New Jim Crow. Mass Incarceration in the Age of Colorblindness. New York: The New Press, 2012.
Correctional Newsfront "Chester Opens New Center for Elderly Inmates." September 29, 2020. https://www.cor.pa.gov/Correctional Newsfront/Pages/Article.aspx?post=1353 [23 September 2021].
Coretta Phillips, The Multicultural Prison. Ethnicity, Masculinity, and Social Relations among Prisoners. Oxford: Oxford University Press, 2012.
Gottschalk, Marie. Caught. The Prison State and the Lockdown of American Politics. Princeton, NJ: Princeton University Press, 2016.
Hurley, Martha H. Aging in Prison. The Integration of Research and Practice. Durham: Carolina Academic Press, 2018.
Jewkes, Yvonne. Captive Audience. Media, Masculinity and Power in Prison. Portland, Oregon: Willan Publishing, 2002.
Stevenson, Bryan. Just Mercy. A Story of Justice and Redemption. New York: Spiegel & Grau, 2015.
Thompson, Jayne and Andrea Zittlau (eds.), N.I.G.H.T. Poems. Pink Gorilla Press, 2016.
Terrance, Personal Correspondence, March 23, 2021.
Russell, Personal Correspondence, August 14, 2021.
Michael, Personal Correspondence, January 4, 2021.
Billy, Personal Correspondence, April 23, 2017.

Acknowledgements

I would like to thank the men who generously shared their thoughts with me in personal correspondence and agreed to the publication of their valuable perspectives. Furthermore, I would like to thank Taneisha Spall and Capt. Lorie Eason for their correspondence and insights into the planning of the Senior Center at SCI Chester. My gratitude goes also to Jayne Thompson for the wonderful collaborative creative writing workshops and for sharing Frank's piece for this article.

Man Plants, Woman Nurtures
Reflections of Older German Men

Lisa-Nike Bühring

Constructions of Masculinity and the Sexual Binary

The unremitting socio-cultural power of the sex binary is astonishing when considering that biological evidence for a division of humans into only two sexes is far from being unambiguous (Feinberg 1996; Kessler 1998; Rubin 1997). Nonetheless, the binary construction of sexual difference is so deeply implanted in the individual from the day one is born that gendering oneself univocally as a man or a woman is essentially the foundation from which one cultivates all other aspects of identity development.

> The division between the sexes appears to be 'in the order of things', as people sometimes say to refer to what is normal, natural, to the point of being inevitable: it is present both – in the objectified state – in things (in the house, for example, every part of which is 'sexed'), in the whole social world, and in the embodied state in the habitus of the agents, functioning as systems of schemes of perception, thought and action. (Bourdieu 2001, 8)

As a consequence, it is practically impossible for men as well as for women to avoid the socio-cultural and largely unconscious process of sexual indoctrination (Bourdieu 2001, 7–33) within which masculinity is associated with predominantly positively connoted aspects such as strength, dominance, rationality and control, while connotations affiliated to femininity centre around notions of passivity, submission, helplessness, emotionality and empathy – characteristics which are, in the occidental world, often valued considerably less than the supposedly male attributes (Schippers 2007, 85–102).

By linking male dominance and female submission to biological predetermination, patriarchy has been defined as representing the 'natural order of things', thus legitimating its rule beyond doubt (Butler 2011, 124–50; Schippers 2007, 85–102). At the same time, and intertwined with the contrasting construction of femininity and masculinity, their interdependence is also assumed, since one narrative gains authority only by referring and comparing it to the other.

Raewyn Connell's now widely accepted definition of masculinity is unique in its reference to precisely this relationality between understandings of femininity and masculinity (Schippers 2007, 85–87). As a cultural construct, masculinity is defined as the result of an interplay between the respective culture, the individual personality as expressed in actions and of positioning oneself in opposition to other men and women. "'Masculinity' [...] is simultaneously a place in gender relations, the practice through which men and women engage that place in gender, and the effects of these practices in bodily experience, personality and culture," (Connell 2005, 71). Understandings of masculinity thus depend on and are affected by the geographical region, by the historical period and its respective values and norms as well as by societal and politico-economic developments (Baur and Luedtke 2008, 9).

However, as context-dependent as constructions of masculinity are, what seems to recur and tie together hegemonic understandings of masculinity across time is the significance attributed to being in control and active, and to displaying and incessantly proving dominance. "The hegemonic definition of manhood is a man *in* power, a man *with* power, and a man *of* power. We equate manhood with being successful, capable, reliable, in control" (Kimmel 1994, 125). Successful performances of masculinity are hence dependent on incessantly establishing and maintaining dominance, control and potency throughout the life-course (Calasanti & King 2005, 10).

Ageing and retirement rob older men of a meaningful role that supported the feeling of all-encompassing agency and linked it to status and individual significance. Older age, therefore, not only seriously impedes men's claims for patriarchal privileges and hegemonic status, but it also challenges their sense of self (Chivers 2011, 99–138; Coston and Kimmel 2012, 99–110; Jackson 2016, 1–26). Therefore, the questions arise as to how men who have retired and who most likely experience a decrease in capabilities handle these age-related changes and how they incorporate aspects linked to ageing into the construction of their older male identity.

Within this context, I was particularly interested in exploring how men, who have during major periods of their adult lives, been part of the hegemonic class of men and who were as a result never forced to find ways of handling marginalisation (Calasanti & King 2015, 193–200; Coston & Kimmel 2012, 97–11; Tarrant 2010, 1580–1591), manage the natural decline in physical and mental abilities and linked reduced level of control and the loss of the identity-constituting professional role in older age. These and linked queries guided the selection of the four interviewees in the focus of this paper.

For above mentioned reasons, it was crucial to select interviewees who used to match a majority of the criteria linked to hegemonic masculinity. The four interviewees selected have been exceptionally successful in their careers, are white, heterosexual and married – criteria which firmly mark them as belonging to the hegemonic masculinity ideal of corporate masculinity promoted in the West (Cheng 1999, 298; Connell 2005, 71).

All interviewees were at the time of the interview between 72- and 79-years old and had been officially retired for some time (Bühring, 2020, XXIX-CXXXI).[1] As a result they witnessed and experienced many societal and politico-economic developments throughout the course of their personal and professional lives which, as highlighted above, instigated alterations in the socio-cultural views of masculinity, particularly

---

1   References regarding the interviews conducted refer to the pages of the transcripts in Bühring, 2020.

of hegemonic understandings of masculinity in the West. To better understand how their lived experiences of, for instance, post war Germany, of the second, third and present wave of feminism (Tasker & Negra 2007, 1–26), of pre and post divided Germany and of professional employment over the course of thirty years and, most importantly, retirement have impacted their view of masculinity (Cheng 1999, 295–315; Connell 2005, 67–81; Connell 1993, 597–623) has motivated the interviews with the participants.

All interviewees participated enthusiastically in the interviews. The openness and willingness of the informants to talk about their experiences, worldviews and the high level of trust they showed towards me, which was emphasised by the fact that only one of three participants wished to be anonymised, allowed me to gain in depth insights into their identity construction throughout their life-course. The inclusion of my father as an interviewee was also motivated by my wish to further my understanding of older masculinity constructions. My father used to fit the hegemonic masculinity ideal in many ways, and given our closeness and my knowledge of his experiences, I believed he could provide particularly crucial and relevant insights into the identity construction of older German men who used to be part of the hegemonic class of men. In addition, it seemed logical to me to include, at least, my Dad in the research since observing my parents' very different approaches towards managing the ageing process has been the main reason for my research focus.

In my view, the high level of cooperativeness the interviewees showed and the combination of similarities and differences of the informants led to a particularly interesting research context which contributed considerably to the depth of the data, and thereby significantly facilitated a better understanding of how these four German men experienced the process of ageing (Haraway 1988, 589–90; Harding 1992, 63–72).

Reflections of Older German Men on Masculinity and Femininity

One of the significant findings of my semi-structured interviews, has been that the perception of the sex binary as genetically predetermined was carried forward into older age (Bühring 2020, 155–164). The informants assigned attributes such as activity, rationality, and determination to men and passivity, emotionality, and of naturally being caring to women; and they drew on this understanding of sexual difference also to construct their identity in older age (Bühring 2020, 105–139). To illustrate this, I will present in the following some quotes from the interviews[2]. Burkhard Rosenfeld defined masculinity as follows:

> To me, masculinity means to have the ability to take part in reproduction and play a crucial role in it. Masculinity is also linked to this traditional understanding of the male respectively female role. That is that the men of the cave people went hunting and the women were responsible for the part, which took care of the family. The man provides the family with protection, and the woman provides emotions and feelings (Bühring 2020, XXIX).

For Lars Bühring masculinity is characterised by:

> [...] drive, determination, well, another word, activity, to be responsible for others. Ultimately to be able to also live with the consequences, which in his surrounding in some way have significance and to identify himself with them and to derive, well, then the suitable consequences and activities. Well, really it is the opposite of passive (Bühring 2020, CVIII).

Burkard Rosenfeld and my father both followed a similar train of thought when the former suggested that masculinity had been determined in early human history when men were the hunters and protectors of the

---

2   Transcripts of interviews can be found in Bühring 2020, xxix-cxxxi

family while the latter named, among other attributes, activity as a core element of masculinity (Fausto-Sterling 2008, 3–12).

Günther Schotten replied, when asked what determined masculinity for him: "Well, masculinity means to me a...the attempt to think stringently and also a certain amount of physical effort and a strong reference to rationality, a highly rational life," (Bühring 2020, LIII). When I then enquired if these characteristics must be viewed as in opposition to female attributes, he confirmed that by saying: "To a certain degree, yes," (Bühring 2020, LIII). Later on, he specified his definition of masculinity by referring to the "problem of masculinity" which he defined as "performance orientation with a strongly systematic approach," (Bühring 2020, LVI). Some minutes later the topic came up again, and Günter Schotten referred to his wife who introduced the idea of the "masculinity gene", which she defined as being "performance-oriented, Yang-excess, to prove oneself, that you can still do it and so on" (Bühring 2020, LXII).

G.B.'s answer to the same question was particularly insightful since he mentioned what others link to masculinity, such as strengths, dominance, roughness, sportiness, but clearly distanced himself from this view since it did not match his own personality. However, he also made it a point to highlight that, although he viewed himself as diverting from conventional understandings of hegemonic masculinity, he did not want to be associated with attributes linked to femininity:

> Honestly, I have never really thought about this. Well, to me masculinity is somewhat a little more linked to a question mark than to an exclamation mark. Since I was -, you need to see the individual situation, so we were four boys at home, and I was the youngest, and I was, let's say, not only by age but also by nature the most sensitive of the four. And the others were bigger, stronger and rougher, I was somewhat more highly sensitive, what then somehow was, yes, somehow perceived, by my social surroundings more than by me, I don't want to say, to have a more feminine touch but it was not the kind of masculinity, let's say, that was embodied by others. [...]. So I had a conception of what masculinity was but, let's say, also some healthy doubts about how sustainable and also justified this was,

let's say, simply because of the discrepancy to my own feelings, to how I viewed myself (Bühring 2020, LXXVII).

Interestingly, although all four men mentioned different aspects of masculinity, they all more or less strongly stressed the differences between men and women which reflects a hegemonic cultural narrative grounded in biology and evolutionary theory (Fausto-Sterling 2008, 3–12). This also became obvious at other points during the interviews.

Burkard Rosenfeld said strikingly little about the specific characteristics of women only when I asked if in his view men or women suffer more by the ageing process, he said: "I think on average women suffer more by the physical signs of ageing, wrinkles, glasses, whatever," (Bühring 2020, XLVIII). This view was also entertained and elaborated upon by my father, who in reply to the same question, said:

> It is much more difficult for women...Yes, because I think that on the one hand, in a different age, they, at least in my view and I think are much more linked to their social environment in a specific way, well, integrated in their social environment, you could also say more dependent and therefore more dependent on the echo of their social surroundings than it is the case with men. And also since the appearance plays a crucial role and the echo naturally becomes less when one becomes a little older. That means they have with ... I think that is; they will have more difficulty in keeping their self-concept (Bühring 2020, CXXVIII).

Neither Günter Schotten nor G.B. agreed with this conception of women, particularly with reference to the women they know. Günter Schotten first said when I asked him whether ageing was more difficult for men or for women: "I have heard that it is more difficult for women," (Bühring 2020, LXXIV). When I then probed for more detail by asking him if he thought that was true, he replied: "I don't know. I don't think so. It's not the case with my wife. She has as little a problem with getting older as I. You hear that regularly but in my circle of friends I cannot confirm that" (Bühring 2020, LXXIV).

Nonetheless, in other parts of the interview both G.B. and Günter Schotten emphasised the differences between men and women. In addition to mentioning the "male gene of performance orientation" (Bühring 2020, LIX), Günter Schotten's view of the natural role division also became apparent when he talked about his wife's professional occupation. He described to me that his wife used to have a lawyer's office with a focus on divorce, inheritance, corporate and criminal law relating to young offenders, which was rather successful "…but small. Very small and it always took backstage. The children had always preference time-wise, and when there was something …That is why it did not play such a big role for her," (Bühring 2020, LX). And shortly after that, he remarked: "My wife worked much but, as said, always completely in the background, and only very little. In comparison to me, naturally very little," (Bühring 2020, LX). I then asked: "And she took care of the children?" and Günter Schotten answered: "Exactly, that always had preference, which was appropriate. That is why she called herself a single mother," (Bühring 2020, LX).

G.B. repeatedly mentioned his high respect for women and especially for his mother. For instance, he said: "Well, I have never met a woman who worked as much as my mother," (Bühring 2020, LXXXI). When I enquired about the gender-specific handling of the ageing process, he even said: "…I also believe that women have much more inner balance…Within this context, I have always been somebody who said that women are the stronger sex," (Bühring 2020, CVI). Nevertheless, as already mentioned above, it became clear in his definition of masculinity that regardless of his high respect for women, he did not want to be affiliated to female characteristics when he said: "…I don't want to say, to have a more feminine touch, but it was not the kind of masculinity, let's say, that was embodied by others" (Bühring 2020, LXXIX).

In my view, the above responses show that the interviewees have incorporated a conception of gender characteristics based on sexual difference into their identity construction, in which characteristics such as activity, performance orientation, being driven by ambition for professional success and the will for domination and winning are attributed to masculinity whilst female characteristics are generally linked to being caring, being more balanced, being emotional and warm, being less interested in career progression but also to passivity and, to a much lesser degree, to dependence (Schippers 2007, 94–95).

The answers, however, do not indicate a general disrespect for women but simply show that women were perceived as a totally different species which has little in common with men. In fact, and despite what is suggested by some scholars (Connell, 2009; Kimmel, 2001; Schippers, 2007), Günter Schotten, Burkard Rosenfeld and G.B. did not appear to link feminine characteristics to negative connotations but instead seemed to, in different degrees, feel admiration for women and their way of handling life. Within this context, it is also particularly interesting that women who in some way display male characteristics were not, as Schippers (2007, 95) believes, categorised as unnatural or social pariahs. In fact, it neither seemed to be something which the interviewees viewed as unlikely nor did it seem to impede their appreciation or respect for these particular women.

Burkhard Rosenfeld said, when reflecting on the fact that his first wife had only found a satisfactory professional occupation rather late in her life, whilst his second wife had continuously worked part-time in a pharmacy during their relationship: "But after all, she[3], she, after all, had additionally[4] had a job, not full-time but part-time. That somewhat gave her strength, and that did not exist for my late wife," (Bühring 2020, XXXV). At another point during the interview, Burkard Rosenfeld described his second wife as "... a little more curious than me," (Bühring 2020, XLV). These remarks and the whole conversation left me with the impression that it was of particular significance for Burkard Rosenfeld to be on an eye-level with his wife, and that he believed that being equal partners in the relationship a prerequisite for a healthy relationship and a working marriage.

Similarly, Günter Schotten stressed that he and his wife were intellectually on the same level and that this markedly increased the quality of their lives, also in older age: "...And yes, my wife and me, we have well, ...

---

3   His second wife.
4   In addition to being a mother and housewife.

We also get on intellectually one hundred percent. We are nearly always of the same opinion. Also critical, very critical. We really are individualists somehow. But also, very critical about all and nothing and as such it[5] has been quite good," (Bühring 2020, LXIV). He also mentioned that he still had contact with two female colleagues who frequently contacted him to discuss legal issues. He clearly held these women in the highest respect and did not at any point indicate that he found it remarkable or inappropriate when women worked in the same profession as he used to do. Referring to one of these two women, he said: "...We are on an absolutely identical wavelength. When she has questions, they are always absolutely justified..." (Bühring 2020, LXII).

G. B. was, except in the instances already quoted above, a little less explicit about his opinion about women, who display characteristics and abilities traditionally linked to men. I, however, believe this was based on him not even questioning that women have the same and perhaps more abilities than men – an understanding which he transmitted throughout the interview (Bühring 2020, LXXIX-CXXXI). The implicitness with which he took the equality of men and women for granted is, I believe, the result of his upbringing on two counts. First of all, he is considerably younger than the other participants and therefore grew up in a time characterised by civil rights movements and feminism, which certainly influenced him and his views on gendered hierarchies (Baur and Luedtke 2008, 13–15; Brown 2013). At the same time, the admiration he felt for his mother, a woman who not only took care of her family and a household, but also helped his father considerably with the administration of the company, very early presented him with a female role model highly unusual for that time. His slightly different view on women became utterly clear to me when he, as the only participant, said quite casually: "That therefore means, everything which was family, what had to do with the children, was her job," (Bühring 2020, XCVI)

At first sight, this might seem to be a rather conservative remark referring to the traditional role division between men and women, and partly this might be true, but to define taking care of the family and the

---

5   It = retirement, respectively the quality of life during retirement.

household as a job and thereby equating it with paid jobs, I find rather unusual.

Although my father, to my mind, provided the most conventional and rigid definition of masculinity, in which he somehow implicitly excluded the possibility of women having the same abilities as men, this was relativised in his answer to my follow-up question. When I inquired if he believed that the qualities he mentioned as being characteristic for men could also apply to women, he admitted that that was possible but not as likely as with men. Precisely, I asked whether his definition of masculinity was also based on a clear demarcation from women and my father answered: "Largely yes, absolutely. But, of course, I also know women to whom this demarcation only applies to, to a limited degree..." (Bühring 2020, CVIII).

Without a doubt and clearly not the least as a result of the historical context they grew up in, all interviewees understand masculinity by and large in contrast to femininity. They entertain a rather conventional view of the male-female role division, whose articulation is nowadays evaluated as politically incorrect which, however, does not mean that men regardless of age do not think similarly. Younger men and women might predominantly just not dare to utter this in public to avoid social sanctions (Bourdieu 2001, 5–53; Hall 2000, 36–53). Nonetheless, the interviewees' views on gender relations and their own embodiment of masculinity are neither quite as black and white and inconsiderate, nor as unambiguous as it may seem at first sight. This became particularly obvious not only in the above comments on their conception of femininity, but also at other points during the interviews, namely when I asked the interviewees about what they thought their conception of masculinity was based on.

Günter Schotten and Burkard Rosenfeld attributed their understanding of gender roles explicitly to their specific situation during childhood and adolescence. Günter Schotten said:

> I think that one is somehow influenced by one's parents, grandparents, by what one experiences. I believe that. Also, by the traditional role model. That was much stronger than one can understand to-

day. ... Yes, my parents stayed together all their lives. And my father worked. He was a notary, too. And my mother took care of the children. She was very extramural, was involved in politics, was in the city council, in the unitary council, but in the end, the role division was absolutely there (Bühring 2020, LIV).

Burkard Rosenfeld elaborated on his view of the man being the provider and protector of the family, when I asked him about his priorities during his professional life:

> I was influenced by my family background. ...So, she had, my mother had, with 29 the war ended, and with 32 she found out that she is a widow, and there she had two boys and had under great privations to bring up these children. That influenced me so that I wanted to become independent as soon as possible; I really wanted to earn my own living. And then could not only earn my own living but I could also together with my brother take care of my mother, who was a fantastic person. And that obviously influenced me ... I take care of the protection of my family. And my wife takes care of the family itself, of the warmth of the family...(Bühring 2020, XXXIII).

In his skepticism of the (hegemonic) conception of masculinity, G. B. expressed the idea that one's understanding of masculinity is primarily influenced by the specific individual situation. As such, I believe it to be justified to say that G.B.'s relatively contemporary and ambiguous perception of masculinity is the consequence of his younger age but also of what he saw exemplified by his brothers, by his parents and particularly by his relationship to his mother. When I asked him with whom he had a closer relationship, his father or his mother, he answered: "Clearly to my Mom. I was somehow her Benjamin[6]...I was very close to her, also later, even as an adult," (Bühring 2020, LXXX). Soon after he described the role division in his family:

---

6   'Benjamin' is a colloquial expression in German which indicates that someone is the youngest sibling and most spoilt child.

> Well, my mother was the centre of the family. My father worked from morning till night...but still had the half hour to play football with his sons when he came home. But my mom was the soul of the family. She managed everything, did everything. She was there for everything and everybody.... a well-fortified woman. But nothing took priority over her family. And, well, I mean, what you might view in a different light as an adult when you look back, for her, the children came first and then there was nothing for a while, then came her husband and then came the rest of the family... (Bühring 2020, LXXX & LXXXI).

When I asked Lars Bühring if he thought his understanding of masculinity was influenced by his upbringing, he denied this possibility and said that the older he became, the more he made his decisions without consulting his parents or siblings. He then continued:

> That's why this conception really formed itself slowly through this development and was not like this from the start. When I look at my mother, then this impression would largely be attributed to the fact that my mother was in some way very passive, but during the war, she incredibly determinedly guided the family's destiny. And with regards to my sisters, they then were in different degrees able to have their own activities ...[but] in the end in some way [they] subordinated themselves to the general standards, that means their respective husbands. Insofar I think that throughout the years it formed itself slowly and well, less during adolescence (Bühring 2020, CVIII & CIX).

Although all interviewees expressed their belief in a gendered role division, their relationship to their wives or female colleagues was not predominantly characterised by the hierarchical structure typical for ultraconservative patriarchy dominant in the nineteenth and early twentieth century (Colvin and Davies 2008, 113–30). Instead, it seemed to me that the participants often viewed women as equal partners, particularly when they displayed characteristics such as being active, rational and autonomous usually linked to masculinity whilst still fulfilling their role as mother and housewife.

Conclusion

The breadwinner model of masculinity is characterised by clearly divided gender roles, in which the woman stays at home and takes care of the children and the household, whilst the man provides for his family by performing a meaningful occupation in the public sphere (Gray 2000). All the participants in some way referred to this rather old-fashioned masculinity ideal popular in the nineteenth and early twentieth century (Gardiner 2004, 115–81; Kessel 2003, 1–31). Simultaneously, the strong emphasis the interviewees placed on activity, performance, personal autonomy and rationality respectively control of oneself are vital aspects in the socio-cultural narratives of modern understandings of hegemonic masculinity (Connell 2009, 237–52). This evidences that these standards have impacted the participants' identity construction throughout their working life and until now which could also explain the ambiguity I identified in their perception of women and their position in relation to men.

On the one hand, my research confirmed that the socio-cultural view which assigns attributes such as activity, rationality, determination and the will to succeed to men, and passivity, emotionality and a natural need and talent for being motherly and caring to women has in the past decades not changed significantly, despite the socio-cultural changes which have taken place. In fact, the view of naturally determined gender relations appears to form one of the most significant and stable markers of the masculine identity the interviewees constructed throughout their life-course. This might be due to its reference to biological predisposition, which is still at the core of many hegemonic narratives linked to masculinity and femininity (Bourdieu 2001, 94–108; Chambers 2005, 325–46; Negra, Tasker and McRobbie 2007; Tasker and Negra 2007, 1–26).

On the other hand, the participants' answers do not indicate a general disrespect for women but simply show that women were perceived as a totally different species which has little in common with men. In fact, and despite what is suggested by some scholars (Schippers 2007, 85–102; Connell 2009, 237–52; Kimmel 2001, 21–37), at least, Günter Schotten, Burkard Rosenfeld and G.B. did not appear to link feminine characteristics to negative connotations but instead seemed to, in different degrees, feel admiration for women and their way of handling life. Within this context, it is also particularly interesting that women who in some way embodied attributes typically associated with masculinity were not viewed as unnatural, nor did it seem to impede the interviewee's appreciation or respect for these women.

This could be an outcome of the loosening of gender hierarchies as a result of civil rights movements and feminism in the 70s, but it certainly is also the outcome of the increasing influence of neoliberal meritocracy, in which outstanding achievement can override social marginalisation caused by gender, sexual orientation or race (Baur and Luedtke 2008, 7–30; Duggan 2002, 175–94). Thus, one could say that the participants utilised and combined masculinity conceptions, hegemonic at different times in their lives which are, however, all based on a binary construction of femininity and masculinity. This allowed the participants of this study to form a consistent and stable identity throughout their life-course expressed in their individual life-course narratives.

In current western industrialised countries, middle-aged and older men still, and despite all public claims of having reached gender equality, occupy a majority of key positions in politics, education, legal institutions and the media. Consequently, they continue the public privileging of men and masculinity. At the same time, through their roles as fathers, grandfathers, brothers, or mentors in the private sphere, middle-aged and older men play an influential role in the socialisation of younger generations. They therefore exert an enormous influence on the construction and reproduction of socio-cultural standards of acceptable gender performances and associated binary hierarchies (Bourdieu 2001, 94–108 ; Griffin 2005, 1–23).

Although my study has found that the interviewees incorporated a more flexible understanding of gendered hierarchies into their identity as older men, their identity construction is still primarily informed by a binary construction of masculinity and femininity. Women were accepted as equals only when they fulfilled their apparently natural biological role as carers, while additionally displaying attributes linked to masculinity constructions such as being physically and mentally in control and active.

This understanding appears to reflect a general societal view in western cultural settings which, in my view, does little to support gender equality. As long as women are viewed as the weaker sex by biologically predisposition, – a predisposition they can only partially overcome by displaying additional male characteristics – gender hierarchies cannot be overcome. Thus, it is essential to not only continue to gain a better understanding of how women perform their gender roles, but it is as crucial to continue exploring male perspectives on gender, since this will allow for a better understanding of how both reproduce and challenge the construction of gender roles and gender hierarchies. This might, in turn, allow insights into the persistence of male privilege and, in the long run, enable changes to current patriarchal structures in western cultural settings.

Works Cited

Baur, Nina, and Jens Luedtke. "Levels of Masculinity Constructions. Current Masculinity Research." *The Social Construction of Masculinity – Hegemonial and Marginalized Masculinities in Germany*. Eds. Baur, Nina and Jens Luedtke. Opladen & Farming Hills: Barbara Budrich, 2008. 7–30.

Bourdieu, Pierre. *Masculine Domination*. Stanford: Stanford University Press, 2001.

Brown, T. S. *West Germany and the Global Sixties: The Anti-Authoritarian Revolt, 1962–1978*. Cambridge: Cambridge University Press, 2013.

Bühring, Lisa-Nike. "The Social Construction of Ageing Masculinities in Neoliberal Society – Reflections on Retired German Men." *E-Thesis*. (2020). Web.

Butler, Judith. *Gender Trouble: Feminism and the Subversion of Identity.* Abingdon: Routledge, 2011.

Calasanti, Toni, and Neal King. "Intersectionality and Age." *Routledge Handbook of Cultural Gerontology.* Ed. Twigg, Julia & Wendy Martin. London & New York: Routledge, 2015. 193–200.

Calasanti, Toni, and Neal King. "Firming the Floppy Penis: Age, Class, and Gender Relations in the Lives of Old Men." *Men and Masculinities* 8.1 (2005): 3–23.

Chambers, Clare. "Masculine Domination, Radical Feminism and Change." *Feminist Theory* 6.3 (2005): 325–346.

Cheng, Cliff. "Marginalized Masculinities and Hegemonic Masculinity: An Introduction." *The Journal of Men's Studies* 7.3 (1999): 295–315.

Chivers, Sally. *The Silvering Screen: Old Age and Disability in Cinema.* 2011.Web.

Colvin, Sarah, and Peter J Davies. *Masculinities in German Culture.* Rochester: Camden House, 2008.

Connell, Raewn. "A Thousand Miles from Kind: Men, Masculinities and Modern Institutions." *The Journal of Men's Studies* 16.3 (2009): 237–52.

Connell, Raewn. *Masculinities.* 2 ed. Cambridge: Polity, 2005.

Connell, Raewn. "The Big Picture: Masculinities in Recent World History." *Theory and Society* 22.5 (1993): 597–623.

Coston, Bethany M., and Michael Kimmel. "Seeing Privilege Where It Isn't: Marginalized Masculinities and the Intersectionality of Privilege." *Journal of Social Issues* 68.1 (2012): 97–111.

Duggan, Lisa. "The New Homonormativity: The Sexual Politics of Neoliberalism." *Materializing Democracy: Toward a Revitalized Cultural Politics.* Ed. Nelson, Russ Castronovo & Dana D. Durham: Duke University Press, 2002. 175–94.

Fausto-Sterling, Anne. *Myths of Gender: Biological Theories About Women and Men.* New York: Basic Books, 2008.

Feinberg, Leslie. *Transgender Warriors: Making History from Joan of Arc to Dennis Rodman.* Boston: Beacon Press, 1996.

Gardiner, Steven Lester. "Masculinity, War, and Refusal: Vicissitudes of German Manhood before and after the Cold War." PhD Dissertation. Cornell University, 2004.

Gray, Marion W. *Productive Men, Reproductive Women: The Agrarian Household and the Emergence of Separate Spheres During the German Enlightenment.* Oxford & New York: Berghahn Books, 2000.

Griffin, Penny "Neoliberal Economic Discourses and Hegemonic Masculinity (Ies): Masculine Hegemony (Dis) Embodied." *IPEG Papers in Global Political Economy*.19 (2005): 1–23.

Hall, S. "Paths to Anelpis: 1: Dimorphic Violence and the Pseudo-Pacification Process." *Parallax* 6.2 (2000): 36–53.

Haraway, Donna. "Situated Knowledges: The Science Question in Feminism and the Privilege of Partial Perspective." *Feminist Studies* 14.3 (1988): 575–99.

Harding, Sandra. "Rethinking Standpoint Epistemology: What Is " Strong Objectivity?"." *The Centennial Review* 36.3 (1992): 437–70.

Jackson, David. *Exploring Aging Masculinities: The Body, Sexuality and Social Lives.* London & New York: Palgrave MacMillan, 2016.

Kessel, Martina. "The 'Whole Man': The Longing for a Masculine World in Nineteenth–Century Germany." *Gender & History* 15.1 (2003): 1–31.

Kessler, S. J. *Lessons from the Intersexed.* New Brunswick: Rutgers University Press, 1998.

Kimmel, Michael. "Global Masculinities: Restoration and Resistance." *A Men's World?: Changing Men's Practices in a Globalized World.* Ed. Pease, R. London: Zed Press, 2001. 21–37.

Kimmel, Michael. "Masculinities as Homophobia: Fear, Shame, and Silence in the Construction of Gender Identity." *Theorizing Masculinities.* Eds. Brod, Harry and Michael Kaufman. Vol. 5. Newbury Park: Sage Publications, 1994. 119–41.

Negra, Diane, Yvonne Tasker, and Angela McRobbie. *Interrogating Postfeminism: Gender and the Politics of Popular Culture.* Durham, U.S.: Duke University Press, 2007.

Rubin, Gayle. "Thinking Sex: Notes for a Radical Theory of the Politics of Sexuality." *Social Perspectives in Lesbian and Gay Studies; a Reader.* Ed. Schneider, P. M. Nardi & B. E. London & New York: Routledge, 1997. 100–33.

Schippers, Mimi. "Recovering the Feminine Other: Masculinity, Femininity, and Gender Hegemony." *Theory and Society* 36.1 (2007): 85–102.

Tarrant, Anna. "'Maturing' a Sub-Discipline: The Intersectional Geographies of Masculinities and Old Age." *Geography Compass*, 4.10 (2010): 1580–1591.

Tasker, Yvonne, and Diane Negra. "Interrogating Postfeminism: Gender and the Politics of Popular Culture." Eds. Tasker, Yvonne and Diane Negra. Durham: Duke University Press, 2007. 1–26.

Health Care and Ageing Masculinity in the Performance of *Notaufnahme – Hospitali*

Pepetual Mforbe Chiangong

Introduction

In the domain of health care, the transnational space emerges as a crucial site of subtle, yet overt confrontation between the global South and the North. Imagining the diaspora as a space of encounters that centralizes critical debates on the reconstruction of narratives on African traditional healing methods, modern medicine is contested. It is significant to note that concerns about medicine and healing have widened the scope of diaspora discourses. If we concur with Leigh Raiford and Heike Raphael that migration, whether forced or voluntary, is a "long and "unfinished" process" as "[d]iasporic subjects plant new roots in each encounter" (2017: 6), new ways of dealing with new conditions of mobility and migration, precisely in a neoliberal era, become relevant. This paper attempts to explore the intersections of health care, elderhood, and African masculinity concerns represented through diaspora theatre. Posing as points of encounter, these intersections are embodied through a performance narrative in a bid to rewrite and archive histories of African traditional health care, deconstruct new narratives of power and also serve as strategies of decolonizing modern medicine. The debates advanced here centre on the performance of *Notaufnahme – Hospitali*, a German-Tanzanian theatre project, written and directed by Christoph M. Gosepath and Robert Schmidt. Performed on its third day on September 24, 2018 at Vierte Welt in Berlin, the play features an elderly male Tanzanian artist, performed by an almost 70 years old Nkwabi Ng'hangasamala. The artist has lived in Berlin for almost a decade. Berlin is portrayed in the performance as a city that echoes complex meanings derived from the challenges associated with migrancy. The artist, however, admits that Berlin had seen better days, but the current reality threatens to estrange the artist from his art, from the understanding of his body, mind, and from his ethnic identification that translate into disillusionment. This situation invokes nostalgic sensibilities towards home that he demands to return to Tanzania. In pursuance of this, we will get to understand the performance space, the artist and his encounter with a younger female medical doctor, which serves as a blueprint to telling the story of mental decline and of resilience. While we pursue an understanding of the diaspora, an elderly African masculinity in the wake of resistance and resulting negotiation is examined.

Knowing the performance space and the artist

The performance space at the Vierte Welt seems to reflect the current, but imagined constellation of Berlin city with its attractive multicultural outlook harboring a slightly bizarre texture. The state of the artist's mind seems to convey these complexities, his reality as a diaspora subject and his health condition. Speaking with the researcher in a Zoom conversation on January 13, 2022, one of the playwrights and directors, Christoph Gosepath, stated that their choice of Vierte Welt for the performance was based on the theatre's preoccupation with political subjects and also the postcolonial thematic concerns articulated on its program. The structure of the Vierte Welt appears to be a fragmentary space and resonates with the unfinished project of the diaspora, belonging, and identity politics associated with post-colonialism, illustrating how the theatre space is crucial to the thematic concerns of *Notaufnahme – Hospitali*. Reverberating with the split structure of the play's plot that could be linked with the unstable mental condition of the artist, one discerns beams of wood that are crisscrossed in squares, serving as the ceiling of the structure from where electric cables and lamps that lighten up the stage and room are hung. At the center of the theatre, four huge pillars are raised to the roof, apparently supporting the building that houses the theatre space. Clearly a nonconventional theater eligible for such themes, the audience sits in the round, reminiscent of traditional storytelling performances across Africa, as they are confronted at all angles with the different conditions of the artist. Depressing illustrations, painted in dark colors by the artist during his psychotic crisis, serve as the backdrop of the theatre, further intensifying and corresponding with the mood of despondency in the play, provoking empathetic but tense expressions from the audience.

In a blogpost of September 21, 2018 Richard Pettifer reviews the premiere of *Notaufnahme – Hospitali* stating that

> The action – centred around a Berlin artist from Tanzania with mental illness – is supplemented by pre-recorded screens which approximate the action (rather like looking at a poorly lip-synced animation, but very effective). We follow the central character through his struggles with the German medical system, as in a maze of bureaucracy – mirrored by the scrawled wallpaper depicting a city skyline – and a fragmented, confused story emerges of the difficulties in addressing mental illness. This is a research-based project that attempts to communicate something very large – the imbalances in medical treatment between people, particularly between Tanzania and Germany...[1]

Concurring with Pettifer's observations about the composition of the plot, the audience encounters the elderly performer as an artist, the storyteller, a restaurant owner and a traditional healer based in Tanzania. Embodying these different identities enable the performer to tell multiple narratives about diasporic experiences, elderhood and masculinity that result in the fragmented structure of the play. Foregrounding a

---

1   Richard Pettifer "Notaufnahme – Hospitali" http://theaterstuck.blogspot.com/2018/09/notaufnahme-hospitali.html, accessed 12. 01.2022.

negotiation of these identities, – artist, storyteller, restaurant owner and traditional healer – essential components that shape diasporic knowledge production, we turn to *Migrating the Black Body: The African Diaspora and Visual Culture*, in which Leigh Raiford and Heike Raphael ask, "in what ways have visual forms functioned as a "diasporic resource" – as raw material, as ore – among, between, and within transnational black communities?" (2017: 3) In response, the construction of multiple identities in the performance privileges visual components of movements, voice, silence, duration, tempo, and rhythm that consider the contradictions and discrepancies in the German-European health care system and indigenous Tanzanian healing procedures and the overall relations between countries, as one explores their impact on an elderly male African artist in *Notaufnahme – Hospitali*.

Inhabiting such a performance space, a trope of Berlin city, and enveloped in a declining mental health condition, the elderly artist seems to be accommodated, yet rejected by the space at the Vierte Welt. This paradoxical condition of existence tallies with the artist's biography, which the storyteller shares with the audience by informing them that "he earned some money with painting and illustrating" and was in good relationship with his neighbors. But as the plot unfolds, the audience is confronted with his mental breakdown, which eventually is not properly attended to at the emergency department of a hospital. While illustrating some designs on a paper placed on an easel (see Fig. 2), the audience lives this mental health condition. The artist screams the following as he breaks down in his atelier in coughing fits;

> No! No! It's the other way around. I found my shadows, ja ... I find ... a continent ... I have turned all the wires, the cardboards, then draw, draw everything, draw everywhere, draw in the corners... Sheisse! The brightness, the light. *(Screams)* What! What is that!!I can't. *(mourning)* Just the voices ... in my head. I want to hear something else *(sings melancholically)*. The voices in his head sounded like they were talking about him ... as if they were monitoring and commenting on everything he did. The only thing he couldn't do was try to describe the voices in his head. *(Illustrating authoritatively)*

Coordinates! Figures! Buildings! Characters! Ok. Storyline! Storyline! Contours! Movements! Figures! Dynamics! *(Screaming and breaking down)* Where am I? Where am I?

In the second part of the utterances, we notice that the artist briefly becomes the storyteller. In playing this role, the artist employs the third person perspective – "his, he" – as if he is talking about someone else. This omniscient point of view enables an accentuation of an important connection between the storyteller and the artist. In these circumstances, the artist, therefore, entertains moments of uncertainty, resulting in the reconfiguration of his art to articulate a chaotic desolation that his new environment dictates to him.

The moment of encounter

In an ensuing circumstance of marginalization, remembering and sickness that the artist eventually is confronted with, the transnational diaspora space becomes complex, conjuring the construction of varied perspectives on ethnic identifications that provoke racialized discourses and behaviours, by the medical doctor for instance, against African and black cultures in the performance. However, an attending negotiation of the diaspora space enables the artist to construct the diaspora as a site of knowledge production and resilience. This latter construction of the diaspora has probably encouraged Anna Rastas and Kaarina Nikunen (2019) to explore the diasporas as spaces of culture rather than engage with "the notion of (black and African) culture" (207) in a bid to centralize the peculiarities of the diverse cultural wealth of African and black communities that is carried across with the migrating black body to Europe. Traditional African health care is one of such areas that this article articulates in order to foreground "... identifications that are more complex and situational..." (208). In this way distorted cultural dialogue between peoples, who include the medical doctor and the artist, may be resolved as epistemic injustice, and accompanying fragmentation of identities are contested through critical pedagogy and interventionist strategies such as theatre.

In Tanzania, 60% of the population resort to traditional healing methods and alternative medicine for the treatment of Non-Communicable Diseases (NCDs) (Stanifer et al: 2015). Across Africa, there have been debates and even measures undertaken to initiate collaboration between traditional practitioners and modern medical institutions, but these efforts have fairly materialized due to divergent views adhering to regulations, places of practice, procedures, approaches to diagnoses and treatment of physical and mental health problems. Therefore, Phares Gamba Mujinja and Pius Happiness Saronga speak of this collaboration by adding that "[i]n Tanzania, the Traditional Medicine Act was enacted in 2002 and a Traditional Medicine unit in the Ministry of Health was initiated" (2022, 1479). Following the preceding accounts from the Tanzanian context, which the artist carries with him to Berlin, prepares us for the cultural conflict that eventually emerges between the younger German medical doctor and the elderly artist in the performance. This conflict presupposes that integrating indigenous African healing methods in major hospitals in the West, is yet to be a major topic of debate. Besides, "African and black diaspora spaces in Europe have always been venues of intersecting transnational and local activism, as well as sites for collaboration among people of different professional and other background" (Rastas and Nikunen 2019, 209). Nevertheless, African and black cultures are nuanced and contested in such spaces underscoring the diaspora as "landscapes of people and agency... [particularly as] diasporas are global and transnational by nature- not only local histories, political and other forces shape the everyday lives of diaspora communities" (2019, 207, 208) when it comes, particularly, to the black diaspora. This paradigm of looking at the diaspora is particularly informative as both Rastas and Nikunen underscore the necessity for cultural flows that should enable the development, and perhaps transformation, of both African and European communities.

Fig. 1: At the emergency unit of the hospital. Photo by P. M. Chiangong

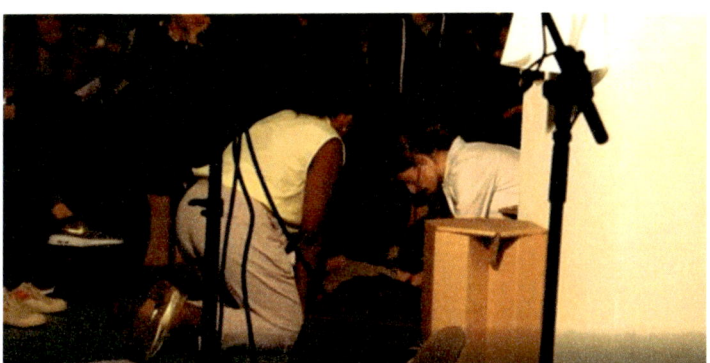

Fig. 2: The artist expressing his mental state through bleak illustrations. Photo by P. M. Chiangong.

That said, the moment of encounter with the artist, during which "transnational activism" and "collaboration" are noted, takes place in an emergency unit of a hospital where we find the artist in a state of unconsciousness (see Fig. 1). He is attended to by a female medical doctor, possibly of German ancestry, whom the narrator, but also the storyteller, informs the audience has an unfriendly personality, which has resulted in the resignation of several other nurses at the hospital. The medical doctor is assisted in her duties by a nurse of African descent, whom the storyteller describes as "the beautiful one." The African nurse also speaks Swahili and serves as the translator to the doctor who speaks neither English, nor Swahili; but to the surprise of the audience, the medical doctor eventually speaks some words of English. The artist, who as stated comes from Tanzania, also speaks Swahili, which is one of the national languages of Tanzania, and supposedly does not speak German.

What storytelling contributes

Storytelling is a key genre of performances in Africa, based on its functionality but crucially on how it creates enlivened spaces for the transmission of history, education, indigenous concepts, the wealth of language and most of all communality. Kudakwashe Tuwe clarifies that "[t]he function of storytelling has been identified as mediating and transmitting of knowledge and information across generations, conveying information to the younger generations about the culture, worldviews, morals and expectations, norms and values" (2016: 2). Further, storytelling accentuates the importance of its performers, the elderly in this case, by affirmation of their role and value. Storytelling is performed by elderly women and men, but C. Chesaina underscores that storytellers or oral artists are generally elderly women who are judged appropriate for the art, particularly because "owing to their age and long experience, they are carriers of values and wisdom of their communities." (1994: 17). It is worth noting that elderly women perform mostly in private settings serving as instructors to children on the codes of conduct and in some cases contest hegemonic relations between humans through the art of storytelling. Elderly men mostly perform storytelling in public spaces with some of them travelling to different towns and villages as itinerant storytellers. Imagining the main performer of *Notaufnahme – Hospitali* as an itinerant performer who has travelled from Tanzania to Berlin as a performer, but also as an artist in the play, he serves as a curator of traditional Tanzanian culture and history. He employs the technique of storytelling in the performance to connect traditional Tanzanian healing methods with Western medicine, and in this process attempts to connect communities and cultures in the diaspora; a function that is central to African orature.

Therefore, elderhood as it unfolds on a diaspora performance space, is guided by the request of "'valuing older people' and the meanings and interpretations people give to their experiences of later life, while trying to maintain an awareness of the structural pressures and constraints, such as wealth and inequality" (Walsh and Näre 2016: 2; see also Prendergast and Saxton 2010:170). In the context of the diaspora, Walsh and Näre go on to identify two groups of migrants in their later life, which include the *"labour migrants 'ageing in place'"* category whose livelihood, as narrated through storytelling in the play, is marked by grave concerns about "social welfare, marginalization, and inequality" (5), where we could situate the artist, as opposed to "affluent retirement migrants" who do not necessarily negotiate their current status to survive in the host country, but abide in wealthy neighbourhoods in their home countries, affording to commute transnational routes. Performing allegories of deteriorating mental health, through storytelling, accelerated by the challenges of the diaspora as lived by the elderly labour migrant in tenuous economic conditions, the plot of *Notaufnahme – Hospitali* offers a narrative of the disintegration of one's subjectivities and cultural identification, but significantly upholding a counter-discourse enacted from the corridors of oppression by racism. An ambiguity sets in as these developments, as observed later in the discussion, also undermine African masculinity.

Telling the story of despair and of resilience

The storyteller – begins the performance of *Notaufnahme – Hospitali* with his narrative, which is prerecorded and played to the audience. In the meantime, the medical doctor and her nurse assistant are occupied with consultations as they move briskly across the performance space. The artist walks unhurriedly in silence across the entire performance space as his prerecorded narration is played as a voice over. The play itself is projected on screen in a delayed format, as indicated earlier by Pettifer, coupled with animations that designate specific scene changes in terms of space, place and of the main performers. The major concerns of the play, the storyteller informs the audience, are the power relations that frame communication between the medical doctor, her assistant, and an elderly African artist who is transported by a rescue service to the emergency unit of a hospital in Berlin. The intersection of the identities of the artist, performer, storyteller and traditional healer are worth noting as it makes the overall performance of elderhood complex, multifaceted and complicated by the diaspora space if we focalize the almost 70 years old body and identity of the artist. In the context of maturity and wisdom, the narration of the storyteller is conveyed through a stable and experienced tone, punctuated with meaningful pauses that resonate with thought. A cheerful youthfulness and euphoria are not registered in the pattern of story narration, making the performer eligible for the role of storyteller and importantly for the play's subject.

Speaking on casting Nkwabi Ng'hangasamala in the role of the artist, Christoph Gosepath remarked that the decision was based initially on his broad career in performance and relevant knowledge in mental health issues. His age, therefore became crucial as "it was indeed helpful to have him as an elderly performer because of his experiences. I think it was good that the protagonist of the play was an experienced older performer and not a young person."[2] He further maintained that it was important for Ng'hangasamala to play the role of the artist and storyteller because he embodied a personality of authority, eligible to contest Eurocentric perceptions on African traditional medicine and masculinity, disparaged since colonialism. That notwithstanding, Gosepath concluded that "in spite of age, in spite of authority and in spite of experience, Europeans tend to be really arrogant in the face of other cultures. And we wanted to show this primary arrogance through the performance" (2022). The pluralistic identity embodied in the performer and the characters that Ng'hangasamala impersonates broadens the understanding of old age to encapsulate esteem that accompanies

---

2 Zoom conversation with Christoph Gosepath, January 13, 2022.

chronological age, but also underscores personal and transnational knowledge and experiences that the actor has accumulated. Therefore, this esteem is seen in the tempo of the storyteller's narration that parallels the movements of the artist on stage, illustrating a certain level of responsibility and ultimately his germaneness as an informed character in the play and the communities, which he epitomizes. Further, evidence of maturity in the storyteller's narrative tone, communicates feelings of reflection, wisdom, and importantly of knowledge. The composition of the character of the artist benefits from Ng'hangasamala's experiences accrued through years of performing, of leading theatre programs in Tanzania and in Germany, together with his expertise in Tanzanian culture, which all emerge as important tools to confront racism and other biases towards an elderly African masculinity in the performance.

Spaces of diasporic encounter: masculinity, old age, and race

African masculinity is varied and specific to different cultures of the continent. Further, masculine tendencies and characteristics are susceptible to societal changes, offering these phenomena not only an inconsistent nature but also a propensity to dynamism. Therefore Lahoucine Ouzgane and Robert Morrell argue that "African masculinities are not uniform and monolithic, not generalizable to all men in Africa, and that masculine behaviour in Africa are not natural or unchanging, suggesting the possible emergence of new (and less violent and less oppressive) ways of being masculine" (2005: 8–9). Arguing that masculinity theory in the West was developed out of the convergences of debates over the objectification of women and gay men by heterosexual men, Sakhumzi Mfecane (2016) underscores that "[s]ocial life varies according to different cultural beliefs, class, race and other variables. This gives rise to the need to construct theories of masculinity that reflect varied life experiences" (205). Mfecane's view suggests that we note the positionality of the elderly male artist when he is undermined by a white, younger, female medical doctor.

In a Black South African context, Mfecane views masculinity, precisely Xhosa masculinity, as a norm that is associated with being a "real man" that is specifically constructed when Xhosa boys successfully complete the circumcision ritual, *ulwaluko*, a requirement, which elevates a man's standing in the society. Central to embodiment, Xhosa masculinity is fundamentally structured on this ritual of circumcision, which all boys are expected by custom to undergo without the intervention of modern medicine. Should the later outcome be the case, a man's status of manhood is interrogated and shunned by the community. "A real man" as an identity is recognized and respected from boyhood to elderhood in many African communities. Some ethnic groups in Tanzania practice male circumcision, which does not only serve as a rite of passage from boyhood to manhood, but importantly it is embedded in the notion of strength and bravery (Mshana et al 2011; Wambura et al 2011), which society perceives as manly traits. While we draw from Connell's theorisation of hegemonic masculinities that underscores the dominance of men over women, gay men, and the establishment of patriarchy, Connell (2005) equally conceptualizes subordinate, marginal, and complicit masculinities. But are complicit masculinities also supported by hegemonic femininities? Carrie Paechter revisits Connell's work on hegemonic masculinity and underlines that theories of gender "treat females and femininity as the Other of males and masculinity [positioning] Femininity ... in opposition and subordinate to it [masculinity], such that femininity cannot be conceptualized at all without a masculinity" (2018: 121). While "emphasized femininity" (Connell 1987; Paechter 2018) is theorized to be the counterpart and subordinate to hegemonic masculinity "performed to men" (122), one deeply ponders where to embed women, such as the younger female medical doctor in the performance, who embodies hegemonic behavioural traits that are shown towards a vulnerable elderly black male, an attitude that seems to resonate with what bell hooks has described as "imperialist ...

capitalist patriarchy."[3] While Paechter keeps female bodies outside her theorization of gender hegemonies, she makes an important point by stating that hegemonic femininity "would need to take into account the ways in which hegemonic gender forms are supportive of the status quo, that they perpetuate an unequal gender regime. It would also account for positions of female dominance, at least with respect to other women and girls" (218: 122) but also over "Other" vulnerable and subordinate masculinities. If Mimi Schippers suggests that hegemonic femininity establishes and legitimises a hierarchical comportment that resonates with hegemonic masculinity that in the end privileges men and objectifies women (2007: 94; qtd in Paechter 2018), it remains crucial for theorists to consider the position of elderly African men in the face of a dominant younger white female behaviour on a transnational diaspora space in order to critically explore claims of infantalising the elderly African male body in spaces of racial encounter. But Connell's exploration of hegemonic masculinities centers on specific experiences that are akin to Western culture and could in many ways parallel the experiences of African men, particularly when they navigate both migration and diaspora contexts.

However, there is a dearth of research on the masculinity of elderly African men, particularly when such masculinity plays out in a transnational migration space (Markussen 2018). Elderhood, health care, race, ethnicity, class, and masculinity embody varied epistemological approaches to understand their formation and materiality, yet it becomes even more complex when these concepts concurrently frame the lives of individuals, groups, and communities. This intersectional epistemology allows for a critical assessment of what Gloria Wekker (2009) has termed "white innocence," which Rastas and Nikunen take up to underpin today's interrogation of the denial of racism, illustrate aptly in the attitude of the younger female medical doctor towards the elderly artist and towards Tanzanian traditional medicine.

---

3   bell hooks and John A. Powell, "Belonging through Connection, Connecting through Love: Oneself, the Other, and the Earth," April 26, 2015, https://www.youtube.com/watch?v=osX7fqIU4gQ, accessed 13.01.2022.

Existing research on ageing in the diaspora is mostly centralized on the impact of migration on elderly women's identities, particularly those allied with remembering, with questions of nationalism and with ethnicity (Markussen 2018; Pasura and Christou 2018). But, given the situation of the artist in the play, one is compelled to agree with scholars of migration studies who have suggested that the diaspora offers more opportunities for women than it does for men as their self-worth is not only endangered but also devalued (Pasura 2014, p. 70), forcing the men to engage in strategies to enable them to construct "respectable masculinities" (Pasura 2014, Pasura and Christou 2017, Markussen 2018) for themselves. The storyteller employs his art in *Notaufnahme – Hospitali* to not only subvert the pejorative treatment of male migrants in some Berlin medical spaces, but equally serves as a platform of remembering and nostalgia evoked by the artist when he sings in his mother tongue at the peak of his mental health crisis (see Fig. 3.).

Fig. 3: The artist attempts to escape from his mental health crisis through the performance of song. Photo by P. M. Chiangong.

Later playing the role of a traditional healer, he unarchives ancestral knowledge on traditional medicine when later in the performance he educates the German medical doctor, who eventually travels to Tanzania, on how to diagnose his health condition, on Tanzanian cuisine and on traditional healing. In the middle of a confrontation between the two (see Fig. 5 below), he advises the medical doctor to return to school in order to improve her overall knowledge of mental health care and probably to learn that about 60% of Tanzanians rely on traditional medicine, a phenomenon that has encouraged the government to initiate a collaboration between modern and traditional healing institutions.

In spite of the values that one associates with the artist in the performance, the medical doctor falls short of employing any honorific address form to speak to the elderly artist. According to a 2011, Help Age International Report on Tanzania, "Older persons [in spite of ageism] play a key role in contributing to the social and economic fabric of the family... (2011:6), but the performance interrogates why such is not the case in the diaspora. Fundamentally, the esteem that many East African societies generally confer on elderly people, specifically men, addressed as *Mzee*, is disrupted when such an identity is relocated to the West. The artist encounters prejudice not only as an elderly man, but also because of his Tanzanian ethnicity and his class as a labour migrant. In an incessant quest to belong to a community and simultaneously feel respected, the elderly African male body and precisely that of the artist in *Notaufnahme – Hospitali* is positioned in the context of contesting masculinity and elderhood.

After gaining consciousness and in a stable condition, the artist, for the most part, remains silent when a string of questions, like in an interrogation, is posed by the medical doctor. Initially, the artist's silence when he is "interrogated" by the medical doctor below, conveys a sense of loss, of not being understood or fundamentally illustrative of a state of internal trauma and self-reflection:

Medical Doctor: *(Muttering to herself as she writes in a note book)* Name wissen wir nicht. Wissen Sie welcher Tag heute ist?
Artist: *(Silence)*
Medical Doctor: Wissen Sie wo Sie sind?
Artist: *(Silence)*
Medical Doctor: Haben Sie Angst für bestimmten Tiere ... für be-

stimmten Dingen?
Artist: *(Silence)*
Medical Doctor: Fühlen Sie mal verfolge... beim Anderen?
Artist: *(Silence)*
Medical Doctor: *(Mutters to herself as she continuous to write)* Uberall keine Aussage. Haben Sie mal das Gefühl kein Gefühl zu haben? *(Again, mutters and writes)* Hm! Auch keine Aussage
Artist: *(Silence)*
Medical Doctor: Sind Sie depressiv?
Artist: *(Silence)*
Medical Doctor: Haben Sie manchmal das Gefühl nicht genug zu sein?...

But the silence conveys defiance, as it is accompanied by a slightly bent head and a stare (see Fig. 4 below).

Fig. 4: The moment of "interrogating" the patient. Photo by P. M. Chiangong.

Although he speaks only in order to voice his opinion on the consequences of anti-psychotics on his body, his silence equally communicates nostalgic feelings that translate into resilience and revolt not only against an individual, but correspondingly against a system that, ostensibly, condones norms that under-privilege his black and elderly body. Remarkably, this debate suggests an ambivalence that encapsulates the thematic of silence as it uncovers a process of negotiating for a respectable masculinity through specific gestures of confrontation and use of space on stage.

The proximal space, distant in this case, that accompanies the stare from the artist detaches the artist from the doctor. These elements play emblematic roles as they differentiate the artist's silence from the rhythm and tempo of the medical doctor's questions. Resisting objectification, the artist through silence assesses the maturity, knowledge and competence of the medical doctor in care and healing, yet her social identity privileges her profession, ethnicity, gender, and class. These intersecting privileges materialize in her impatient tone, fast pace and rhythm in which her questions are delivered, in assigning instructions and in her occupation of the performance space. Stressing that a pyramidal relation marks this encounter, we recall the storyteller's earlier assessment of the medical doctor when he stated that an element of power was present whenever she took over "the command in those moments"; her command of her profession, but also of the performance space, an attitude, which the narrator reveals was not appreciated by everyone.

Further, the duration in this scene expresses the positionality of the artist and shapes a hierarchy that ruptures the platform for him to communicate crucial knowledge about his health condition that could enable precise diagnoses and treatment. Therefore, the duration that the doctor accords the patient is expeditious, significantly limited, and resonates with the conclusions she draws on the mental condition of the artist. In this context, she informs the artist that the source of his illness lies in his head, while the artist contests her diagnosis by emphasising that the cause of his health condition is located in his stomach. Walther R. Volbach's perception of duration in the theatre is still relevant today as he sees it "as the limited extent of an event or the time required for the execution of an event, i.e., on stage, of an action, speech (music), transition of lighting, or shifting of scenery" (1967:137). These observations about duration, rhythm and tempo put the medical doctor in a position of authority and even more so because her encounter with an elderly African man on this space becomes the dominant discourse in the entire narrative of the performance. The emerging power dynamics at the hospital scene locate the doctor and her profession on a privileging spot that seemingly guarantees her control over the space and over her interlocutors.

Fig. 5: Confrontation between the medical doctor and the artist. Photo by P. M. Chiangong.

Concluding remarks

In *Notaufnahme – Hospitali*, an ageing African masculinity is in conflict with a conceited attitude of a younger female medical doctor that objectifies the elderly African artist in the performance. This paradigm of marginalization, as portrayed, in the performance is in the process of being deconstructed, resulting in a counter-discourse that contests dominance and creates a platform for the emergence of what Pasura and Christou (2018) have addressed as a respectable masculinity. The major question of interest in the performance of *Notaufnahme – Hospitali* has been the parallelism that marks the performer and the various roles that he impersonates in the play. While elderhood connects the performer and the character, the multiple identities that he embodies in the play offer the space to conceptualize ageing from different angles. His chronological age has provided a convincing trope for the depiction of the complexity that frames mental health issues and the experiences of the diaspora, as they weigh on one's corporeality and psychology. On the one hand, wisdom and knowledge normally associated with old age and particularly how they are conveyed through a 70-years-old African performer, on the other hand, permits one to wonder whether performance as an aesthetic component employs the ageing body as constructive metaphor to depict biological ageing. Could the challenges of the diaspora, testing economic conditions, mental health issues, including the loss of self-esteem through racial prejudice age the body? This supposition does not dare to disparage old age, which is a normal process of human development, but allows one to critically reconsider the role of theatre in portraying old age, and in portraying the impact of prejudice on a male ageing body, as one seeks to unravel the possible avenues for resistance that emerge thereafter.

Works Cited

Chesaina, Ciarunji. *Oral Literature of the Kalenjin*. Nairobi: East African Educational Publishers LtD, 1994.

Connell, R. W. *Gender and Power*. Cambridge: Polity Press, 1987.

Connell, R. W., and J. W. Messerschmidt. "Hegemonic Masculinity: Rethinking the Concept." *Gender and Society*, 19.6 (2005): 829–859.

hooks, bell and John A. Powell. "Belonging through Connection, Connecting through Love: Oneself, the Other, and the Earth, April 26." 2015. https://www.youtube.com/watch?v=osX7fqIU4gQ. Accessed 13.01.2022.

Markussen, Kristin Gullbekk Marith. "'Nobody Comes to Baba for Advice': Negotiating Ageing masculinities in the Somali Diaspora." *Journal of Ethnic and Migration Studies* 2018: 1–18.

Mfecane, Sakhumzi. "'*Ndiyindoda*" [I am a man]: Theorising Xhosa Masculinity," *Anthropology Southern Africa*, 39.3 (2016): 204–214.

Mshana, Gerry, Mwita Wambura, Joseph Mwanga, Jacklin Mosha, Frank Mosha and John Changalucha. "Traditional Male Circumcision Practices Among the Kurya of North-eastern Tanzania and Implications for National Programmes," *Psychological and Socio-Medical Aspects of AIDS/HIV* 23.9 (2011): 1111–1116.

Mujinja, Gamba Phares and Happiness Pius Saronga. "Traditional and Complementary Medicine in Tanzania: Regulation Awareness, Adherence and Challenges," *International Journal of Public Health Management* 11.8 (2022): 1496–1504.

Ouzgane, Lahoucine and Robert Morrell. "African masculinities: An Introduction" *African Masculinities: Men in Africa from the Late Nineteenth Century to the Present*. Ed. Lahoucine Ouzgane and Robert Morrell. New York: Palgrave Macmillan, 2005. 1–20.

Paechter, Carrie. "Rethinking the Possibilities for Hegemonic Femininity: Exploring a Gramscian Framework", *Women's Studies International Forum* 68 (2018): 121–128.

Pasura, Dominic and Anastasia Christou. "Theorizing Black (African) Transnational Masculinities," *Men and Masculinities* 21.4 (2018): 521–546.

Pasura, Dominic. "'Do You Have a Visa?' Negotiating Respectable Masculinity in the Diaspora," in *African Transnational Diasporas: Fractured Communities and Plural Identities of Zimbabweans in Britain*, London: Palgrave Macmillan, 2014: 69–85.

Prendergast, Monica and Juliana Saxton. "Reminiscence Theatre" in *Applied Theatre: International Case Studies and Challenges for Practice*, Bristol: Intellect, 2010. 169–171.

Raiford, Leigh and Heike Raphael-Hernandez. "Introduction." *Migrating the Black Body: The African Diaspora and Visual Culture*. Ed. L. Raiford and H. Raphael-Hernandez. Seattle: University of Washington Press, 2017. 3–9.

Rastas, Anna and Kaarina Nikunen. "Introduction: Contemporary African and Black Diasporic Spaces in Europe", *Open Cultural Studies*, 2 (2019): 207–218.

Schippers, Mimi. "Recovering the Feminine Other: Masculinity, Femininity, and Gender Hegemony." *Theory and Society*, 36.1 (2007): 85–102.

Stanifer, John W., Joseph Lunyera, David Boyd, Francis Karia, Venance Maro, Justin Omolo and Uptal D. Patel. "Traditional Medicine Practices among Community Members with Chronic Kidney Disease in Northern Tanzania: an Ethnomedical Survey." *BMC Nephrology*, 16.170 (2015), 1–11.

Tuwe, Kudakwashe. "The African Oral Tradition Paradigm of Storytelling as a Methodological Framework: Employment Experiences for African communities." *New Zealand, African Studies Association of Australasia and the Pacific (AFSAAP) Proceedings of the 38th AFSAAP Conference: 21st Century Tensions and Transformation in Africa, Deakin University, 28th-30th October, 2015*, (2016): 1–18. https://www.ecald.com/assets/Resources/Assets/Tuwe-African-Storytelling-Research-Method.pdf. Accessed 13.01.2022.

Vice President's Office-United Republic of Tanzania, "Ageing and Poverty in Tanzania: Country Position Paper," http://www.tanzaniagateway.org/docs/Ageing_and_Poverty_in_Tanzania.pdf. Accessed 14.04.2021.

Volbach, R. Walther. "Time and Space on the Stage." *Educational Theatre Journal*, 19.2 (1967): 134–141.

Walsh, Katie and Lena Näre. "Introduction: Transnational Migration and Home in Older Age" *Transnational Migration and Home in Older Age*. Ed. K. Walsh and L. Näre. London: Routledge, 2016. 1–22.

Wambura, Mwita, Joseph R Mwanga, Jacklin F Mosha, Gerry Mshana, Frank Mosha and John Changalucha. "Acceptability of Medical Male Circumcision in the Traditionally Circumcising Communities in Northern Tanzania", *BMC Public Health*, 11.373 (2011): 1–8.

Wekker, Gloria. "Another Dream of a Common Language. Imagining Black Europe." *Black Europe and the African Diaspora*. Ed. Darlene Clark Hine, Trica Danielle Keaton and Stephen Small. Champaign, Ill.: University of Illinois Press, 2009. 277–289.

Contributors

Lisa-Nike Bühring's research focusses on the analysis of the socio-cultural frames of ageing and gender in the West and on gaining a better understanding of how these narratives affect older people and particularly older men. She is employed as a research assistant at the private University of Applied Sciences Fresenius in Cologne where she continues her researches and is a lecturer for qualitative research and cultural studies. While her passion for teaching remains unbroken, she is also increasingly motivated by her interest in the socially and culturally constructed narratives and the way in which these influence individual lives. Lisa, therefore, pursues her development as an early career researcher actively and has contributed an entry to the *Encyclopedia of Gender, Media and Communication*. She is a member of the Centre for Women, Ageing and Media (WAM), the European Network in Ageing Studies (ENAS), Ageing + Communication + Technologies (ACT) and the North American Network of Ageing Studies (NANAS) as well as of the ERA Gender-Net Plus Project Masculine Ageing (MASCAGE).

Pepetual Mforbe Chiangong is Assistant Professor of African Literatures and Cultures at the Department of African Studies of the Humboldt University in Berlin, Germany. She holds a Ph.D. in theatre and drama studies from the University of Bayreuth, Germany. Among her publications on African drama and performance are the monograph *Rituals in Cameroon Drama: A Semiological Interpretation of the Plays of Gilbert Doho, Bole Butake and Hansel Ndumbe Eyoh* (2011), an edited volume *Old Age in African Literary and Cultural Contexts* (2021), the co-edited collection *Alter und Geschlecht: Soziale Verhältnisse und Kulturelle Repräsentationen* (2018) with Elizabeth Reitinger and Ulrike Vedder, and "'Transgressing' Wisdom and Elderhood in Times of War? The Shifting Identity of the Elderly Queen in the Performance of Women of Owu" in *Under Construction: Performing Critical Identity* (2021) by Marie-Anne Kohl (Ed). Her current areas of research and teaching include intervention theatre, old age in African drama and performance, the Kenya Schools and Colleges Drama Festival and the literariness of colonial letters in British Southern Cameroon.

Katharina Fuerholzer: Originally a translator (Spanish), Katharina studied Scandinavian Studies, Comparative Literature, and American Literary History in Munich and London. In 2017, she obtained a Joint-PhD from the Universities of Münster and Ghent for a thesis on the ethics of pathographies. Afterwards, she worked at the Institute of History, Theory, and Ethics of Medicine, Ulm University. In 2019, she joined the Program of Comparative Literature & Literary Theory, University of Pennsylvania as a postdoctoral visiting scholar. Since her return in 2022, she has been working at the Department "Ageing of Individuals and Society" at the University of Rostock. Recent publications: *Lyrik und Medizin* [Poetry and medicine]. Ed. with Florian Steger. Heidelberg: Winter 2019; *Das Ethos des Pathographen* [Ethics of pathography]. Heidelberg: Winter 2019; "Living oblivion: Poetic narratives of dementia and fatherhood in Pia Tafdrup's *Tarkovsky's Horses*." *Ageing Masculinities, Alzheimer's and Dementia Narratives*. Ed. Heike Hartung, Rüdiger Kunow and Matthew Sweney. London: Bloomsbury, 2022, 73–90.

Dagmar Gramshammer-Hohl is Senior Lecturer in the Department of Slavic Studies at the University of Graz, Austria. She studied Slavic and Romance languages, literatures, and cultures in Graz, Moscow, and Rouen and holds two master's and a doctoral degree from the University of Graz. She specialises in literary and cultural studies with a focus on twentieth- and twenty-first-century Russian literature, gender, and ageing studies. In her Ph.D. thesis (2002) she analysed representations of women's ageing in Russian literature. Her current research project focuses on narratives of homecoming in Slavic literatures of exile. Dagmar Gramshammer-Hohl was granted the Prof. Paul Petry Award in Ageing Studies in 1998; she is an alumna of the Austrian Academy of Sciences and a member of the European Network in Aging Studies (ENAS). Among her recent publications is the essay collection *Foreign Countries of Old Age: East and Southeast European Perspectives on Ageing*, co-edited with Oana Hergenröther (Bielefeld 2021).

Renate Hansen-Kokoruš is a retired professor of Slavic literatures and cultures at the Department of Slavic Studies at the University of Graz in Austria. Her PhD (*The Prose Works of Bulat Okudjava*) and post-doctoral degree in Slavic Studies (*Intertextuality in Ranko Marinkovic*) she completed at the University of Mannheim where she worked in several positions. She taught at the Humboldt University in Berlin, the University of Waterloo in Canada, the University of Zadar in Croatia, the State University of Tomsk in Russia, the University of Frankfurt/M in Germany as well as the University of Innsbruck in Austria. Her research interests include intertextuality and intermediality, narratology, representations of identity in literature in film, satire and humour, chronotope of the return, and memory. She is co-editor of the journal *Anzeiger für Slavische Philologie*.

Heike Hartung is an independent scholar who holds a PhD in English Studies from the Freie Universität Berlin and a PhD habil. from the University of Potsdam, Germany. She is affiliated as senior researcher at the Center for Inter-American Studies, University of Graz, Austria. In her publications she applies the methods of literary and cultural studies to the interdisciplinary fields of ageing, disability and gender studies. Recent publications include the monograph *Ageing, Gender and Illness in Anglophone Literature: Narrating the Bildungsroman* (2016) and the co-edited collection *Ageing Masculinities, Alzheimer's and Dementia Narratives* (2022). She is a founding member of the European Network in Aging Studies (ENAS) and co-editor of the Aging Studies publication series with transcript, Bielefeld.

Rüdiger Kunow is a retired Full Professor and Chair of the American Studies program at Potsdam University. He is a founding member of the European Network of Aging Studies (ENAS). He served as speaker of the international research project "Transnational American Studies", a co-operation of the University of Southern California, Dartmouth College, the Freie Universität and Humboldt University in Berlin, and Potsdam University. Furthermore, he was the speaker of the European Union research and teaching project "Putting a Human Face on Diversity: The U.S. In/Of Europe". He also served as Director of the interdisciplinary research project "Cultures in/of Mobility" at the School of Humanities of Potsdam University. Until 2008 he held the position of the President of the German Association for American Studies. His major research interests and publications focus on cultural constructions of illness and ageing, transnational American Studies and the relations of human biology and culture. He is the author of *Material Bodies* (2018).

Annette Leibing is a medical anthropologist (PhD U Hamburg), who had her first academic position at the department of psychiatry at the Federal University of Rio de Janeiro. There she founded and directed the CDA, a multidisciplinary centre for mental health and ageing, with a special focus on dementia. After a postdoctoral fellowship at McGill University, she is now full professor at the Nursing faculty at the Université de Montréal. Her research focuses on issues related to ageing, by studying – as an anthropologist – Alzheimer's and Parkinson's disease, ageing and psychiatry, pharmaceuticals, elder care and, stem cells for the body in decline, among others. At the moment, her research focuses mainly on the prevention of dementia in different national and social contexts – a topic about which an edited volume recently came out (Leibing, A. and S. Schicktanz (eds.). *Preventing Dementia? Critical Perspectives on a New Paradigm of Preparing for Old Age*. New York/Oxford, UK: Berghahn, 2020).

Roberta Maierhofer is Professor of American Studies at the University of Graz, Austria, and Adjunct Professor at Binghamton University, New York. Since 2007, she has been directing the *Center for Inter-American*

Studies of the University of Graz. Her research focuses on (Inter)American Literature and Cultural Studies, Feminist Literature and Research, Gender Studies, Transatlantic Cooperation in Education, and Age/ Aging Studies. In her publication *Salty Old Women: Gender, Age, and Identity in American Culture*, she developed a theoretical approach to gender and ageing (anocriticism) and was one of the first within the European context to define her work within the field of Cultural/ Narrative Gerontology.

Christian Schmitt-Kilb teaches English Literature at the University of Rostock. He received his MA from the University of Keele (UK), PhD from the University of Frankfurt/Main on early modern rhetoric and poetics and habilitated at Rostock University with a thesis that resulted in a monograph on the theme of absent fathers in the contemporary novel. His current research interests, editorships and essay publications are in the field of ecocriticism, ecopoetry and New Nature Writing.

Kristina Weber is a PhD candidate at the University of Rostock. She received both her Bachelor's and Master's degrees in British and American Studies (the M.A. with a Transcultural focus). Her research focusses on asexuality in Anglophone postcolonial literatures and is funded by Rostock's scholarship for the university's best alumni.

Yumin Zhang is a Researcher and assistant professor in the School of Journalism and Culture Communications at Zhongnan University of Economics and Law. She received her PhD in American studies from Humboldt University of Berlin. Her fields of interest include comparative literature and culture (Chinese, American and German) and gender poetics. She is the author of the monograph *Masculinities in Transcultural Spaces – Negotiating of Masculinities in Ang Lee's Films* (2017) and the edited collection *Creative Writing Course* (2022).

Andrea Zittlau teaches at the department of North American Studies at the University of Rostock. Her monograph *Curious Exotica* (2016) explores the display of othered bodies and associated material culture. Her current work looks at poetry and marginalized communities and its dynamics to reveal and twist dominant discourses with a continuous focus on absence and the invisible. She frequently teaches poetry in community outreach contexts such as prisons and nursing homes and has connected those communities with her research.

Index

A

adolescents, 160, 161, 201, 203

ageing, 9–16, 18–20, 25–29, 34, 38, 69, 70, 77, 87, 88, 91–93, 95, 99, 100, 103–105, 132–134, 193, 194, 197, 198, 219, 224, 228

    Chinese fathers, 88

    double standard, 11, 133

    father, 92, 93, 95, 99, 100, 103, 104

    in India, 27, 34, 37, 38

    in prison, 58, 174–181, 184–186

    multi-generational, 12, 13, 26

    non-normative male, 132

    parents, 34, 35

agency, 98, 193, 216

B

Bolsonaro, Jair, 13, 45–51, 53, 55–61

Bosnia, 15, 17

    film, 15

Brazil, 13, 43, 45–50, 53, 55, 56, 58–62

C

chosen family, 135, 136, 139, 140

chosen family, 135

Clifford, James, 10, 32

coming out, 17, 128, 133, 134, 137–143

Confucian fatherhood, 15, 88, 94–96, 99, 104

Connell, Raewyn, 17, 130, 152, 192–194, 199, 204, 205, 222, 223

constructions, 11, 13, 19, 192

    of masculinity, 192, 194, 206

    socio-cultural, 191, 193, 204, 205

control, 54, 58, 191–193, 204, 206, 228
COVID-19, 10, 13, 50, 59

D
da Silva, Luis Inácio Lula, 46
dementia, 13, 16, 113–116
demodernization, 53, 54
desexualisation, 129, 134, 135
    of old age, 129, 134
diaspora, 9, 15, 38, 211, 212, 215, 216, 219, 220, 223–225, 229
    Indian, 9, 25, 31, 34

E
Eat Drink Man Woman, 15, 88, 100
emigration, 69, 83, 84, 163
    Russian, 70, 75, 84
Everyday Life, 17, 152, 153, 156, 162, 165, 166, 171
exile, 11, 14, 69, 70, 77, 83

F
family, 12, 15–18, 28, 30, 49, 50, 52, 58–60, 81, 83, 89, 91–96, 98–100, 104, 112, 118, 122, 128, 129, 137, 139, 141, 143, 152, 177, 178, 184, 195, 196, 200, 202–204, 225
    biological, 137, 140, 143
    nuclear, 32, 137
    relations, 96
    the sacred, 48, 49

father-son relationship, 14, 95, 99, 100
Father Trilogy, 14, 87, 104, 105
femininity, 18, 19, 45, 47, 72, 134, 192, 196, 201, 204–206, 222

G
gender, 9, 11, 14–16, 18–20, 27, 32, 33, 43, 49, 51, 57, 60, 70, 74, 83, 84, 87, 130, 131, 133, 136, 142, 174, 198, 205, 206, 222, 223, 227
    equality, 19, 44, 51, 102, 205, 206
    expression, 130, 131
    hierarchies, 200, 205, 206
    identity, 19, 140
    masculine, 56, 130, 131
    norms, 104, 134, 181
    relations, 192, 201, 204
    roles, 17, 33, 201, 203, 204, 206
generations, 12, 17, 25, 28, 30, 32, 33, 38, 82, 91, 109, 154, 167, 205, 218
Gilroy, Paul, 34
Great Indian Joint Family, 34
Greece, 112, 115

H
heteronormative, 13, 47, 50, 53, 60, 139, 140, 143
homecoming, 71, 74, 75, 77

homeland, 14, 72–74, 76–80, 83, 112
homesickness, 14, 71, 84
homophobia, 17, 48, 61, 127, 132, 136, 137, 143
  internalised, 17, 132, 136
house, 72, 73, 77, 90, 92, 100, 101, 104, 115, 140, 187, 191
hypermasculine, 129, 134
hypermasculinity, 181
hypersexuality, 129

I

identity, 15, 17, 19, 27, 31, 33, 52, 58, 59, 98, 100, 101, 104, 111, 117, 120, 123, 128, 135, 138, 142, 174, 180, 191, 193–195, 198, 204, 205, 212, 220, 222, 225, 227
  male, 17, 151, 193
illness, 13, 17, 19, 52, 109, 114–116, 118, 213, 227
incarceration, 57, 173, 177, 178
infantilisation, 117, 223
intercultural kinship, 110
intergenerational, 12, 17, 26, 29, 30, 32, 34, 35, 109, 123
  differences, 26, 32
  interactions, 17
  migration, 109, 123
  relations, 12, 29, 30, 34, 35
intersectionality, 20
interviews, 19, 193–195, 197
  qualitative, 194, 201

L

Lahiri, Jhumpa, 12, 28–35, 38
Lamb, Sarah, 28, 34, 35, 38
Lebedev, Viacheslav, 75, 76
Lee, Ang, 14, 15, 87–89, 93, 94, 103, 104

M

masculinity, 9–15, 17, 18, 20, 43–46, 52, 57, 59, 60, 62, 87–91, 93, 95, 96, 99–105, 127, 128, 130–134, 140, 143, 173, 181, 187, 191–193, 195–198, 201, 203–205, 213, 220–225, 227
  African, 19, 211, 212, 219, 221, 228
  caring, 15, 18, 101, 102, 105
  Chinese, 14, 88, 95
  complicit, 222
  hegemonic, 17–19, 56, 60, 130, 131, 133, 193, 194, 196, 202, 204, 222, 223
  toxic, 17
  wen-wu, 88–93, 104
masculinity models, 44, 45, 47, 50, 51, 53, 55, 56, 58–60, 62, 204
mental health, 138, 214, 216, 219, 220, 224, 229
  care, 225
migration, 9, 12, 14–16, 19, 20, 25–29, 34–38, 84,

109–111, 115, 118, 122,
  211, 223, 224
literature, 84
Mother Russia, 69, 74, 77
Mr Loverman, 17, 127–129, 132, 136,
  138, 141, 143

N

narration, 17, 111, 113, 116, 118–120,
  122, 130, 131, 219, 221
neo-pentecostal or evangelical
  male, 59
Not Another Second, 138

O

obscene politics, 46
old age, 11, 12, 17, 25, 26, 30, 32, 38,
  45, 52, 76, 88, 93, 95,
  104, 132, 133, 135, 138,
  139, 141, 143, 173, 186,
  220, 221, 229

P

patriarchy, 56, 87, 192, 203, 222
performance, 19, 45, 52, 128, 181,
  196, 198, 204, 211, 212,
  214–216, 219, 220, 222,
  224, 225, 227, 228
physical health, 99, 177
poverty, 61
prodigal son, 14, 72, 74, 75, 83
Pushing Hands, 15, 88, 100

Q

queer community, 128, 141–143
queerness, 16, 130, 131, 137–139,
  141, 142

R

racism, 61, 173, 219, 221, 223
re-traditionalisation, 150, 158
resilience, 61, 141, 212, 215, 219, 226
return, 153, 160, 162, 163
reversion, 13, 43–45, 50, 53, 55,
  57–61
Russian émigré literature, 70, 73,
  75, 84

S

Senior Center, 174, 179–183, 187,
  189
Sevela, Efraim, 69, 70, 75, 78–82,
  86
sevā, 12, 25, 28, 30, 35, 36, 38
sex binary, 191, 195
silence, 19, 214, 219, 225–227
storytelling, 213, 218, 219
Sweden, 16, 74, 109, 111, 112, 115, 118
symbolic spaces, 163

T

Tanović, Ines, 17, 149, 151, 152
Tanzania, 19, 211–214, 216, 218,
  219, 221–223, 225, 231
the life review, 139
The Wedding Banquet, 15, 88, 94, 95,
  100, 106
Turoverov, Nikolai, 75–78

U

Unaccustomed Earth, 12, 29, 32

V

violence, 13, 16, 46, 48, 54, 55, 59, 60, 62, 90, 134, 150, 161, 164, 167, 183, 184, 186

W

war, 17, 50, 111, 114, 153, 154, 158, 162–164, 182, 194, 202, 203

Windrush generation, 17, 127, 129, 130, 141, 143

womb, 73, 80